Pet
NATION

Pet
NATI🐾N

The Love Affair That Changed America

MARK L. CUSHING

AVERY
an imprint of Penguin Random House
New York

AVERY

an imprint of Penguin Random House LLC
penguinrandomhouse.com

Most Avery books are available at special quantity discounts for bulk purchase for sales promotions, premiums, fund-raising, and educational needs. Special books or book excerpts also can be created to fit specific needs. For details, write SpecialMarkets@penguinrandomhouse.com.

Library of Congress Cataloging-in-Publication Data
Names: Cushing, Mark L., author.
Title: Pet nation : the love affair that changed America / by Mark L. Cushing.
Description: New York : Avery, an imprint of Penguin Random House LLC, [2020] |
Includes bibliographical references and index.
Identifiers: LCCN 2020000681 (print) | LCCN 2020000682 (ebook) |
ISBN 9780593083864 (hardcover) | ISBN 9780593083871 (ebook)
Subjects: LCSH: Pets—United States—History.
Classification: LCC SF411.36.U6 C87 2020 (print) | LCC SF411.36.U6 (ebook) |
DDC 636.088/70973—dc23
LC record available at https://lccn.loc.gov/2020000681
LC ebook record available at https://lccn.loc.gov/2020000682
p.   cm.

Printed in the United States of America
1   3   5   7   9   10   8   6   4   2

Book design by Laura K. Corless

For Natalie, Meredith, Caitlin,
Jillian, Mark Patrick, and Annelise . . .
and the menagerie of cats and dogs
we've served over the years

CONTENTS

1. IN THE BACKYARD NO MORE:

The Transformation of Pets in American Society

1

2. HOW PETS WENT VIRAL

37

3. THE WHOLE DAMN COUNTRY HAS RUN AMOK:

The Pet Land Grab

75

4. THE SECRET TO PET NATION:

The Human-Animal Bond

113

5. DOG SHORTAGES AND CANINE FREEDOM TRAINS

139

6. THE GOOD, THE BAD, AND THE UGLY:

Legal and Political Fights Are Just Beginning

175

Contents

7. PET HEALTH CARE WILL NEVER BE THE SAME AGAIN
209

8. "IT ISN'T ONLY DOGS AND CATS"
239

9. PET NATION:
Is There More to Come?
273

Acknowledgments
287

Notes
289

Index
299

Pet
NATION

·1·

IN THE BACKYARD NO MORE
The Transformation of Pets in American Society

Two strangers meet in a park, each walking with a dog on a leash. They don't ask each other where they work, or live, or went to college; or about the kind of car they drive, or their favorite football team. They say one, perhaps, two things: "What kind of dog is that? What's her name?" Twenty minutes later, they know everything about each other's pet and then part ways as friends. Not have-each-other-over-to-dinner friends but friends who look forward to seeing each other, and their dogs, again.

When you consider the condition of pets in America before Pet Nation, it seems as if everything was photographed in black-and-white or sepia, all stills and no video. Pets were scattered here and there, nearly invisible, as if they didn't matter. Then they began to appear *everywhere*. Before long, pets were transformed from a diversion to the center of our culture and so many lives. This wasn't a purely personal experience; pets became *social* glue, the common bond between people with little else in common, who would never otherwise have spoken to each other. That's the essence of Pet Nation, and why I wrote this book.

I majored in medieval and renaissance history at Stanford (how's that for spotting a trend?), went to law school, and became a business trial lawyer. I figured I'd spend my life in a courtroom, raise a family, and see the world. If you had asked me for a thousand scenarios that might unfold in my life, building the Animal Policy Group and becoming a leading advocate and adviser in the pet world would not have made the list. Not even close. Fortunately, that is what happened. In 2005, I received a phone call from Banfield Pet Hospital's founder, asking me to lead a pet lobbying effort with our federal government in Washington, DC. This was possible then because everything was changing with pets in America.

Dogs and cats went from the backyard to the bedroom, and then dogs headed out the front door of the house to every corner of the United States, every town, suburb, and city. Pets stepped into political and legal arenas, stirring up issues and passions we'd never thought about before. My daily world became the dramas at the intersection of pets and American society. My career as a trial lawyer and DC-based lobbyist morphed into a full-time, national practice, fighting battles and advancing causes related to pets. No one else had the job I created or, rather, shaped for myself. This job had never existed, and I've battled, cajoled, lobbied, and persuaded ever since.

Pet Nation reveals that something about *us*—not about dogs and cats—has changed without our realizing what happened. Pets aren't a fad. They are more like the medicine America needs now for individuals and communities to feel better, and to do better. This is the story of *what* happened, *how* it happened, *where* it happened, and *why*. We explore issues challenging Pet Nation today and a culture that wasn't prepared for dogs and cats to move center stage. We study the human-animal bond, legal restrictions, political conflicts, colorful history, cutting-edge research, and a pet health-care system that's turned upside down. What I have discovered is often entertaining, occasionally surprising, and sometimes shocking. It's an insider's account of what no one saw coming twenty years ago, or could stop if they tried.

Now, let's begin with a few stories about dogs and cats.

March 14, 2019

The flight to Orlando, my third red-eye of the year, was delayed but not without diversion. Besides the usual suspects tapping away on their iPhones and laptops—business travelers, Palm Beach dowagers, and families bound for Disney World—there was a new and decidedly more exotic passenger in the American Airlines Admirals Club that night. Well groomed, with a jeweled necklace, a Louis Vuitton case, chestnut-brown coat, and long eyelashes, Suzette made a stir. From time to time, she sampled a few candies proffered by her traveling companion, a woman in her thirties with a similarly understated fashion flair, took a sip of Tasmanian Rain bottled water, then sat back and closed her eyes, waiting for the flight to board. Three years old, this long-haired Chihuahua was accustomed to the comforts of business class. Seated across the aisle from her owner / pet parent / friend on the flight from Phoenix, I learned that Suzette had a busy social calendar, a passport of her own, more Instagram followers than I will ever have, and a full, pampered week ahead of her in Boca Raton.

November 16, 2018

A Huffington Post article by Elyse Wanshel tells a different story, in which two beautiful cats became the fulcrum for a modern

Seattle wedding of two women that would make any ailuro-phile* purr. In the article, Wanshel describes the efforts of two newlyweds—Colleen, 27, and Iz, 26—to entertain their guests at their wedding. Since the ceremony was performed at a Quaker meetinghouse, they were not allowed to serve alcohol while a photographer took their post-wedding portraits. Inspired by their two older, disabled rescue cats Ladybird and Pangur, Colleen and Iz devised a plan. As Colleen told Wanshel, "When we were brainstorming something alcohol-free for our guests to do while we took family pictures, kittens came up and things flowed from there." Instead of a "cocktail hour," they invented a "kitten hour," starring six kittens from the Seattle Animal Shelter that were made available.

While Ladybird and Pangur were otherwise engaged at home, "sleeping on the couch, watching squirrels out the window and thinking about killing them," the kittens entertained the wedding guests, and all the kittens eventually landed adoptive homes. Encouraged by Iz and Colleen to donate to SAS (from which they foster cats) as wedding gifts, several guests filled out adoption papers. Perfect wedding toasts in the form of "Ladybird" and "Pangur" cocktails brightened the reception.

Welcome to Pet Nation.

---

* Ailurophile: A person who loves cats.

WHAT IS PET NATION?

We live in a brand-new country, one with new codes of behavior, social mores, and artifacts—iPhones, Facebook, texting, Tinder, emojis, tattoos, cars that drive themselves, fake news, miniature helicopters called drones that deliver pizza to your doorstep, virtual assistants who schedule appointments and remember birthdays. And pets; lots of *pets*. It's as if American society said, "Let's toss out the nineteenth and twentieth centuries and start over. Let's invent a new world." Pet Nation is a country where 75 percent of our pets sleep on their owner's bed, and where millions of dogs and cats have their own social media accounts, receive birthday cards they cannot read, and wear expensive Halloween costumes only once. And it's not just cats and dogs, as you'll see in chapter eight. The range of species in Pet Nation is breathtaking.

America has a whopping 185 million cats and dogs. That's more than one for every two people, or 1.4 per household. Two of three dog owners consider their dog their "best friend," and this trend is not relenting. As more people acquire their first dog, 26 percent of existing dog owners have two dogs, 10 percent have three dogs, and 7 percent have four or more. The sign above the door to a local groomer's shop reads, "Dogs are like potato chips. You can't have just one." Today, 30 percent of millennial couples acquire their first dog before their first child. In 2000, there were seventy-three million cats and sixty-eight million dogs in America; now there are ninety-five million cats and ninety million dogs.

After two centuries on the margin, as likely to receive a kick in the ribs as a holiday treat, dogs and cats rose to the status of children in less than thirty years. How did this happen? And why is this fervor focused on cats and dogs? There are other kinds of pets (birds, ornamental fish, ferrets, snakes, turtles) in Pet Nation, all loved and fussed over by their owners, as I discuss later in the story, but dogs and cats "rule the roost." The national mantra became "If it's good enough for Mom and Dad, or the kids, then Rover and Mittens deserve the same."

Dogs and cats free people from the emotional labyrinths that have cut them off from other people. In the words of Temple Grandin, the author and animal behaviorist, "Animals make us human." My friends know the names of neighborhood dogs but not the names of their neighbors themselves. On city and suburban sidewalks, dogs are "connective social tissue." A dog walker wearing headphones and a jangle of apartment keys strolls down the street, texting as she goes, bouncing off other pedestrians like digital bumper cars. Then she sees an Irish Setter pulling its owner down the block. They meet and the dog walker: stops; smiles at the stranger; admires the dog; asks its age, name, and provenance; snaps a picture; and then moves on. If cats are question marks, dogs are exclamation points.

THE PET REVOLUTION

It was a long and treacherous journey from the backyard to the bedroom for American pets in the twentieth century.* It took that long for people to work through a culture of abuse and indifference that consigned dogs and cats to a second-class status in America. The word "pet" first entered the English language around 1500 as a term for "a

---

* From 1950 to 1995, approximately ten million dogs were euthanized annually in America, many of them strays, because they were a nuisance, "in the way," caught by a local dogcatcher, or unclaimed at the local pound.

spoiled child," then assumed a second meaning in 1530 as "an animal kept as a favorite." This was not a word commonly heard during the next three hundred years, since few domestic animals enjoyed that status during the period. The rare exceptions were those animals belonging to royal households, other members of the European aristocracy (who prized dogs for hunting and, secondarily, companionship), and the rare families who treated pets (dogs, cats, parrots, and sometimes more unconventional species such as squirrels or crows) as beloved members of the family.

During the Victorian era (1837–1901), the concept of "kindness to animals" entered public discourse. This prompted the establishment of the first English animal charities, such as Our Dumb Friends League,* in London, in 1897. Today this organization is known as the Blue Cross; it finds homes for unwanted animals and educates the public in the responsibilities of animal ownership. There were also pockets of animal compassion in America during that period, both public and private. Animal-welfare organizations took shape, like the ASPCA in Manhattan, in 1866, and SPCA in Buffalo, in 1867, to protect animals and to rescue those in need. Those initiatives eventually led to the revolution that has unfolded over the past twenty years, which has unleashed social and economic forces (not to mention actual four-legged dogs and cats) with astonishing results for both people and pets. In short:

1. After gestating for one hundred years, Pet Nation exploded in the 2000s, a complete and radical reversal of every part of the human-pet dynamic.
2. While it wasn't a political coup d'état, in the literal sense of a subordinate party unseating a ruling power, dogs and cats ended

---

* This organization was the inspiration for the Dumb Friends League in Denver, Colorado, founded in 1910, still one of America's leading animal shelters, discussed at length in chapter five. Animals cannot talk, hence the name.

up *on top*. Previously, people owned and dominated dogs, treating them as chattel, working beasts, or disposable household accessories. Through no effort of their own, pets have become royalty, at least for the 65 percent of American households that own them.

3. Pet Nation has produced dramatic changes in the socioeconomic order of the United States.

4. Pet Nation was ignited by a shift in the way people think about pets. Who these change agents were, and how they became the architects of the new pet *paradigm*, will be revealed in chapter two.

An Accidental Revolution

If Pet Nation was revolutionary, it was only by accident. Dogs and cats didn't conspire, plot resistance, wage battles, or dethrone a king. There were two "oppressors"—people and a social norm that declared that animals have no intrinsic value beyond the work they do (herding, hunting, ratting) or are throwaway companions, to be replaced at will or euthanized if they become a financial or logistical burden. This revolution simply happened, for multiple reasons: technological, sociological, and behavioral. Pet Nation could be the first revolution in history in which the oppressors voluntarily stepped aside for the oppressed.

PET CULTURE

The Internet has splintered society into thousands of separate communities, on- and offline, each a mini culture with passionate devotees and behavior systems. For fifty years, American television—with three channels and a handful of programs people liked or didn't like—was a conversational template; today, there are thousands of entertainment channels on television, phones, and computers. Music, sports, and movies are temporary cultural markers but don't meet the definition of a full-blown culture. Social media and digital paraphernalia have hijacked our collective free time; digital culture is sprawling, all-consuming, and occasionally dangerous.

Pets are emotionally nourishing, so important that people orient their day, plan their week, and schedule holidays and weekend encounters with their dog or cat in mind. They choose cafés depending on their dog policy; they swear off IKEA when the store bars the door to dogs; and they bless The Home Depot and Bed Bath & Beyond for their enlightened embrace of our four-legged companions.

Pet culture is respectful, lowercase democratic, and grounded in the American ideal of *equality.* No one measures a pet by the wealth, appearance, or social status of its owner—it's all about the animals. Whether at a dog run, on the sidewalk, or on Facebook, a Cavalier King Charles Spaniel is a Cavalier King Charles Spaniel, a mutt is a mutt, an Abyssinian cat is an Abyssinian cat, nothing else matters. It is not a question of privilege, family name, accent, education, job, or lack of a job. "One nation, indivisible, with cats and dogs and parakeets for all." Dogs and cats are equal, and people with pets meet as equals. My cat is the most beautiful Ragdoll cat on earth, and yours is also the most beautiful Ragdoll cat on earth—illogical but true. Pets are loved, no matter how much they cost: Americans earning $30,000 per year own and love their dogs, just like those earning $100,000 or more.

Yet many Americans still don't see the charm of a 150-pound New-foundland in the next office, or care to stand in line at a bakery behind a Doberman Pinscher. They would rather not limbo their way through a gauntlet of dogs and dog leashes on the sidewalk on their way home from work as neighbors meet and trade news about their dogs. Many people are allergic to animals, or have lasting childhood memories of encounters with pets that didn't end well. Roughly one-third of American households do not have a pet. What does that mean? How does it feel for people who once inhabited a world where pets were invisible? Where every other TV commercial didn't feature a dog? Literally and figuratively, pets are impossible to ignore. It is said that 25 percent of all American dinner-table conversations involve dogs.

A French acquaintance of my brother, newly arrived from Paris, found it tricky to build a social life in New York without a dog: "My English isn't the problem. I do not have a dog, so I can't join in elevator stories or texting. When we go out for drinks from the office, I have nothing to talk about when everyone wants to talk about their French Bulldogs. I *am* French, but that doesn't seem to be good enough." Pet lovers are surprised, or taken aback, when someone doesn't like their dog or cat, or is simply indifferent to them. Apathy is harder to accept than antipathy, which can be countered with photographs and anec-dotes.

A frequent Google query today is, "Why do some people hate dogs?" The chosen word is "hate," a powerful verb, not "dislike." I've summa-rized the responses, which, you'll notice, have more to do with the owner than with the dog:

1. The dog owner doesn't clean up after their dog.
2. The dog owner doesn't control their dog.

3. The dog owner doesn't take responsibility for their dog.

4. The dog barks too much and too loudly.

5. The dog roams off-leash.

6. The dog invades my personal space.

7. The dog destroys property.

8. The dog owner brings the dog to innappropriate places.

9. The dog is annoying at the park or other public places.

10. The dog owner never stops talking about their dog.

There are several possible explanations for the cultural pet divide. Some people are afraid of animals. Others were raised in no-pet households and find the notion of sharing a home with an animal absurd, a regression to the Middle Ages when European farmers lived upstairs in their houses and livestock downstairs. Maybe it's their nature: some scientists believe that the disposition to like dogs and cats is genetic: you're either born to like animals or not. And those who don't like animals, don't.

Do the naysayers have a say in the direction of our society? Relatively little. In chapter three, "The Whole Damn Country Has Run Amok: The Pet Land Grab," I discuss the daily march of pets into more public real estate and private work spaces, and the millenial drive for pet-friendly housing. Pets are here to stay.

What Changed?

Every element of pet culture has changed: from food to boarding, medicine, play, shelters, sleeping, training, travel, surveillance, getting lost, getting found, to the number of pets in the United States, now more dogs and cats than Americans ever imagined was possible. Consider a few examples:

1. It's Raining Cats and Dogs

Historically, the number of dogs in America was relatively stable until 2000, when the dog population exploded, increasing from 68 million to 90 million by 2017. If the rate of growth continues at this pace, America will have 135 million dogs by 2039, and I will show why 135 million dogs won't be enough.

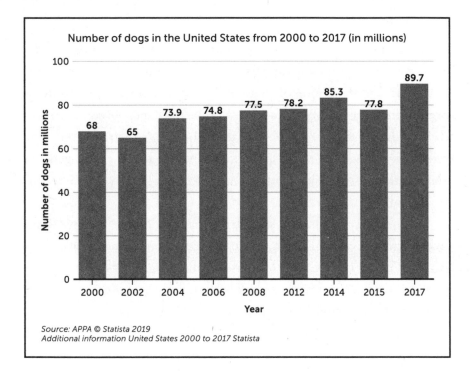

Number of dogs in the United States from 2000 to 2017 (in millions)

Source: APPA © Statista 2019
Additional information United States 2000 to 2017 Statista

From 2002 to 2004, as the United States human population increased 1.7 percent, the dog population increased 13 percent, from 65 million to 73.9 million. From 2006 to 2008, the human population rose 2 percent, dogs 3.6 percent, from 74.8 million to 77.5 million. The numbers kept rising. From 2012 to 2014, as the United States human population increased 1.5 percent, the dog population increased 6.5 percent, from

78.2 million to 83.3 million. From 2015 to 2017, the human population rose 1.2 percent, dogs 15 percent, from 77.8 million to 89.7 million, after a dip in 2014 to 77.8 million.

Cats were equally reproductive, their population increasing 31 percent during the same period, from 73 million to 95.6 million (not counting feral cats).

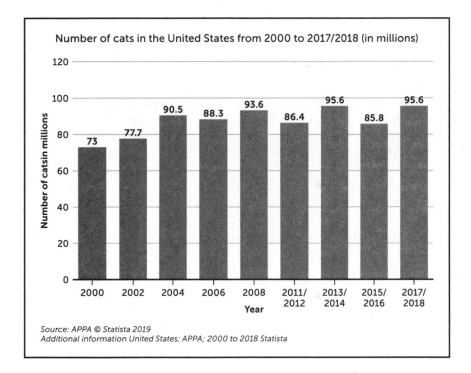

Number of cats in the United States from 2000 to 2017/2018 (in millions)

Source: APPA © Statista 2019
Additional information United States; APPA; 2000 to 2018 Statista

More public than cats, dogs are ubiquitous. While they once lived on the periphery, skulking from yard to yard, they are now everywhere: on airplanes, at work, in stores, in pet-friendly cafés, in Catholic churches on the feast day of Saint Francis of Assisi, in city parks, on trains and city buses, and even at memorial services (for people and other pets).

THE ONLY ELECTED DOGCATCHER IN AMERICA

The dismissive political epithet "He couldn't get elected dogcatcher" is both misleading and condescending, since it is a challenging job and rarely an elected position. Most city governments appoint their town's animal-control officer.

One historical exception was Duxbury, Vermont, population 1,802, where Zeb Towne held the elected position for fifteen years, and was quoted on NPR in March 2018, saying, "I'm the only person in the country who gets elected as a dogcatcher. So, I'm awesome, I guess." Annual salary: $500. Term: one year, limiting the possible abuse of power. Number of annual calls: twenty to thirty. Dogs only? Not at all: dogs, cats, deer, ermine—whatever runs, creeps, hops, or flies, provided it is in some kind of trouble. After the NPR coverage, Duxbury changed the dogcatcher position to appointee, retaining Zeb, reputedly the only person in town who wanted the job, and a capable dogcatcher at that.

2. A Day in the Life: Then and Now

As the stories that opened this chapter showed, life has changed dramatically for pets in the last half century. Imagine for a moment that you are a dog in 1956—choose your breed. Daily life was simple. You'd wake up, cold and hungry, indoors, if you were lucky, but, generally, outdoors, in the garage, on the patio, or in the doghouse, tethered to a post or a tree. Then wonder where food would come from. Depending on how neglected you were, you could roam the neighborhood during the day, getting into mischief, avoiding the dogcatcher, one of the least-respected, though most dangerous, jobs in mid-century America, apart from that of mail carrier.*

---

* In 2018, 5,714 American postal workers were bitten by dogs, versus 6,214 in 2017, and 6,714 in 2016. New technology, including mobile delivery scanners and a package-pickup app, which link dogs to delivery addresses, has lowered the number of attacks. Per capita, Texas is the most dangerous state for mail carriers, with four cities in the top ten, in descending order of bites:

Days were long and bleak for dogs in America then: you lived alone; you were not fussed over by strangers as you ambled down the sidewalk; you were not coddled by Mom and Dad; in winter, you didn't wear a shearling jacket with pockets for water bottle, treats, and polka-dot waste bags, with the words "Service Dog" embroidered in gold to announce your status. Your daily routine traced and retraced the confines of your backyard, the run of ten to fifteen feet from your tree or doghouse, or the neighborhoods where you were safe from the pound and possible euthanasia.

Now, on average, the numbing *monotony* of a dog's life in the nineteenth and twentieth centuries has been traded for a different set of nouns: "adoration," "adventure," "affection," "challenges," "change," "comfort," "possibilities," "royalty," "surprise." Today, the life of a typical American dog is radically different, and how a dog (be it mutt or pedigree) spends the day depends on its answers to several questions. The variety of answers dogs could give to these questions—if they could speak—reveal the diversity of experiences and lifestyles enjoyed by today's pampered pets. Imagine Rover filling out this questionnaire.

Where do you live, Rover: City or country? The answer to this question could betray your exposure to the elements and other animals (canine or otherwise) and your wardrobe (coat, booties, hat, sweaters, rain slicker). *Are you part of a family?* This will tell if you have siblings, canine or otherwise; one parent or two, married or otherwise, and if you shuttle from one house to the other. *Where do you spend most days?* There are choices: If home, house or apartment? If work, big office or small, alone or with other dogs? *Do you have a walker?* How many times a day? How many dogs? Your size or a mix? Just your breed?

This litany of questions will determine how much, where, and in

---

Houston (seventy-five), Dallas (forty-nine), San Antonio (forty-seven), and Fort Worth (thirty-five). The statistics are reported each year during National Dog Bite Prevention Week, the second week of April.

what degree of luxury Rover sleeps, eats, walks, plays, shares, day-dreams, and spends time being the most fabulous canine or feline on the planet, according to Rover's Mom and Dad, if questioned under oath.

3. Let's See: The Doghouse or the Bedroom?

The forlorn, chocolate-brown Boxer dog in a nineteenth-century German illustration titled *Boxer vor seiner Hütte* has the saddest face imaginable. He enjoyed few possessions: a crudely built and crumbling wooden doghouse, a water bowl, and a bone or two. The eighteen-inch chain tying him to the doghouse signaled his daily ambit, which was severely restricted. The word *"Hütte"* is uppercase because nouns are capitalized in German, not because his "hut" was an impressive structure. For centuries, if dogs were sheltered from the elements, this was their home. What could a dog do inside a doghouse? Next to nothing: sit up, lie down, bark, wait, wait some more, chew on the old bone, or drink water, provided it wasn't frozen.

Marie Antoinette's turquoise, velvet-cushioned dog kennel, once the home of her favorite dog, Coco,* a Papillon, or Toy Spaniel, as the breed is sometimes called, now resides in the permanent collection of the Metropolitan Museum of Art, in New York City. Today, it would be considered too decorative, too formal, for most American dogs, but it was an *indoor* kennel, which is where most dogs now live. The master bedroom has replaced the doghouse as the place to sleep, on top of

---

*Historians believe that, minutes before her execution, Marie Antoinette handed Coco to her children's governess, Madame de Tourzel. And that Madame de Tourzel took Coco to Austria, where she lived in the Hofburg until the Bourbon monarchy was restored. At the age of twenty-two, Coco returned to Paris and died shortly thereafter, to be buried in the gardens of the Hôtel de Seignelay, a private residence in the 7th arrondissement, near the site of Marie Antoinette's execution. Lucky Coco, a Papillon, escaped the fate of Bichons, considered a symbol of royal power, who were released onto the streets of Paris, where they earned a few sous and treats by performing acrobatic tricks on the city sidewalks.

the bed, sometimes with a miniature three-step staircase for easy access. Doghouses are still marketed, but they are more architectural follies or playhouses than primary dwellings. Cats never required their own houses, although cat towers have become common in American homes, enabling our feline masters to survey the world beneath them.

Sleeping indoors in the master bedroom (on the bed) is now standard practice for three of four American dogs and cats. This was unthinkable thirty years ago. For much of the nineteenth and twentieth centuries, married couples slept in separate, single beds, with animals outdoors. Fortunately for dogs and cats today, most American couples sleep together on large mattresses.

4. What's for Dinner?

Dogs love to eat. They rarely leave food in a bowl, and will eat for hours if we let them. Cats eat when they want to, *if* they want to, and at a pace that people will never comprehend (although many chow down like dogs, as if they haven't been fed in months).

Americans spent approximately $36.9 billion on pet food in 2019, triple the 2000 level, by far the largest category of pet expenditures. Like everything in Pet Nation, food is changing—in how it is researched, designed, manufactured, bought and sold, marketed, and, most of all, eaten. Surprisingly, what *people* eat, how they eat, and the human birth rate are reshaping the American *pet*-food industry.

Pet-food trends and human-food trends have naturally converged in California, where the farm-to-table and local food canon of Alice Waters, and the organic food movement, revolutionized the American diet. After the appearance of a single, French-infused restaurant named Chez Panisse on a Berkeley side street in the early 1970s, along with the Zen breads of Tassajara, and a few organic farms near Santa Cruz, people began to think about the nature, quantity, and origin of the foods they and their family consume. Amazon (pure commerce) now owns Whole Foods (pure foods), where people buy organic everything. The pet-food industry is duplicating these two trends: (1) healthier, organic foods; and (2) corporate ownership of on-trend food makers.

Wild Earth, a Berkeley-based pet-food company cofounded by vegan Ryan Bethencourt, and partially funded by Mars (whose products span from M&M's to dog treats), is developing vegan food for dogs (fungi-derived "clean proteins" called koji) and cats (bioreactor-produced mouse meat). If people feel better on a vegan diet, should German Shepherds switch from lamb chops to cauliflower? Where is the evidence? In her recent article in *The Atlantic*, Sarah Zhang quotes Tony Buffington, a veterinarian at the UC Davis School of Veterinary Medicine, who acknowledges that cats and dogs *can* be healthy on a vegan diet. However, Dr. Buffington questions the approach: "There's an ethical challenge to making others the means to one's end. To me that's what people are doing. When they're feeding dogs and cats vegan foods, they're making dogs and cats abide by their own personal philosophical beliefs." Do dogs crave kale treats? The jury is still out.

A larger related trend pervades pet food, mimicking the trajectory of human food over the past fifty years: human-grade and non-GMO ingredients; ethical farming; organic components and production; probiotics; fresh food (people cook for their dogs daily, or feed them raw, uncooked chicken, a canine twist on the paleo diet, echoing "life in the wild"); and an understanding of allergies and food compounds.

Pet owners knew little about pet nutrition before Pet Nation, but they're learning. If your Cocker Spaniel has a sensitive tummy, should you feed her the prescribed canned food that has forty-odd ingredients with periodic table names, everything from powdered cellulose to L-threonine, potassium chloride, water, pork liver, turkey, chicken, colorant caramel, five or six different vitamins, calcium, psyllium seed husk, various minerals, beta-carotene, on and on? Many households still shop the old-fashioned way, buying the most nutritious diet that is easily replenished, affordable, vet-approved, and tolerated by young or old Tristan. This is sensible, time-tested advice for most animals, and there are specific diets for specific breeds, as well, both meat protein and vegan.

Dogs and cats don't care about Michelin stars, but you'd never know it from the growth in premium pet foods reported in the *Washington Post*. In 2019, Americans spent $19.6 billion of disposable income on premium foods. As the pet population expanded post-2000, traditional food companies like Smucker's pivoted from jams and jellies to "kibbles and bits." In a few years, Smucker's spent $4 billion buying pet-food brands, including Big Heart Pet Brands, trying to catch up with Mars Petcare (with brands such as Royal Canin, Eukanuba, IAMS, WHISKAS, Pedigree, and Greenies).

Who would have thought that dog and cat food could become so

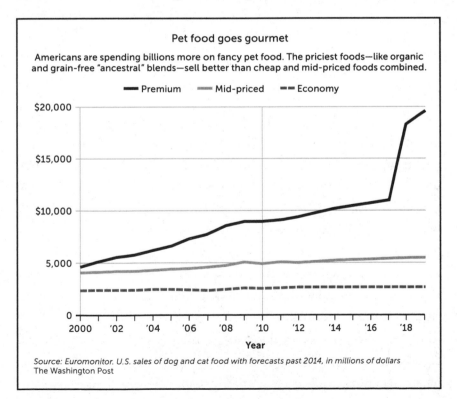

Pet food goes gourmet

Americans are spending billions more on fancy pet food. The priciest foods—like organic and grain-free "ancestral" blends—sell better than cheap and mid-priced foods combined.

Source: Euromonitor. U.S. sales of dog and cat food with forecasts past 2014, in millions of dollars
The Washington Post

complicated? The common knowledge that has structured dog and cat diets for two hundred years holds true:

- Domesticated dogs and cats are carnivores.
- Dogs (and some cats) will eat too much if we let them; how often and how much they eat depends on their age, breed, and size.
- Dogs can thrive on a pure kibble diet, or a mix of kibble and rice or cooked/raw meat, or vegetables.
- Chocolate, onions, garlic, and citrus fruits are all off-limits.
- Every dog is different; therefore, diets vary.

And so, when the dinner bell rings, and Rover or Mittens asks, "All right, what's for dinner?," if you answer, "Quinoa, koji, and blanched parsnips. And for dessert, some marigold petals," do they answer, "Yum yum yum," or "Are you sure? How about a nice, juicy, thirty-two-ounce porterhouse, or a salmon steak . . . ?"

5. "We're Having a Baby . . ."

Approximately 30 percent of millennial couples choose to have a dog before a child. Once a spontaneous act—"Let's get a puppy"—only slightly more considered than buying Easter chicks at the local pet shop, the pet decision can now involve months of discussion. The decision to get a pet approaches the solemnity, and the drama, of when and whether to start a family. Simultaneously obsessed with student debt but strangely happy to pay for lavish vacations, millennial couples view their first pet as: (1) a serious, long-term commitment, not a temporary or frivolous purchase; and (2) a surrogate child or training vehicle for their first child (which they perhaps can't yet afford), therefore, a way to assume responsibility for another living being before having an actual baby.

Three of four millennials own a dog and one of two own a cat. Many manage their dog or cat as they would their first child, celebrating milestones and giving them the focus, attention, and medical care typically reserved for children. That's why the Dog Starter Kit is so long. There is little difference between outfitting a nursery for a baby and a home for a puppy. Like an infant, a pet needs many things, and every need must be addressed. Convenience is critical, which explains the growth of online businesses like Chewy, which deliver supplies to millions of homes daily. Chewy carefully chose the words of its tagline "Where Pet Lovers Shop," to enfold the pet, the pet owner, and the purchase process in one loving and lucrative embrace.

DOG STARTER KIT

1. Dog	9. Food–wet	17. Sweaters
2. Blanket	10. Foot cream	18. Toothbrush
3. Booties	11. Harness	19. Toothpaste
4. Brush	12. Kennel	20. Toys
5. Coat	13. Leash	21. Training pads
6. Dog bone	14. Pillows	22. Treats
7. Food bowl	15. Placemat	23. Water bowl
8. Food–dry	16. Raincoat	

Quality matters, whether in the animal's diet, with nutritious ingredients and environmentally correct production, or in all-cotton blankets, coats, and accouterments. It is a given that pets are expensive. The decision to acquire a pet bears on finances, vacations, time allotment, commitment, and residence. If you choose to live in an apartment building, it could affect your choice of a residence, since many apartments don't allow pets, or dogs above a certain size. If you have your heart set on a Golden Retriever, you might have to switch to a Highland Terrier or find another apartment. If your building only allows service dogs or emotional support animals, you will need certification from a doctor, but few people worry about the validity of these certificates (although litigious neighbors are increasingly common), believing that nothing can stand in the way of their right to have a dog and knowing that apartment buildings rarely test dog owners armed with a certificate.

6. Lost and Found

Every year, according to the American Humane association, approximately ten million dogs and cats are lost or stolen in the United States (1.5 million of them stolen). Of that number, an estimated 93 percent of dogs and 75 percent of cats reported lost are returned safely home. One in three pets will get lost at some point during their life, a meaningful percentage. How do dogs and cats get lost? A few ways, none of which are new to man, they: slip off their leash; run out the back door; jump from an open car window or door; are tied to a post outside a store or restaurant and either are stolen or escape from their leash before their owner returns.

Dogs rely on familiar scents to find their way home—a ten-mile journey homeward bound is not uncommon, provided wind conditions are right and it isn't pouring rain. Dogs construct mental maps, which orient them. Cats are also natural navigators. Memory plus a powerful olfactory sense point the way home.

How are Lost Dogs and Cats Found?
A recent ASPCA survey of one thousand dog and cat owners nationwide found that:

- 49 percent of dog owners find their dog by searching the neighborhood.
- 15 percent of the dogs are recovered because they are wearing an ID tag or have a microchip (an identifying integrated circuit placed under an animal's skin).

- 30 percent of cat owners find their cat by searching the neighborhood.
- 59 percent of cat owners recover their cat because it returns home on its own.
- 6 percent of dog owners and 2 percent of cat owners find their lost pets at a shelter.

A study published in the *Journal of the American Veterinary Medical Association* (including fifty-three animal shelters across the United States) confirmed the high rate of return of microchipped dogs and cats to their families. "When an animal is found and taken to a shelter or veterinary clinic, one of the first things they do is scan the animal for a microchip. If they find a microchip, and if the microchip registry has accurate information, they can quickly find the animal's owner." Consider:

- 22 percent of lost dogs in the shelters were reunited with their families. However, the return-to-owner rate for microchipped dogs was 52 percent.
- 2 percent of lost cats in the shelters were reunited with their families. The return-to-owner rate for microchipped cats was dramatically higher at 38 percent.
- Only 58 percent of microchipped pets were registered in an online recovery database.

There are two solutions to the lost-and-found problem: more vigilance on the part of pet owners, and microchips at a reasonable cost of thirty-eight to forty-five dollars. Though microchipping is required by law in some countries, such as the United Kingdom, it is not in the United States. If microchips double the chance of a dog being reunited with its owner, and raise the odds of a cat being reunited with its owner by a factor of twenty (yes, twenty), it puzzles supporters that the technology isn't required by states, like the rabies vaccine is, or at least uti-lized more uniformly.

I met the pet industry through a successful battle to use open tech-nology for microchips, rather than proprietary systems that make it impossible to read a chip without a compatible, proprietary scanner. That was in 2005, but interest has waned in the pursuit of state-by-state laws mandating microchips. Pet owners have not demanded a political solution, partly because it's easy to get a microchip at a veterinary clinic, and partly because most lost pets are found. Microchipping goes into the basket of good ideas that never materialize into laws.

7. Isn't It About Time You Get a Job?

There are three ways to consider this question given the contribution of pets to the American economy: (1) people who work *with* and *for* pets; (2) pets at the office; and (3) pets on the job. In twenty years, the pet economy has grown from $23 billion to $95.7 billion. At the current rate of growth, it will reach $120 billion by 2027, and pet-related employ-ment will approach two million people. If the next twenty years were to repeat the growth curve of Pet Nation (from 1998 to 2018), the pet economy would reach $285 billion by 2038. By any measure, this is a substantial industry.

As in human medicine, a significant percentage of pet workers share a goal: to increase the affection, love, and social bonding produced by pet ownership. If the looming question of pet supply (that is, do we have enough dogs and cats, but primarily dogs) is addressed, the numbers could exceed the current forecasts. More dogs and cats in more loving homes means more jobs, more commerce, more economic stability for the overall industry, and more science and research dollars to solve pet wellness and supply problems. These three facets of the pet economy knit together to create a galaxy that keeps expanding, comprising pets, companies, and people interacting in commercially innovative ways to solidify the foundation of Pet Nation.

- People who work with and for pets. Some 1.3 million Americans make a living in the pet economy (to compare: Walmart has 1.5 million American employees), servicing animals in professions that mimic those of humans, such as neurologist, trainer, surgeon, dermatologist, psychiatrist, pet hotel concierge, or costume designer. Historically, the animal-based employment opportunities were limited: veterinarian, farrier, blacksmith, jockey, dogcatcher, cowboy, shepherd, rancher, lion tamer, and breeder. The list is longer now and more colorful, including, to note a few:

  ◦ Pet-food tester (not "taster"): evaluating food on various metrics, including smell, flavor, texture, palatability, nutritional content. PhD often required.

  ◦ Animal colorer: an artistic endeavor, akin to a makeup artist, found in film, television, and advertising: the person who paints the ring around the Target dog's eye.

  ◦ Relocation expert: someone who moves dogs safely and efficiently from one place to another—from a shelter to a new country, from a city street to its natural habitat (as with a wild animal), from a breeder to a new home, or from an abusive environment to a safe one.

  ◦ Animal rights lawyer: lawyers specializing in cases involving alleged animal cruelty, breeding restrictions, or the organizational mistreatment of animals.

  ◦ Guide dog trainer: training dogs to help the blind, before adoption and upon introduction of the dog to its new owner.

- Pet adoption counselor: popular with millennials seeking their first dog or cat, counselors work with shelters and prospective owners to find the perfect pet.

- Talent agency: a fast-growing field, representing dogs, cats, and exotics for traditional advertising, digital branding, and influencer work on social media, with some animals earning in six figures (dollars not treats).

- Veterinary acupuncturist: veterinarians who use acupuncture in their practice.

- Pet tracker: a person-and-dog team that tracks lost or runaway pets, using scent and artifacts connected to the lost animal, at distances of five to ten miles.

- Pet psychic: sometimes called "pet communicators," pet psychics help people and pets communicate, addressing problems that vets cannot always solve. They help people understand what their pets are thinking, with some communicating telepathically with the animals.

- Dogs in the corner office. In the old days, dogs and cats stayed at home, in the backyard. Today, a surprising number of dogs (not cats, who are hard to control and perhaps too clever to be put to work) go to work, treats in tow, with Mom and Dad. This is a mini revolution that started quietly, one dog at a time, which has now spread across the country in companies small and large. You will read more about this phenomenon in chapter three.

  - The economic effects of pets in the workplace are both direct and indirect. As the *Los Angeles Times* reported on June 21, 2019, seven thousand dogs "go to work at Amazon facilities each day" with their owners, out of a total Seattle workforce of forty-nine thousand people. That is one dog for every seven people. Unsurprisingly, a "host of dog-oriented enterprises, including doggy daycare and trendy pet-friendly bars and restaurants, contribute to the beehive of activity in the neighborhood where Facebook and other tech firms are also opening offices."

- Pets on the job. Dogs have always worked (hunting, herding, ratting, security), while cats have avoided employment, except for chasing mice on seventeenth-century sailing ships, in eighteenth-century German breweries, nineteenth-century American streets, and in Lower East Side delicatessens.* The job market is evolving in serious ways, witness: psychiatric service, seizure alert, cancer detection (lung cancer, melanoma), allergy detection (especially peanuts), guide dogs, TSA airport security, drug-sniffing dogs, entertainment, TV advertising (with every other ad including a dog or cat, pet influencers are in demand), search and rescue (hurricane and building-collapse rescue), water rescue (Newfoundlands, as big as lifeboats, are great swimmers and good at seaborne rescue), bedbug detection, truffle sniffing, and cadaver detection.

8. "Until Death Do Us Part . . ."

Further proof of the maxim "A dog is man's best friend" lies in the trust men and women place in their dog's or cat's reaction to people, whether casual dates or potential mates. An entire Nissan commercial centered on one test: Did the owner's dog like her new boyfriend? A survey in *Bustle* found that a poll of 3,500 dog parents from the walking service Wag!, conducted by OnePoll, "found that four out of five people think their dog's reaction to a potential partner is an important factor in de-

---

* A South African proverb says that monkeys know how to talk but don't let on to people for fear of being put to work. It is entirely possible that cats know this story.

termining whether or not it's a love match, and 86 percent said they would break up with someone who didn't jive with their dog." And then, what happens when "I do" changes to "I don't"? Pets are considered common property in most states. Alaska and Illinois allow a judge to consider the pet's welfare in a divorce proceeding. In some jurisdictions, judges will grant visitation rights or partial custody.

Who will care for a pet after the owner's death, maintaining the dog or cat or African gray parrot (who can live to one hundred) in the lifestyle to which they've become accustomed? This is not a frivolous question, and a caretaker should be specified in any will and testament. Karl Lagerfeld, the German fashion designer, died February 19, 2019, with an estate estimated at $300 million, which he had said he might leave to his cat. As a German citizen, Lagerfeld could leave all or part of his estate to Choupette, his beloved Birman cat. If Lagerfeld had become a French citizen, poor Choupette would have been "cut out of the will," as they say in the movies.

Why Do We Love Them?

1. Best Friends

If you drive cross-country today, it's worth a stop in Warrensburg, Missouri, to see the statue of Old Drum on the Johnson County Courthouse lawn. In 1870, a man shot and killed a farmer's hunting dog, a foxhound named Old Drum. A lawyer named George Graham Vest represented the farmer in a lawsuit against the killer. In his closing argument, Mr. Vest said, "The one absolutely unselfish friend that a man can have in this selfish world, the one that never deserts him and the one that never proves ungrateful or treacherous is his dog. A man's best friend is his dog." Mr. Vest won the lawsuit, and, in 1958, a memorial melding a statue of Old Drum with Mr. Vest's words was built with donations.

"My dog is my best friend." Today, two out of three dog owners make this assertion. What are they saying? What is rare, unusual, and powerful about a dog? Is this degree of friendship specific to a dog, or can a cat be a best friend, too? Is this the path to human happiness? Does the intensity of an animal's gaze cement this bond?

There is historical precedent for this statement, starting with the poet Homer in the eighth century BC, with his epic poem *The Odyssey*. After twenty years of travel, Odysseus returns home to Ithaca, and his dog, Argos, is the only one to recognize him. To protect his identity, Odysseus cannot acknowledge Argos, and the dog, who has been neglected during his absence, is confused and as heartbroken as Odysseus. King Frederick of Prussia (1740–1786) is the first person on record to say, "A dog is man's best friend," referring to one of his Italian Greyhounds. The French philosopher Voltaire might have scooped him, though, since, in 1764, he wrote in his *Dictionnaire philosophique*, "It seems that nature has given the dog to man for his defense and for his pleasure. Of all the animals it is the most faithful: it is the best friend man can have."

The transformation from vicious guard dog to man's best friend is complete. The qualities that inspired Homer, King Frederick, and Voltaire (although not recognized by the public in early cultures) are the same adjectives quoted in conversation and hundreds of blogs today: "loyal," "trustworthy," "nonjudgmental," "affectionate," "uncomplicated," "amusing," "steadfast," "loving," "unconditional in their love," "unwavering," "comforting," "unquestioning," "uncritical." A random sampling of quotations underlines the singular nature of a dog's companionship:

> **"Dogs love their friends and bite their enemies,**
> **quite unlike people, who are incapable of pure love**
> **and always have to mix love and hate."**
> ~SIGMUND FREUD

> **"To his dog, every man is Napoleon."**
> ~ALDOUS HUXLEY

> "Until one has loved an animal a part of
> one's soul remains unawakened."
> ~ANATOLE FRANCE

Why do people talk to their pets? Because pets listen. They don't argue or interrupt, unlike friends, family, and business colleagues. How many times a day does the average pet owner tell their pet, "I love you"? Twenty, thirty, perhaps forty? Do pets answer? Yes, as Martin Buber wrote in *I and Thou*: "An animal's eyes have the power to speak a great language." There is a modern digital-pet paradox: even as people retreat *into* their phones and adopt digital animojis, or talk to Amazon's Alexa as if she's an old family friend, they want more real, breathing dogs and cats in their lives. Though millennials may be characterized as being especially allergic to chance, there is one zone in life where they are willing to take a leap—pets. They buy a pet and everything changes.

Helicopter moms and dad are now everywhere, monitoring pets as well as children. As the human birth rate declines, people transfer the mothering and fathering tendency to pets. Pets connect the dots between people, between people and themselves, and between people and society. Pets and people forge a new identity: my friend Ashley is no longer "Ashley," she's become instead "Ashley and Bailey and Toby" (her two Shih Tzus).

2. "My Cat Is My Best Friend . . ."

Do people say this? They do, but not as often as dog owners declare allegiance. Why? When people make this cat statement online, they sometimes wonder aloud if it is odd to say so, as if there is something innately different about cats and dogs. They quote many of the same qualities: dependability, unconditional love, nonjudgmental, loyalty, but other words enter the vocabulary: "independence," "wisdom," "freedom," "superiority," "philosophical," "focus." Their love is no less fervent, but they calibrate their relationship differently. While man's control of dogs underlies the dog owner's declaration of love, cat people enjoy admitting that cats are smarter than they are, and, having been anointed by cats, they themselves are, therefore, somehow superior to *cynophilists.**

"Children, old crones, peasants, and dogs ramble;
cats and philosophers stick to their point."
~H. P. LOVECRAFT

"Owners of dogs will have noticed that,
if you provide them with food and water and shelter
and affection, they will think you are God.
Whereas owners of cats are compelled to realize that,
if you provide them with food and water and affection,
they draw the conclusion that they are God."
~CHRISTOPHER HITCHENS

"As anyone who has ever been around a cat
for any length of time well knows, cats have enormous
patience with the limitations of the human kind."
~CLEVELAND AMORY

"No, I never thought I would like cats."
~KARL LAGERFELD

"I have studied many philosophers and many cats.
The wisdom of cats is infinitely superior."
~HIPPOLYTE TAINE

---

* *Cynophilist:* A person who loves dogs.

ECONOMICS

The proof that Americans love pets is in the spending. From 1998 to 2018, the total annual amount of money spent on pets in the United States increased from $23 billion to $90.5 billion, an astonishing 393 percent increase. In 2019, it reached $95.7 billion. During this period, the dog population increased from sixty million to ninety million, and cats from seventy-three million to ninety-five million. People spend more on dogs than cats, primarily for veterinary visits and boarding, but dogs also receive more treats, toys, and visits to the groomer (2017–2018 National Pet Owners Survey, from the American Pet Products Association [APPA]).

- On average, American families spend $1,125 per year on their pets, a 393 percent increase from 1998. According to an August 2019 study, their annual spend, by species (including food, litter, and medical costs), is:

  - Cat: $1,140

  - Dog: $1,836

- If pet spending continues at the current pace, it will be more than a $120-plus billion industry in 2027 and will exceed $240 billion by 2035, nearly the size of the smartphone industry. This is a new way of life for two of three households, with pets in the middle of everything. "Talk to any pet owner and they'll tell you how difficult it is to put a dollar limit on what they'd spend to give their loyal companion a happy life," says APPA president and CEO Bob Vetere, "and it's this outlook that continues to drive growth."

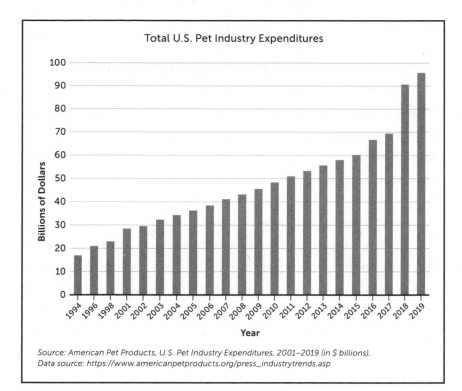

Total U.S. Pet Industry Expenditures

Source: American Pet Products, U.S. Pet Industry Expenditures, 2001–2019 (in $ billions).
Data source: https://www.americanpetproducts.org/press_industrytrends.asp

The steep grade of this graph says it all. The climb is measured in billions of dollars. The regularity of the increases is pegged to the steady increase in the pet population. People shop everywhere it is efficient and economical: pet shops, big-box retailers, though online rules.

How do pet owners spend this money? Food is the clear winner.

Pet Spending by Category in the United States, 2016–2019 (in $ billions)

Year	Food	Supplies/ Live Animals/OTC Med	Vet	Other**	Total	Year Increase %
2019	36.90	19.20	29.30	10.30	95.70	5.0%
2018*	34.50	18.60	27.70	9.70	90.50	30.0%
2017	29.07	17.21	17.07	6.16	69.51	4.1%
2016	28.23	16.81	15.95	5.60	66.59	

National Pet Owners Association Survey for American Pet Products Association
* 2018 figures have been restated using APPA's new research methodology.
**"Other" includes grooming, boarding, walking, training, and other services.

IMPLICATIONS

The tsunami of changes that have occurred in two decades (economic, social, legal, and political), and their combined effect on the American psyche, is the story of this book—how and why they occurred, and the implications for American society in the future. Chapter six delves into these issues, in depth, and the surprising and controversial results spread across the Pet Nation map.

Apart from the size of their populations, the animals themselves have not changed—dogs still chase balls and cats still chase string. They still don't live as long as we wish they would. *We* are the ones who've changed. People have fundamentally changed in the way they consider pets, treat them, and live with them. This behavioral shift set in motion a juggernaut of changes in the lives of all Americans, both the "haves" and the "have-nots."

Are Americans happier today with more dogs and cats and tropical fish? Unquestionably yes. That is, those who have pets. Emotionally. Physically. Perhaps even spiritually. Every year, the number of pet owners rises, as does the number of people who acquire a second, third, or fourth pet.

Are pets happier? Science says so, as you'll see in chapter four. A significant percentage of our 185 million pets would preface their answers to this question with a gobsmacked "Duh? You can't be serious?"

"Would you like to be tied to a tree?"

"We live indoors now and do not miss the rain."

"Some say we are 'pampered.' We say, 'We are loved at last. Appreciated for who we are.'"

"Most of us live in loving homes with plenty of food, heat, and TV."

"Doghouses are for museum exhibitions. Why don't you turn them into kindling?"

"No more euthanizing! It's about time!"

"No more running from dogcatchers."

The pet revolution is in full swing. The pet paradigm has changed. We think differently about pets today. Who they are. What they do. What they mean to us. How they should live. How our lives intersect. How they affect our relationships with other people. People who never thought about pets are now obsessed with them. Dogs and cats went from a position of subservience—animals with little inherent value in society—to a position of privilege and dominance. The pet economy rocketed from $23 billion to $95.7 billion in twenty years, while many industries stagnated or retreated.

Pet Nation tells two interlocking stories: the transformation of pets in American society and the radical changes Americans themselves have undergone due to pets. In chapter three, I explore the advance of pets into public and private spaces that were previously off-limits. In chapter four, I discuss the human-animal bond. In chapter five, we confront the surprising news that we are running out of dogs in America. Then, in chapter six, we examine the strange, but common, legal and political battles of Pet Nation, followed by a study of pet health care in chapter seven. I wrap up our story with a look at exotic pets—birds and fish and many other animals—then tell you where I think Pet Nation is going next.

But before we get to all of that, in the next chapter, I will reveal how this happened in the first place. Who flipped the switch on Pet Nation? Why did it blast off so suddenly and flamboyantly? You'll have to wait until the final chapter to see if it will ever slow down.

· 2 ·

HOW PETS WENT VIRAL

I f you lived in Europe before the 1860s, there were three reasons to get a dog: (1) to hunt game birds, such as ducks, pheasant, grouse, and woodcock; (2) to herd sheep and cattle; and (3) to catch rats in barns, granaries, and breweries. Cats were also put to work. Although they didn't herd sheep or find partridge in the English forest, they were excellent mousers and ratters. If you visit the historic Jameson whiskey distillery in Dublin today, you will see their legendary eighteenth-century mouser Smitty displayed in all his taxidermied glory. Dogs worked on farms, estates, and industrial sites; cats were freelance, *non-union* workers. It was only in the mid-nineteenth century, in London, that people began to acquire dogs for companionship and pleasure. Initially a fashionable pastime of the well-to-do, the practice soon spread to the middle and working classes, promoted by annual dog shows in major English cities, which attracted thousands of paying visitors.

America emulated England in the use of dogs, employing them for hunting, herding, and even catching mice in breweries (in 1898, there were forty-eight breweries in Brooklyn alone). However, during the twentieth century, the need for working dogs declined. In 1920, 32 percent of Americans lived and worked on farms, dropping to 2 percent in 2018. Today, the 98 percent of Americans living in cities, suburbs, and small towns rarely go pheasant-hunting, and breweries are gleaming, high-tech facilities, often located in bland, suburban shopping malls, sending mice scurrying for new lodging.

As the American human population jumped from 106 million in 1920 to 249 million in 1990, did life improve for dogs? Paradoxically, as dogs became civilized, city animals, technically part of the family, became less important. Where did they go? Outside. To the backyard. For much of the twentieth century, dogs were often tied to trees and lived in small, wooden doghouses, exposed to the cold. Even then, it was understood that the doghouse was not a good place to be; husbands who came home tipsy from the Christmas office party would land in the metaphorical doghouse. The inferior status of dogs lasted well into the final decades of the twentieth century. Consider that, in the early 1990s, more than ten million American dogs were euthanized each year. Today, with thirty million more dogs in America, the number of dogs euthanized annually has shrunk to 770,000.

Seemingly oblivious of people, cats had their own behavior codes.* They, too, were second-class citizens, though even less a part of the household. Cats spent their first one hundred years (1775–1875) in America catching rats and mice. Then, after the stray-cat population spun out of control and public sanitation evolved in large Eastern cities (1875–1925), mass euthanasia became common. It wasn't until the mid-1900s that these independent animals began to change into pets. They lived on the periphery, cozying up to people when they felt like it, often bonding with only one family member. Still, cats were low-maintenance and less expensive than dogs. (For many years there was a popular myth

---

* A friend's tabby cat in Oxford, Mississippi, died in 1972 at the age of twelve, was buried by the whole family in a backyard ceremony, and then, three days later, marched into the house during Sunday dinner, alive and in a foul mood from that day forward.

that cats could heal themselves, so owners rarely took them to the vet.) Cats roamed the neighborhood, where backyard birds were easy to catch, a delectable, low-cost treat.

EUTHANASIA

The word "euthanasia" is derived from the Greek prefix *eu*, meaning "well, easily" and *thanatos*, which means "death." In Greek mythology, *Thanatos* was the personification of nonviolent death, with a gentle touch like that of his brother, Hypnos, the god of sleep. Violent death was the province of their sisters, the Keres, spirits of slaughter and disease.

The modern meaning of "euthanasia" is to painlessly put to death the hopelessly invalid (human or animal). While the process of putting a dog or cat to sleep is mechanically easy, via the injection of an overdose of pentobarbital, a drug used in surgery to induce unconsciousness, there is nothing emotionally easy about it for either the person or family saying goodbye to their beloved pet, or the veterinarian, who often grows close to an animal during long years of care and treatment.

AN EXPLOSION THAT
ROCKED THE PET WORLD

In the twentieth century, with more Americans trading farm life for the city, one would expect the rate of dog acquisition to decline. Dogs were a legal and logistical challenge, and many apartment buildings outlawed pets, especially big dogs. With longer work commutes and fragmented schedules, people had less time to walk, feed, and play with their pets. As their lives became more complicated, why would people assume an additional financial burden? Still, despite these demographic trends, dog ownership remained stable. From 1975 to 1998, the American dog population hovered around sixty-two million, while the human population grew 1 to 1.5 percent annually. Then, the remarkable rise in pet ownership began. What drove this growth?

If you google "Why get a dog?" today, you'll find many answers, but no mention of grouse hunting, herding Dorset sheep, or chasing mice around the hayloft. Instead, the answers sound like an advertisement for a yoga studio. The collective wisdom of the Internet tells us that dogs will: (1) keep you "happy, healthy, and help you lose some weight"; (2) keep your mind "engaged and active"; (3) teach you to "relax and be Zen"; (4) "make you laugh"; and (5) "be your loyal friend for life." Given the low esteem in which dogs were held for most of the twentieth century, this is a surprisingly upbeat response.

SOCIAL MISFITS

The word "dysfunctional" is frequently applied to many aspects of modern American life: family, personal relationships, marriages, corporations, Congress. Some apply this label to American society in general, arguing that any culture in which a meaningful percentage of the population is isolated, alienated, and lonely should be classified as *dysfunctional*. Are Americans lonelier today, more isolated? Has that changed our relationship with pets? Are dogs and cats the beneficiaries of our discomfort?

Though the divorce rate in the United States has dropped 18 percent since 2008, in part a function of a declining national marriage rate, the underlying statistics remain discouraging. Fifty percent of all marriages fail within eight years. More people live alone. Both marriage and co-habitation are slowing. College graduates live with their parents into their thirties. Millennials wait longer to get married, or simply don't marry at all. Countries all over the world, including the United States, have declining birth rates, a frequent outcome of deferred marriage patterns.

TELE

The Greek word *tele* means "far." It is the key to several English words that permeate modern life, which have contributed to the high level of dysfunction in our society: "telephone," "television," "telecommunication," "telecommute." *Tele* words are magical, since, with each one, something (a message, a voice, a photograph, a movie, or a person who works from home) travels a distance instantaneously, even thousands of miles. Unfortunately, distance = separation from people, who cannot be touched or seen without an electronic intermediary. Many of these *tele* words have created opportunities for pets, who are present, here and now, to satisfy the human need for companionship. As we will see later in this chapter and in chapter three's analysis of pets in the workplace, pets would soon come to replace or to "stand in" for people, closing some of the emotional gaps that technology unintentionally creates.

Doubtless, the instability of modern social life contributes to this reluctance to settle down. My father, a country lawyer, lived to the age of eighty-three and worked for two law firms in forty-five years of practice. This wasn't unusual from 1900 to 1975, when Americans often worked at a single company throughout a career. Today, the average American will work for ten to fifteen companies in their lifetime, according to the US Bureau of Labor Statistics. People are no longer rooted in a company or a community, geographically close to their immediate and extended families. In 2018, seventy-eight thousand Americans died of an opioid overdose, an astonishing one out of every four thousand people. It's not a surprise that the national suicide rate—129 each day and rising—is at its highest level in history.

If pets make people happy, or save people from loneliness, then, in an era of rising depression or uncertainty, it could make sense to get a dog or cat. As Simon Kuper wrote in the *Financial Times*, describing political tribes today, "In our atomised societies, ever more adults are single, don't identify with their jobs and don't belong to a clear economic class, religious grouping or trade union." Pets provide friendship, diversion, amusement, identity—someone to watch TV with, even if the furry companion sleeps fifteen hours a day and slumbers through the complete cycle of *The Crown*.

But social dysfunction alone is perhaps too simple an explanation. While all forms of social dislocation are disruptive—divorce, low marriage rate, declining birth rate, depression, job shocks, drug abuse, alienation, suicide—none of these factors individually is sufficient to explain the rapid growth of Pet Nation. After all, people were unhappy long before 1998, and America has experienced previous eras of social upheaval.

THE RISE OF PET NATION

You might blame it on Lassie.

To be fair, it wasn't entirely her fault. It was a joint effort uniting that fictional Collie, arguably the most famous dog in history, and technologies from a constellation of nineteenth-century scientists, inventors, and entrepreneurs, including Alexander Graham Bell.* But how could Lassie share a sentence with eminent scientists who transformed the way the whole world communicates?

The answer lies at the intersection of certain Victorian obsessions: electricity, the telephone, the telegram, the encyclopedia, the typewriter, the paperback book, letter writing, and the dog show. The descendants

---

* At the age of seventeen, before inventing the telephone, Alexander Graham Bell taught his Skye Terrier, Trouvé, to say "How are you, Grandma?"

of these nineteenth-century obsessions (the Internet, Apple, Google, Facebook, YouTube, Instagram, Amazon, the Westminster Kennel Club Dog Show), coupled with America's unbridled love for dogs and cats, enable eighty-five million American households today to: find, study, discover, acquire, outfit, feed, medicate, surveil, microchip, photograph, and show off pets in greater numbers, at all hours of the day and night, at home, at work, on the subway, with people like themselves all over the world, faster, at greater expense, and with greater abandon than ever before.

THE VICTORIAN EIGHT

1. **Electricity** → the Internet → Amazon
2. **The telephone** → iPhone
3. **The telegram** → Text messaging
4. **The encyclopedia** → Google → Wikipedia
5. **The typewriter** → Computer → iMac → Smartphone
6. **The paperback book** → Movies → TV → YouTube → Instagram → Snapchat
7. **Letter writing** → Facebook
8. **Dog shows** → Westminster Kennel Club → Petfinder

How and Why Did Pet Nation Happen?

Though they didn't realize it, Americans in the mid-1990s were on the cusp of a tectonic shift in behavior intertwined with the Internet and the digital tools it spawned. From 1992 onward, the pace of change quickened, as astonishing new products migrated from academia to industry to the general public. The abundance of innovations gave people new opportunities and new problems, shaping their behavior—new things to remember (passwords, keystroke commands) and old things to forget (phone numbers, directions). Cameras, printed road maps, photo albums, letter openers, file cabinets—all familiar objects—were rendered obsolete by the Internet and digital media.

In 1991, the Internet belonged to academics and the US Department of Defense; in 1992, it broke loose. Suddenly, it went from being a place to occasionally go, hence the phrase "to go online" (with "@" or ".com" replacing the postal code), to being inseparable from daily life. Walking down the street changed; talking to people changed; what people did before falling asleep at night or upon waking changed. No one understood how radically their lives would change. And it all changed for dogs and cats, too. Ironically, both the good and bad ramifications were beneficial to pets.

MEDIA PETS: Dogs and Cats and Mice and . . .

As it turned out, the liberators of dogs and cats were a different set of dogs and cats altogether, along with some other two- and four-legged creatures. And they were hiding in plain sight—in neighborhood theaters, on network television, in the funny papers, in comic books, picture books, and later in video games—wherever people went for thirty minutes to forget their troubles, to laugh or to get lost in a good story.

Media dogs and cats, plus some mice, ducks, a skunk, a bird or two, a frog, and a female pig with platinum-blond hair and a flashy wardrobe, had been slowly domesticating pets since the 1920s. And none more than Lassie, the Victorian heroine who blossomed in the 1940s and became the first true "media pet."*

---

*If a pet is defined as a "domestic or tamed animal kept for companionship or pleasure," a media pet is its first cousin, broadly, "a pet created by the media, whether a book, cartoon, movie, or software program, adopted or enjoyed for companionship or pleasure."

Together, these fictional animals had a profound effect on the public imagination and the lives of people during the twentieth century. This was a function of the intangible treasures they brought to the world. These media pets provided audiences with heroes, laughter, companions, dreams, memories, and a big dose of attitude. When everyday life is difficult, people want distractions and, as the twentieth century descended into chaos, they fell for movies, animated films, cartoons, and television.

Media pets emerged in the first half of the twentieth century, a dark period in history. In the space of twenty-five years, the world suffered two world wars and the Great Depression. These cataclysmic forces redrew maps and changed the world's political, financial, and religious status quo. Laughter and fun went missing from the world. People needed a tonic, and they found it in mass entertainment. Dreamers like Walt Disney came to the rescue, inventing a cast of unforgettable animal characters who made people laugh, cry, and forget their troubles, if only briefly.

Anthropomorphized animals became Walt Disney's cinematic troupe, and these spirited creatures found themselves playing and scheming in the world of humans, far from the farms and fields and factories where beer was brewed and rats were rampant. It was a radical break from the persona that dogs and cats had been shoehorned into in the previous century. These stories transformed the way we think about animals and, by extension, pets. They reframed our perception of what a dog or cat is, or can be. It was a skillful, if completely accidental, public relations campaign for pets.

Heroes

We begin with real-life animals, heroic, flesh-and-blood dogs with waggly tails, who were bigger than life on TV and movie screens. These brave pets became famous for saving people, running, jumping, and doing the heartwarming things that real dogs can do. People all over the world fell in love with canine heroes like Lassie, Strongheart, Rin Tin Tin, and later with Benji, Hachi, and many others.

"Hie thee, Lassie, hie thee home!"

Lassie was the first canine superstar, but she was no overnight success. It took her eighty years to become a media sensation, yet she is still a commanding figure. Her creator, Elizabeth Cleghorn Gaskell, was an English novelist, the first biographer of Charlotte Brontë, and a confidante of Charles Dickens. When she published *The Half-brothers* in 1859, Mrs. Gaskell could not have imagined that the fictional Lassie and her descendants would build a bridge from printed books to motion pictures. Lassie's story is told in fifty books, eleven films, two radio shows, and sixteen television series, including an Emmy Award–winning franchise that ran for nineteen years. Lassie-branded product merchandising continues to this day.

The Half-brothers is fraught with action and suspense—storytelling elements that became Lassie's narrative signature. Two teenaged half-brothers, Gregory and the unnamed narrator, are lost in the mountains in a dangerous snowstorm. The boys realize that their brave Collie, Lassie, is their only hope of rescue from the ice and snow.

The Half-brothers

"'Oh, Gregory, don't you know the way home?'"

"'I thought I did when I set out, but I am doubtful now. The snow blinds me . . .'"

"'I can go no farther . . .'"

"'It is of no use. . . . Our only chance is in Lassie.'"

"'I pulled out my pocket-handkerchief . . . Gregory took it, and tied it round Lassie's neck.'"

"'Hie thee, Lassie, hie thee home!'"

"'And the white-faced ill-favoured brute was off like a shot in the darkness.'"

The boys lie down, huddling together for warmth, remembering their departed mother . . .

Three hours afterward, . . . Lassie came home, with the handkerchief tied round her neck. They knew and understood, and the whole strength of the farm was turned out to follow her, . . . I lay in chilly sleep, but still alive, beneath the rock that Lassie guided them to. I was covered over with my brother's plaid . . . He was in his shirt-sleeves—his arm thrown over me—a quiet smile (he had hardly ever smiled in life) upon his still, cold face.

Gregory has died, but Lassie has saved the day, as she will in a thousand future incarnations.

It's worth noting that there is an alternate (or companion) theory to the Lassie legend, proposed by Nigel Clarke, in his book *Shipwreck Guide to Dorset and South Devon*. This nonfiction account illuminates the power of the human-animal bond. Clarke tells the story of a half Collie named Lassie, who revived Able Seaman John Cowan after a German torpedo attack on the Royal Navy battleship *Formidable* during World War I that took five hundred lives. Lying among the bodies in a makeshift morgue in the Pilot Boat, a pub in Lyme Regis, South Devon, John Cowan was presumed to be dead. Sensing that he was still alive, Lassie, the pub owner's dog, found Cowan, licked his face repeatedly, lay on top of him, and kept him warm. John Cowan recovered fully. The incident was widely reported, an indication that animals have powers we can't always explain.

Lassie is perhaps the most enduring, best-loved dog in history. The original Lassie story was inspiring—showcasing powers unique to a dog—and invented a character whose appeal has spanned three centuries. Lassie 2.0 had a long gestation, beginning in 1938 with *Lassie Come Home*, first as a short story, then a novel in 1940, then the 1943 film with Elizabeth Taylor. Lassie had arrived in the twentieth century with bravado. She then captured the American imagination via television, a new medium that needed a constant supply of heroes and heroines. From 1954 to 1973, through 591 episodes, people tuned their TV sets to CBS every Sunday night to watch Lassie run through the fields to rescue Timmy and other characters. It became the fifth-longest-running show in television history, with nine different dogs playing the part, all descendants of Pal, the original TV Lassie.

Some Dogs Don't Talk and Some Never Stop Talking

There are twenty fictional animal characters with stars on the Hollywood Walk of Fame, seventeen of whom are cartoon or puppet characters, such as Mickey Mouse, Donald Duck, Snoopy, Godzilla, and Kermit the Frog (Miss Piggy is strangely absent). Only three are live-action animals: Lassie and two male German Shepherds—one named Strongheart, an abandoned German police dog, and the other Rin Tin Tin. Both German Shepherds came to America after World War I and became silent film stars in the 1920s. These were brave and charismatic dogs who helped popularize the German Shepherd breed in the United States.

Rin Tin Tin

A powerfully built German Shepherd who could jump eleven feet high, Rin Tin Tin was born to be a movie star. A nursing puppy, he was rescued by an American serviceman who named him Rin Tin Tin and took him home to California. In his first film, Rin Tin Tin was a stand-in for an ornery wolf who misbehaved on set. His first starring role, in 1923, was in the movie *Where the North Begins*, which helped save Warner Bros. from bankruptcy. All of his twenty-seven films were successful. His renown was international; Anne Frank wanted a dog like him and wrote about him in her World War II diary. When Rin Tin Tin died in

1932, there was great sadness around the world. His longtime owner, Corporal Duncan, sold his home so he could afford to return Rin Tin Tin to his native France, to be buried in a pet cemetery outside Paris.

"Mommy, can we get a puppy?"

Working dogs like Rin Tin Tin and Strongheart were formidable creatures, with extraordinary physical powers, surviving on farms, in breweries, in saltwater marshes. Schnauzers, Terriers, Affenpinschers, Dachshunds—these were not cuddly breeds. They were fast, explosive, aggressive dogs doing rough work. Collies and Retrievers were at the gentle end of this spectrum, but they were almost exclusively dogs for men—shepherds, farmers, grown men in deerstalker caps and tweed jackets shooting guns at defenseless birds, and big guys in leather aprons brewing beer. These dogs hadn't been groomed for indoor living or a stroll in a manicured city park.

Children watching brave dogs like Lassie or Rin Tin Tin wanted to have a dog of their own. Suddenly, the question, "Mommy, can we get a puppy?" became a popular refrain in American homes. Parents resisted, perennially questioning the cost and inconvenience of owning a house pet, but they started to come around. It sometimes took an entire generation for this change to occur, as in my own family. Sometimes, people needed another kind of pet altogether.

Laughter

Cartoon animals have had a different, but no less hypnotic, effect on people. They began their lives in animation studios, painted into existence by talented artists. They entered the entertainment world in the 1920s, in animated films contemporaneous with Rin Tin Tin. While live-action dogs were brave and protective, the Disney dogs (Pluto and Goofy) and the rest of their menagerie were whimsical characters who made people laugh with antic, slapstick, side-splitting, therapeutic humor. It began with Mickey, and it never stopped: Minnie Mouse, Donald Duck, Daisy Duck, Pluto, Goofy, Garfield, Woody Woodpecker, Bugs Bunny, Tom and Jerry, the Road Runner, Wile E. Coyote, Snoopy, Porky Pig, Miss Piggy, on and on . . . making people happy as animals do.

In 1928, a little mouse named Mickey, wearing red shorts, yellow shoes, and white gloves, replaced Oswald the Lucky Rabbit in a cartoon called *Steamboat Willie* and changed the entertainment world forever. This little creature with the squeaky voice was Mickey Mouse. The world fell in love with Mickey Mouse from the first animated cell. Inspired by a real-life tame mouse at Laugh-O-Gram Studio in Kansas City, Missouri, where Walt Disney began his career, Mickey has since entertained the world in nearly every entertainment medium. It is impossible to quantify the economic effect this cartoon mouse has had on the company and the larger industry. An international hero, the subject of museum exhibitions, Mickey celebrated his ninetieth birthday in 2018 and is still going strong.

Companions

Kids love pals, and what sidekick is better than a dog they can sneak through the window into their bedroom? Smaller dogs, more their size, offset their stature with spirit and loyalty. Hollywood delivered them with plenty of attitude, like Pete the Pup in *The Little Rascals* and Toto in *The Wizard of Oz*, Dorothy's feisty and loyal companion.

To save poor Toto from Miss Almira Gulch's dastardly euthanasia scheme, Dorothy runs away with her little dog. Adventures ensue in the Land of Oz. Ten of the most chilling words in movie history involve Toto, when Margaret Hamilton, the Wicked Witch, cackles to Dorothy, "I'll get you, my pretty. And your little dog, too!" When Dorothy finally wakes up at home in Kansas, safe at last, Toto is beside her as she says the famous words, "There's no place like home," and, for her, home means Toto. Terry, the brindle Cairn Terrier who played Toto, earned $125 per week, double the salary of a Munchkin. A memorial honoring Terry for her work is found at the Hollywood Forever cemetery in Los Angeles. Fittingly, it is also the resting place of Judy Garland, Toto's movie friend and companion.

Dreams

Why did 350 million people around the world love Snoopy for fifty years and beyond? Sure, he loved cookies. Almost as much as he loved Lucy, who, alas, spurned him. No, people loved Snoopy because this cheerful, good-natured beagle was a dreamer. Dreaming is a fundamental part of human life and, clearly, animal life, too. He had a wild imagination: one moment he is in college, Mr. Joe Cool; the next a famous writer; and then a flying ace in World War I. It didn't matter that most of Snoopy's fantasies came to naught, it was the fact that he dreamed big. In a 1997 interview, Charles Schulz said of Snoopy's character: "He has to retreat into his fanciful world in order to survive. I don't envy dogs the lives they have to live." If Charles Schulz were alive today in Pet Nation, he would likely soften his opinion of Snoopy's plight.

Attitude

People laugh when little dogs or ten-pound cats go after big dogs. They see a five-pound Yorkshire Terrier tear into a massive, muscular Bullmastiff twenty-five times his weight. Legs spin, cartoon-style, as he hammers the Mastiff in his best Yorkshire accent. Confusing the Yorkie with a wind-up toy, the Mastiff barely notices. We can learn a lot from this fearless behavior.

In the long-running television series *Frasier* (1993–2004), Frasier

Crane pontificated, Niles dithered, Daphne tempted, Roz fooled around, Martin sounded off, and Eddie, a Jack Russell Terrier with a major attitude, taunted and stared at Frasier, sometimes eating meals that Frasier had prepared for his would-be girlfriends. Eddie wasn't bashful about sharing his opinions, behavior we have all experienced with dogs and cats. After a long and successful career, including an autobiography, *My Life as a Dog*, by Brian Hargrove, Moose, the real-life Eddie, retired in Los Angeles, where he died at the age of fifteen.

Memories

After a family's first trip to Disneyland, a young girl returns home with her Mickey Mouse hat. It finds a special place in her bedroom, a talisman and a memory, for her a link to Mickey, for Mickey a foot in the door. Through merchandising, media pets slipped inside the home. Since 1930, merchandise has been an important part of their profile (hats, coffee mugs, notebooks, sunglasses, T-shirts, et cetera). All manner of products followed the books and movies that featured our favorite four-legged stars, reminders of a happy trip and of what a great friend a pet can be.

SUSIE

George Edward Stanhope Molyneux Herbert, 5th Earl of Carnarvon, was an English aristocrat who financed the excavation of Tutankhamen's tomb in Egypt in the 1920s. On March 19, 1923, Lord Carnarvon suffered a mosquito bite, then septic poisoning, and died on April 5, 1923, in Cairo. At 2:00 a.m., the moment of Lord Carnarvon's death, his faithful dog, Susie, back home in England at Highclere Castle, the site of the television series *Downton Abbey*, let out a howl and died. Lord Carnarvon and Susie are buried on a hill overlooking Highclere.

Lassie created a template that media pets have followed ever since: cinema, television, books, then branded products. Some of the media critters turned that platform into entire industries, such as Mickey Mouse, Snoopy, Garfield, the Muppets. These are formative influences in American culture, anchored in childhood storytelling and the digital swagger of cartoons.

Pets made their way into American lives with people of all ages. Pets became less foreign. People found that pets comfort the soul. The health and social benefits of having pets would come later. But even then, cartoons were fun, unpredictable; films followed the same lighthearted formula. Movies like *Beethoven* and *Beverly Hills Chihuahua* are lighthearted family comedies, a far cry from Strongheart's first movie *The Silent Call*, the story of a dog-wolf mix accused by ranchers of killing sheep and sentenced to death, that, luckily, ends on a happier note.

Picture books and animated films make people happy. The archetypes who populate them (dogs, cats, mice, rabbits, frogs) and their real-life equivalents (dogs and cats from the pound, the pet shop, or the neighbor's litter) underwent a gradual transformation in public media, a social and personality makeover. They became safer—positive, welcome, and uplifting—fit for socializing, ready to enter the front door of the house. Still it would take seventy-five years for the marriage of pets and the media to jell.

WELCOME TO 2020

We have enjoyed a century of theatrical animals from live-action to animated and comic-strip. Toward the tail end of this period, in the 1980s, computer animation began to evolve. New pets and pet memes appeared on YouTube in 2006, and then on Instagram. It isn't that the social media platforms created genetically new animals, it's that pets journeyed into a new and different universe, a world of pixels, texting, likes, followers, LED screens, and tweeting, far from city parks and grassy meadows. Are they dogs and cats or marketing constructs? Is a "meme cat" a cat, or is it a meme? Is a meme cat a new kind of cat altogether?

PET NATION TAKES SHAPE

Pet Nation is not simply a function of pets and people. Without three additional factors—tech, media, and commerce—it would not have happened so fast, at such a scale, or been sustained. It might not have happened at all. It isn't pure technological innovation that changed people's lives, it is the corresponding changes that tech brought, directly and indirectly, to the lives of pets and people. As animal welfare improved, the emotional lives of pet owners did, too.

Tech

Pet data, resources, stories, and information can be summoned with a few mouse clicks, then shared instantly between households around the world. This is thanks to the communication infrastructure that began with the inventions of Alexander Graham Bell and Samuel Morse. Without their work, which led to the Internet, messaging, and the iPhone, the process to find a modern Lassie could take months. There was too much random, unreliable information to gather from disparate sources. However, on an iPhone, this exercise would take thirty minutes today, delivering a Lassie surrogate that has been vaccinated, house-trained, and socialized, ready for a loving home.

From 1998 to 2018, the rise of Pet Nation coincided with the commercial growth of the digital world. There were gains in every segment of the pet economy, aided by digital tools. And, yet, Facebook didn't *make* people adopt more cats and dogs. Nor did Instagram *force* people to buy a Halloween pirate suit for their three-year-old Collie. More people began to do more pet things with more digital things: read, research, rescue, buy, walk, train, go to the dog run, share photos, on and on. Yes, shopping became simpler, since you could sit in bed at 2:00 a.m., after your three-month-old had finally gone back to sleep, and shop online for bulk dog food. But it wasn't only the efficiency, since many industries, such as travel, music publishing, and office products contracted during this era.

Dogs and cats didn't change, *people* changed. And social media was the change agent, linking people across their passions, in endless permutations, gathering them into tribes: Pug to Pug, Pembroke Welsh Corgi to Pembroke Welsh Corgi. Suddenly, people could meet hundreds of people online to talk about pets. The world unfolded into a broader, more textured online community. Yet it was still online, with correspondents who could vanish with a keystroke, without a physical trace. For people who didn't want commitment, that was a plus; for others, sadly, most online relationships never traveled offline.

Bring on the Kittens and the Puppies

The technical foundation of Pet Nation unfolded in three stages, from 1984 to 1998, 1999 to 2007, and 2008 to 2018. Each period gave people more and better tools that made the pet world easier to navigate. This allowed potential pet owners to: (1) become fully aware of pets; (2) figure out where pets were; and (3) get pets quickly, now, no matter the cost, along with whatever else they needed.

Entrepreneurs overlaid pets onto tech. Before long, iPhones and pets would sync, yielding the pet selfie, texting would emerge in all its twisted glory to celebrate pets, and the American cityscape would change. Goodbye, doghouse; hello, bedroom.

Stage 1 (1984–1998): Typewriter → Digital Vacuum → Computer → Internet → Email → DIGITAL HEAVEN

1984 was a prophetic year. Not only is 1984 the title of George Orwell's harrowing novel of a totalitarian state, it is also the year a band of Apple warriors launched the Macintosh computer in the iconic Super Bowl commercial. If you were born in 1984 or after, you may never have used a typewriter at all or considered it a relic from the analog past. The Macintosh, which democratized computing, sounded the death knell for this machine. Nevertheless, without this ingenious 1868 invention, the personal computer and, later, the iPhone, would not have unlocked the gates to Pet Nation, with the new global addiction: *instant access to all information in the entire world.* Today, everyone is a typist.

The Internet, email, and the personal computer (more design and publishing instrument than office machine) were the components of a new way of life that changed pet life. People began to "go online," but it still wasn't that easy. Desktop computers were bulky and needed power cords. Brick-like mobile phones were a relative rarity. The process of finding and acquiring pets and supplies was still analog: drive to the local shelter, pet shop, or breeder, if you could find one, to buy your dog, cat, or parakeet. Then drive to the local store, Safeway, Petco, or PetSmart, the evolving pet superstores, to shop for pet food and supplies. Walk, drive, and carry it all home yourself. Online delivery was not an option.

Stage 2 (1999–2007): Digital Heaven → Human Isolation → INDIVIDUAL LONELINESS

With a cascade of innovations, the digital world erupted. It changed color. Sped up. Flowered. Shifted into high gear: Google (1998), Facebook (2004), YouTube (2006), and then, a watershed year, the iPhone in 2007. The earth was suddenly mobile, the smartphone pervasive, *The Whole Earth Catalog* went online. Pet Nation could begin to scale. The iPhone was the tool, and Google Search the routine, the path to knowledge, yielding everything about dogs and cats you could ever want to know, understand, process, and ultimately purchase:

- Pets for sale or adoption
- Medical services of veterinarians and pharmacies
- Supplies, from ordinary cat litter to diamond-studded dog collars
- Other services like groomers, kennels, and dog walkers

As well as engaging in other ways:

- Social media: A community, with people as crazy about Pulis as you are. Connect with them via their pets, at any hour, at home or at work, through the iPhone.
- Entertainment: A few hours to burn? Switch off the TV, YouTube is waiting with millions of crazy cat videos and do-it-yourself programming. Curate your own shows, no matter how lowbrow, with your own cats starring on your own YouTube channel.

From 2002 to 2004, as the United States human population increased 1.7 percent, the dog population increased 13 percent, from 65 million to 73.9 million. From 2006 to 2008, the human population rose 2 percent, and dogs went up 3.6 percent, from 74.8 million to 77.5 million. Almost every element of pet life was in place. The tools were all there, but tech was running faster than commerce and the media. They had to catch up. People wanted more stuff, more websites. They wanted it faster. And they wanted it delivered with precision.

The websites came quickly, with more choices and information. Soon, people could communicate expansively and obsessively with like-minded people. If you raise Bernese Mountain dogs and want to meet other Bernese Mountain dog people, it happened in seconds. More than any other single app, Facebook helped to jump-start Pet Nation, by connecting Mary in Idaho with Mary Anne in Iowa to share and celebrate their passion for Maine Coon cats.

Stage 3 (2008–2018): Individual Loneliness → PET NATION → HUMAN HAPPINESS

Digital mania was raging. In twenty-five years, people had gone from typing reports one page at a time on a mechanical typewriter to sending documents with complex graphics (from their laptop computer) to their colleagues on earth below, while aboard a 737 at thirty-five thousand feet. Every day, legions of teenagers sent hundreds of messages to their friends down the block, while Mom and Dad sent their own emails over family dinner, without conversation.

This era was unquestionably better for dogs and cats. The previously unpredictable, ad hoc process of pet acquisition became simpler and more streamlined. On Petfinder, you could search for a dog or a cat, using a broad range of criteria, matching a particular breed or mix to your lifestyle before making a complex, life-altering decision. Petfinder would qualify you for purchase, coordinate the transaction with the shelter, and then fly the dog to your home for $300 to $400. Safe, easy, and precise. People swapped the proverbial school snapshots of young Sarah and Johnny in Dad's wallet for the pet selfie, the identity card of Pet Nation citizens. Billions of photos of our dogs and cats at home, at play, on holiday, enhanced with Hollywood-quality photo-editing tricks, traded like baseball cards, languishing inside our phones, waiting to be admired, offering anyone we meet our own slice of Pet Nation.

All good. Perfect? Well, not yet. But dogs didn't mind, for they had moved out of the doghouse. And numbers kept moving in the right direction. From 2012 to 2014, as the US human population increased

1.5 percent, the dog population increased 6.5 percent, from 78.2 million to 83.3 million. From 2015–2017, the human population rose 1.2 percent, dogs up 15 percent, from 77.8 million to 89.7 million, after a dip in 2014 to 77.8 million.

And then slowly, without warning it seemed, our social fabric began to unravel. After several heady years, the iPhone, the *great enabler*, subtly, almost imperceptibly, began to pull people apart with addictive apps that deepened their personal alienation, gelding the English language, forging new ways to communicate or to avoid communicating at all. The author Sherry Turkle labels this condition "Alone together." People are physically close but emotionally distant, protected by digital moats. Luckily for dogs and cats waiting in crowded shelters, people continued to acquire even more pets and pet accoutrements, spending increasingly more time with young Jack and Sugar Candy.

The text message app was the offender: It was simply too addictive. A workhorse communicator, launching 8.3 trillion global messages each year, it turned into a social inhibitor, a way to keep the world at bay. People retreated into their phones, shunning human contact and conversation—a boon for pets. Human intimacy receded from daily life. Communities need a balance of online and offline resources. Post-2007, people needed real people in their lives. And real dogs and cats.

PETS: To the Rescue

Pets were happy to accommodate. Remember the answer to that Google query: "A dog will: (1) keep you 'happy, healthy, and help you lose some weight'; (2) keep your mind 'engaged and active'; (3) teach you to 'relax and be Zen'; (4) 'make you laugh'; and (5) 'be your loyal friend for life.'" The idea is not so farfetched after all. Science has demonstrated it, and peer-review journals validate the benefits of pet ownership. Anthropologists find evidence in old burial sites, looking for bones and clues to the origin of dogs. There are theories galore surrounding the human-animal bond, which I cover in depth in chapter four, and all have merit, but ultimately it comes down to this: dogs and cats give us two things that people rarely surrender: (1) true, free, and unconditional love, for as long as they can breathe; and (2) deep, long-lasting trust and loyalty.

The following quotations underscore this thought:

> "My little dog—a heartbeat at my feet."
> ~EDITH WHARTON, AMERICAN NOVELIST

> "A house is not a home until it has a dog."
> ~GERALD DURRELL, NATURALIST, CONSERVATIONIST,
> AND AUTHOR OF *MY FAMILY AND OTHER ANIMALS*

> "The love of a dog is a pure thing.
> He gives you a trust which is total. You must not betray it."
> ~MICHEL HOUELLEBECQ, FRENCH NOVELIST

If Gerald Durrell is correct, many Americans lived in *houses*, not *homes*, for most of the twentieth century. Edith Wharton, a portraitist of Gilded Age interiors and the human interior, prized the emotional intensity of her dogs, Sprite, Mouton, Mitou, Miza, Nicete, and, by extension, honored all the dogs who sit beside us, their tails wagging like metronomes, as we work away on our computers. It is fitting that Michel Houellebecq, a serious man by all accounts, emphasizes the gravity of the commitment a person makes when a dog enters their life. The bond is reciprocal: *We* depend on *them*, and *they* depend on *us*. Lonely Americans were ready for a change of pace.

Pets stepped into the void, effortlessly entering the lives of people all over America, supported by a massive, 24-7 on-demand emporium of dogs and cats and an endless array of goods, services, and information at their fingertips on the web. Before long, people could buy paraphernalia for their new best friends at any hour of the day or night.

Soon, dogs would bring people out of their homes and apartments and into the world, onto the street. They were offline. Real, tactile, breathing beings, they weren't made of pixels, or a thousand miles away. People rediscovered the sidewalk, then their neighborhood, then city parks filled with dog runs, leading them to a long-lost world called "my community" that had vanished from many cities and towns as people burrowed into their computers.

Natural communicators, dogs and cats began to fill the emotional void created by the digital world. They offered an easy-to-learn language of barks and meows. *Beginner Shih Tzu* has only eight elemental barks: "Cookie." "Pay attention to me. Now!" "I'm hungry." "I have to go out!" "Let's play." "Why are you putting on a jacket? Are you going to leave me here alone?" "Time for a massage!" and "I need to go see Dr. Rubin." *Beginner Bengal* has even fewer meows: "Pet me." "Stop petting me." "You've been gone for months." "Is there anything edible to eat?" "Let me go outside and I promise not to run away." For anyone uncomfortable with human communication, these are much better conversations than ones with layers of commitment and emotional land mines.

Who can say no to unwavering love throughout a ten- to fifteen-year relationship (depending on the breed, or the age of the pet at adoption) with few demands (food, water, bed, sunlight, toys, play, twice-a-day walks, and veterinary care)? If 50 percent of American marriages end in divorce before the eighth year, then, in some ways, a Tibetan Terrier is a safer bet. Not the same as a husband or wife, with children, certainly, but a true, loving companion who will never desert you for the Toy Poodle or the Russian Blue down the block.

MEDIA

Brand "P" for Pets

Though people today are drowning in a sea of brands and marketing lingo ("brand equity," "brand image," "brand architecture," "brand experience"), branding is not a twentieth-century invention. In 2700 BC, the Egyptians branded cattle to distinguish one herd from another and to keep track of their property. Today, branding is a way to express identity. Individual pets have their own personal branding, the microchip implant, which is placed under the skin of a dog or cat and serves as their "identity card." The second branding iteration is embedded in traditional media and social media. After Facebook opened its membership to the world in 2006, social media switched on the pet/love machine. To understand the interplay of pets and the media over the past few decades, we will look at three areas where pets are now center stage: (1) consumer product advertising generally and automobile advertising specifically; (2) celebrity marketing; and (3) social media. Cue dogs and cats, and their talent agencies.

Pets Can't Drive, or Can They?

No, they can't. Which is why the tagline that Pets.com (an early dotcom start-up) ran at the 2000 Super Bowl was superficially clever: "Pets .com. Because Pets Can't Drive." Since pets can't drive, pet owners would buy food and supplies online, right, obviating the need to drive? The logic was sound, but the timing was off. Pets.com was a few years early. In 2000, in an industry with 3 percent profit margins, it was prohibitively expensive to ship fifty-pound boxes of kitty litter to consumers. Pets.com burned through $100 million in two years and eventually closed their doors. It would take Amazon a few more years to sort out the logistics, but they and several online pet retailers have managed to sell tons of kitty litter since then.

Good marketing often turns on simple insights. In the 1980s, Howard Schultz laid the cornerstone for the modern American coffee industry, realizing that while Italians drink small shots of espresso standing at tall, round marble café tables, Americans would prefer to sit in comfortable chairs and drink good coffee in larger cups. If Starbucks had traded chairs for stand-up tables, it might not be around today.

In 2010–11, nine years after the Pets.com flameout, the Carmichael Lynch advertising agency in Minneapolis had a Starbucks moment with dogs that turned the "Pets can't drive" mantra on its head. Rather than make a standard public-service ad for animal behaviorist Cesar Millan's reality TV show *The Dog Whisperer*, the agency's creative director Randy Hughes made a car commercial with a family of dogs trying to parallel-park a Subaru (Cesar's sponsor). Tagline: "Dog Tested. Dog Approved." Mr. Hughes realized that while pets don't drive, 40 percent of Americans have dogs, and 71 percent of Subaru owners have dogs. People connected with the ad. The tagline stuck. It polished the Subaru image and changed automobile advertising for Subaru and other car manufacturers—indeed, it changed all television advertising, by casting dogs in a leading role. They became the *good guys*, the *fixer*. If you need to warm up an ad, to humanize your brand, cast a Golden Retriever or an English Bulldog. More than a decade later, dogs are still driving Subarus, and I assume Subaru will continue dog commercials well into the 2020s. Today, 40 percent of television commercials feature dogs, no matter the product category.

In the process, pets themselves became a brand with a boatload of brand equity.

Who's the Star of the Show?

Elizabeth Taylor, who played a leading role in two of the greatest animal movies ever made, famously said, "Some of my best leading men have been dogs and horses." She was referring to her parts in *Lassie Come Home*, in 1943, and *National Velvet*, in which she played the part of Velvet Brown alongside the racehorse the Pie, in 1944. During her life, Taylor had many dogs, ranging from Spaniels to Pekingese to Maltese to Lhasa Apso to, poetically, a Collie descended from Pal, the original Lassie.

The canine and feline stars of Pet Nation enjoy a celebrity that rivals the most well-known human entertainers. The biggest of them all, Grumpy Cat, a Snowshoe Siamese, earned $100 million in her short life and had millions of devoted followers on social media.

Jiffpom the Pomeranian, the Instagram Dog

Jiffpom the Pomeranian has thirty million followers across all social media channels. His owners claim that Jiffpom is the "most famous animal in the world," not the "most famous dog," which would be Lassie or Snoopy, both fictional characters. Though Jiffpom *is* a real-life dog, a Teddy Bear Pomeranian, he could be confused with a plush toy, or an animated character, more at home on-screen than on green grass. He is, perhaps, a new breed, an "Instagram dog," which the American Kennel Club has not yet recognized. Naturally, Jiffpom has a YouTube channel.

After stealing the show in Katy Perry's music video for "Dark Horse," in 2014, he entered the Guinness World Records twice, for the fastest ten-meter run on hind legs and the fastest five-meter run on front paws. He seems to be happy and makes children across America happy. *Best in Show* in the Instagram Dog class, Jiffpom is a sign of pooches to come, hovering between natural pets and media pets. Now, repeat after me, "CUTENESS IS REAL."

Taylor Swift has three beautiful Scottish Fold cats, Olivia Benson, Meredith Grey, and their brother, Benjamin Button, who are nearly as photogenic and famous as she is.

The Internet is filled with articles about the pets of famous people, the animals celebrities follow on social media, and celebrity pets themselves. People want to know about them, to see them at home, at play, to know their names. Does it change the way people think about celebrities, adding dimension to their profile, burnishing their image? Perhaps. Does it inspire people to acquire more pets?

In the last years of his life, Karl Lagerfeld, one of the world's great fashion designers, shared the limelight with a beautiful, snow-white Birman cat named Choupette. She, in turn, became a celebrity. Sharing a birthday (August 15) with Emperor Napoleon Bonaparte, Choupette could be considered a feline empress, with two maids who keep her diary and manage her health regimen. Choupette has a growing presence on social media with her own Twitter and Instagram accounts. She earned $3 million in 2014 alone from marketing ventures, and prompted Mr. Lagerfeld to say that he would marry her if it were legal. A gift to Mr. Lagerfeld from a friend, Choupette is now a bona fide celebrity and part of the Karl Lagerfeld legacy.

Sign In

There are 2.2 billion registered Facebook users, roughly 28 percent of the earth's population. There are common threads that run through most personal Facebook accounts: posts about boyfriends, girlfriends, old boyfriends, old girlfriends, children, parents, and siblings. And Dogs and Cats. Dogs and Cats are *capitalized* because of their prominence on social media. Some people join Facebook simply to share pictures of their pets. The statistics are eye-opening:

- On average, America's dog owners post photos of their pet on social media six times per week, and watch dog videos three times per week.
- Ten million American dogs have their own Instagram account.
- Every holiday, 54 percent of pet owners hang a Christmas stocking for their dog or cat, and 29 percent send them cards.
- 33 percent of pet owners post about their pets as often as they do about their human family.
- 13 percent of pet owners post about their pets more than they do about their human family.
- 15 percent of pet owners have a social media profile specifically for their pet.
- 50 percent of pet owners admit that their pets get more coverage than they do.

Social petworking is inescapable and habit-forming. Everything from photos, videos, veterinary advice, and adoption to online shopping, rescue stories, Animal Planet, and celebrity pets can be shared by people—at work, at lunch, anywhere with an Internet connection. What accounts for the addictive quality of this pet content? Here are three possible reasons for the American pet obsession: equality, control, and commonality.

Equality reflects the democratic nature of America's love for pets. It's all about the animals—the owner's status, net worth, job, residence, or family pedigree doesn't matter in the slightest. Two Cairn Terriers meet at the corner of Union Street and Webster in San Francisco, and they meet as equals. It doesn't matter where they live or whether their owners work at Apple or the Apple Bagel Shop around the corner. Focus is squarely on the animals. This is the first time they've met, and people recede into the background.

Control separates children from pets. Though cats have a mind of their own, owners are still in charge; by the time a child is seven, they begin to move on. Dogs are partners, but they belong to people. The nomenclature is foggy: owner, parent, partner, guardian, friend, but it doesn't matter. People control their pets, in the disposition of food, heat, comfort, exercise, and medical care. There is an undeniable satisfaction in feeding a dog or cat, or helping them recover from an illness. Making them happy, watching the rush to the bowl.

Commonality is perhaps the most important aspect of social media for pets. "Commonality" means shared traits. A person in Aptos, California, who owns a Himalayan cat, sees a video of a Himalayan cat in Black Rock, Connecticut, and knows exactly what the East Coast doppelgänger of their cat is doing and thinking, how it behaves, the physical and emotional problems the cat might have. The owners can trade photos, information, diet ideas, anecdotes, rescue stories. Though more than three thousand miles apart, they bond. The cats never meet, but the people become friends.

Every person on social media effectively has their own broadcasting channel inside their smartphone or laptop. They can publish photos, videos, and stories about their pets as often as they like. Many do little else but trade photos of their dogs and cats. A high percentage of text messages contain pets: a few words and pictures of your Westie, Sam, then a return text with a comment or recent photos of your friend's Havanese, Manolo.

Pets are part of a community, the lifeblood of Facebook. If your mutt, Francisco, wanders out of the yard, you post a picture, then a stranger five blocks away sees your neighborhood post, finds him, and brings him home. Need the name of a good, affordable vet? Here are three recommendations. The seventh annual French Bulldog Walk needs volunteers—here are details. The information wheel keeps spinning.

The Facebook computer home page is Spartan, stripped down, without pictures, a handful of words and three icons, resembling the cover of a government report. Considering the absence of copy, each word matters:

- *Connect with friends and the world around you on Facebook.* Two definitions for the word "friends": people and pets. You will connect.
- *See photos and updates from friends in your news feed.* No worries—millions of times each day.
- *Share what's new in your life on your timeline.* And that would be Trixie, Cooper, Sunny Jim, Deli, Millie, Marly, Coral, Tsu-Tsu, Buddha, Gus, and so many more. "Oh, and did I tell you about . . ."
- *Find more of what you're looking for with the Facebook search function.* It doesn't matter what it is. Breed. Shelter. Dog walker. Groomer. If it has a tail (sorry, Manx) and barks or purrs, you will find it.

Try Not to Laugh

YouTube is compulsive and fun. Why else would millions of otherwise sane individuals watch three billion hours of videos each month? It makes them laugh. Silly? Sure, but who cares? Pure amusement: the same reason people have gone to the movies since the 1920s. A healthy percentage of those three billion hours feature dogs and cats. Especially cats. Cats chasing cats. Cats chasing dogs. Dogs chasing cats. People with cats and dogs.

Dog and cat memes are ubiquitous on YouTube. Coined by Richard Dawkins in his book *The Selfish Gene,* the word "meme" has acquired a less lofty, though fanatical, following on the Internet, thanks to dogs and cats. Anyone can publish these impromptu Internet commentaries, which are compiled and shared via dozens of ranked lists: "Top 50 Dog Memes," "Top 50 Cat Memes," "Top 50 Dog and Cat Memes," and so on. Though impossible to count, there are perhaps as many dog and cat memes in America as there are dogs and cats.

Internet entertainment is instant and constant. When I was young, we were allowed to watch a ration of TV before bedtime during the school week, then wait for the Saturday matinée at the movies. This included plenty of cowboy movies and cartoons, featuring Tom and Jerry, the Road Runner, Yosemite Sam. It was the same kind of knock-about humor that is playing endlessly on smartphones all over the world today in memes, videos, and text messages. Today, however, no Hollywood studios are needed—you are the producer, the casting agent, and young Mimi is the star. Who knows, she could be the next Jiffpom with thirty million followers. Now it's your turn. Sign in and start posting.

COMMERCE

Media changed the way people look at pets, think about pets, and communicate about them. It's time to complete the equation: People + Pets + Tech + Media + Commerce = PET NATION. How and where do I buy the right dog or cat? And the myriad products I will need to manage young Theo? What do I do when I travel? During the period 2010–2018, several conditions meshed to make owning and maintaining a pet effortless and almost automatic. Digital tools and resources were the key to this transformation.

With the exception of taking your dog or cat to the vet (and tele-veterinary medicine is slowly becoming an option) or the groomer, every commercial pet purchase today can be managed online, with a smartphone or laptop, at any time of the day. That includes the adoption process, and online adoption options are as rich and varied as in the other categories. While many people go to local shelters, that is only one source of dogs and cats, and your choices there are limited by supply. If you prefer a specific breed or mix, it is more efficient to go online through a service like PuppySpot to find your ideal dog or cat. You can get exactly what you want, with precise and predictable delivery routines. There will be no surprises in delivery. The precision and process control that millennials cherish dovetail in these routines. Online services are thorough, fairly priced, and comprehensive. The differences between purchasing a dog today and thirty years ago are revealing:

1. **1988:** In the eighties, you had to drive to a local pet shop or pound to see the available dogs and cats. Those animals were your only choices. Period. You could find a half-dozen breeds, if you were lucky, depending on the day. Unless you were wealthy and part of the dog-show world, it was difficult and expensive to buy a purebred dog. The paraphernalia supporting a dog or cat was also limited to your local resources. You did the homework yourself and searched specialty shops, pet shops, or large grocery stores on foot for leashes, collars, and other accoutrements. It was a homemade, improvised process without a predictable path to adoption. It took time, money, considerable shoe-leather research, and driving to find your dream dog or cat (and all the other things you needed to care for them) and drive them home.

2. **2020:** Today, you can go to PuppySpot, Petfinder, or hundreds of other sites to find a dog. Select your breed. Sort through the different features: size, color, age, disposition. Once you've contacted the shelter or breeder, you'll undergo an exhaustive purchase process, comprising an application form, personal ref-

erences, photos of your home and yard, a phone interview, and credit references. If you pass muster and are formally approved, you will sign a legal contract and make payment. Once the shelter or breeder completes vaccinations, documentation, and a complete medical check on the animal, you can start shopping for paraphernalia. The shelter will arrange transport of your dog or cat, which you will track like any Amazon purchase. Then race to the airport and meet the newest member of your family.

Serendipity has evaporated from the purchase process. Choices expand as the process becomes simpler and more controlled. Build a profile of the dog or cat you want, and then find your dream pet quickly, dependably, and safely, at a local shelter, breeder, rescue group, or online. It is a serious purchase, a commitment in years, as millennial couples decide between a mutt and a purebred.

Services are no different. Whether you use Rover, the largest dog-walking service in America, or a local provider, the process is as digital and methodical as you want: from scheduling to daily pickup to monitoring with pictures and posts to walking summary. A one-billion-dollar industry that was once entirely ad hoc (nonexistent in most small towns) now allows you to curate every step in the process. If you want your Standard Poodle, Pandora, to walk only with other Standard Poodles, that can be arranged. Need a dog walker or cat sitter/companion? Relax, and follow the steps, just specify: dog or cat; walking, boarding, house-sitting, drop-in visit, or playdates; size of dog; and "extras" (hourly check-in, walking summary, video feed).

Rover maintains that they accept fewer than 20 percent of sitter applicants. New sitters must pass a background check, with a detailed personal profile and approval by a team of sitter specialists. When you entrust your dog or cat to a complete stranger for daily walks or visits, you want to be sure that your pet is safe, with a responsible companion. In large cities, teams of independent dog walkers divide up neighborhoods and parcel out the dogs in multiple buildings, coordinating coverage, attentive to both the dogs and the owners.

In every category of service, successful online sites share best practices. They are thorough, easy to use, dependable, predictable (they've done this a thousand times), and verifiable, since you can monitor every step of the service.

Where do you buy all the amazing products that your pet (or you) can't live without? In every category, there are several channels, in no particular order of importance. People have a wide range of choices, at a good-quality level, depending on the purchase:

1. For pet accoutrements and services only (not pets): local groomer, pet shop, online store
2. For cats and dogs: local breeders, PuppySpot, Petfinder, and shelters
3. For supplies, food, cats for adoption: pet superstores like Petco and PetSmart
4. For supplies, toys, and food: Amazon
5. For food, kitty litter, apparel, toys, et cetera: the dominant online merchant in each category, e.g., Chewy

If you want to find it, whatever it is, and whenever you want it, you can, and quickly.

Pets Went Viral and It's Been Quite a Ride

Pets didn't change, but we, the American public, did and never looked back. The social world atomized. We grew lonelier, while a media and technology environment evolved that shared and celebrated media pets and real-life pets—funny, companionable, clever, cute, and emotionally supportive animals. As nineteenth- and twentieth-century technologies shifted into the digital age, our pet obsession simultaneously lifted off. Technology and pets *grew up* together. Pet Nation was the product of this coevolution.

The story is still being written, but the data is remarkable: a $75 billion industry, 1.3 million pet people at work, with ninety million dogs and ninety-five million cats running all over America, who continue to outsmart us day after day. In chapter three, we'll see where they go next.

· 3 ·

THE WHOLE DAMN COUNTRY HAS RUN AMOK
The Pet Land Grab

No Dogs Allowed: these three words in the Atlas Bakery window in McMinnville, Oregon, my hometown, said it all, in 1967. They encapsulated America before Pet Nation. In 2019, the sign on the front door of Bedford Cheese Shop on Irving Place in Manhattan tells a different story: "We know your dog/iguana/savannah cat/ocelot is awesome, but they can't come into the cheese shop. Thank you for understanding!"*

The land grab took some time to get started, roughly 9,980 years for dogs to trade the outdoors for the indoors and to discover the civilized, physical world beyond the back fence. Evolutionary anthropologists believe that dogs arrived in North America ten thousand years ago, crossing a land bridge over the Bering Strait from Siberia to Alaska with human emigrants. A few dogs at first, a pack here and there, and now we're a nation of ninety million dogs, in every town and state. However,

---

* Having just spent $5,000 for a specialty veterinarian to treat our cat Oscar's penchant for Tillamook sharp cheddar, I appreciate Bedford Cheese's caution.

until the epoch we define as Pet Nation (1998–2018), dogs largely lived outdoors, restricted by their owners to a defined set of private spaces (backyard, front yard, barnyard, field, farm, brewery), and, occasionally, a few public spaces (the Greyhound race track, the park). The rest of the world was off limits. Today, dogs enjoy a life of comparative luxury and a free pass seemingly everywhere.

American dogs—and most European dogs—are fortunate to have crossed the threshold into the home. Dogs in certain European countries, such as Romania, Poland, and Russia, live a less pampered life than French and English dogs and are often smuggled into the United States to be sold clandestinely. Approximately 50 percent of the world's dog population still live in developing countries and spend their days and nights outdoors as feral or community dogs, exposed to the heat and cold, sometimes fed and sometimes hungry, often abused. Ironically, until recently, *Ancient Dog* enjoyed a more symbiotic relationship with humans than *Modern Dog*. How did these two species connect?

Descended from a species of wolf that is now extinct, dogs began the long, complex process of domestication by living with tribes of hunter-gatherers as guard dogs, or hangers-on, in their camps. The first animal species to be selectively bred and fully domesticated, dogs helped people in multiple ways: *hunting* (with their acute sense of smell); *protection* (barking at invaders or strangers); *hygiene* (scavenging camp food); *pest control* (catching vermin); and *heating* (providing warmth on cold nights). The phrase "three-dog night" wasn't coined by the eponymous 1970s rock group; the phrase comes from either the Aboriginal people of Australia or the Inuit tribes of the Aleutian Islands, for whom a "three-dog night" is a night so cold that three dogs are needed in bed to stay warm. The band's 1971 hit song "An Old Fashioned Love Song," written by Paul Williams, could be applied to America's relationship to dogs (and cats) today, since two of three domestic dog owners consider their dog their best friend.

The original relationship between hunter and dog was good for the animals, too. In camps, dogs were safer, enjoyed more food, and could breed more. Early man used tools to hunt animals and build fires to cook them, which fed hungry dogs. This relationship helped both species to survive. Still, for thousands of years, the majority of American dogs lived outdoors as second-class citizens.

INDOORS AND OUTDOORS

After pets charmed their way indoors, there was no more subzero weather, old bones, or days and nights mousing or tied to an apple tree. No ice and rain. Hello, master bedroom and central heating. Wall-to-wall carpeting. Cartoons on television. Dining on demand. Human servants (excuse me, "owners") to refill the water bowl. Who could complain? The significance of the journey from backyard to bedroom cannot be downplayed. A four-legged animal that had been feared and disdained for centuries, considered unclean and kept at bay, was welcomed into the home to share a bed with clean sheets, blankets, pillows, and Mom and Dad—a full-fledged member of the family. Indoor-pet life was a cultural watershed, which involved the rewiring of the American persona.

In Pet Nation, the movement of pets indoors began on private property, with a single dog or cat entering its owner's private house. If you want to paint every room in your own home pink or chartreuse, or put a Che Guevara poster on the dining room wall, that is your constitutional right. If you want to bring your dog or cat indoors, it is your choice, provided it doesn't hurt anyone or infringe on your neighbor's rights or way of life. The emergence of Pet Nation fundamentally changed the American lifestyle, but, until recently, it was still a private behavioral change, limited to an individual or a family's house and property, not a public act with repercussions for the village. After all,

55 percent of American households (still) choose not to have a dog and 35 percent have no pets whatsoever.

Then something unexpected happened. The new status quo, with Bailey indoors, sleeping by the hearth, curled up on a Persian rug all day long save for bathroom breaks, didn't last long. It seems that Bailey was ready to go back outside, but not through the back door this time, exiled to the backyard like a rogue uncle on the run from the law. No, Bailey stepped triumphantly through the front door and out onto the sidewalk, into civilization, with a bigger basket of access passes and a twenty-first-century itinerary. Out into society with new places to visit.

With little hesitation, dog owners said, "Let's go!" and dogs led the charge, leashes flailing in the wind. In twenty years, America turned into Pet Nation, with pets everywhere: the workplace, airplanes, nursing homes, farmers markets, shops, weddings, even the halls of Congress. The rise of Pet Nation has witnessed a veritable land grab by dogs (with cat cafés increasingly dotting the cityscape). You could now insert your dog into the middle of daily life, where it would interact with neighbors, strangers, shopkeepers, policemen, flight attendants, other dogs, trucks, taxis, buses, bicycles, in short, the ebb and flow of cities and towns across (and above) America. No one can tell you that your shelter mutt, Ginger, isn't equal to every other dog on the block, with a mixed heritage like most American dogs, and she's ready to ramble.

America caught up with France—where the sight of a Standard Poodle perched on a velvet pouf in a *soigné* Parisian restaurant gnawing on a juicy lamb chop was once a selfie moment for American tourists—and then leapfrogged it. Tolerant of dogs in public places, whether restaurants, markets, or hotels, the French are more utilitarian in their pet relationships. More employees than best friends, guard dogs, or fashion accessories, dogs have a place in French society and a fixed set of rights. America went bigger and bolder, granting dogs privileges and access to an ever-expanding network of approved public places to romp.

The number and types of dogs that people encounter on a typical day has skyrocketed from mid-century America, when you could go for days or weeks without seeing a dog, unless your family owned one.* No longer. With 98 percent of Americans living in towns and cities, dogs are unavoidable in modern life. They greet you in the apartment elevator or on your doorstep as you leave for work. Tangling leashes as they meander down the street, they dominate the sidewalk. Outside the office or in a shopping mall, you'll see one or two nestled into carrying cases or soft shoulder pouches, the modern papoose. Stop at your local café for a latte and there's a Labradoodle in line with her owner. Depending on your company's size and canine policy, you could encounter a half-dozen dogs before lunch, snoozing or roaming. The universe of dog-friendly venues would astonish your grandparents. In this chapter, I'll examine the most important public places and weigh the consequences of change for society as a whole, for companies and employees, dog lovers, and those who do not in any way enjoy sharing spaces with the four-legged angels.

I'll observe how America embraced 185 million cats and dogs, and its effect on the 35 percent of Americans who don't own pets. How do they feel about the pet invasion? Do they enjoy sharing sidewalks, parks, hotels, workplaces, even some cafés, with furry little beasts with their own ideas of hygiene? Millennial pet owners are pressing for more pet-friendly rental housing, and the battle is gearing up. *Pet Nation* poses the ultimate question: Should we control where and how pets roam, or is there nowhere that America will post a "Pets Not Wanted" sign in the future?

---

*Since 1977, my brother has lived in Manhattan and remembers that, until the mid-1990s, neither he nor his wife was aware of any dogs in the five apartment buildings where they lived—some with as many as 330 apartments. It was only after 2001 that dogs began to be ubiquitous in the city.

∴

AND IN THE CORNER OFFICE . . .

Prior to 2000, you never saw a dog in an office or workspace, except for a service dog shadowing a person with physical or sight limitations. Granted, the random small-business owner might bring his trusted Retriever to the shop on Main Street like Dad before him, but that was atypical. Offices were for people: conventional wisdom held that dogs were too messy, disruptive, or annoying to fellow employees, potentially dangerous; in a nutshell, dogs were a nuisance. It was the rare employee who'd muster the courage to ask her boss if she could bring her "perfectly well-behaved Norwich Terrier" to work even one day a month.

Once dogs escaped from backyards and doghouses, it was inevitable that they'd want to go to work with Mom or Dad. Dogs are social beings, and who wants to stay at home alone ten hours a day? Pet Nation is changing the workplace like everything else it touches—pets are on the move from the backyard to the boardroom. This land grab is only beginning. I'll examine the rationale for pets (basically dogs) in the workplace, the options that organizations are testing, the issues pet-friendly policies trigger, and the direction of this trend. Pets won't stop until every workplace in America is saturated, unless a bona fide health or safety concern stands in the way. I'm of the view that this movement is healthy for society at large (even, counterintuitively, for those who don't like dogs, as we'll see later in this section).

Many companies have adopted detailed pet-friendly policies, particularly in the tech industry, where quality-of-life benefits often trump salary considerations for their many millennial employees. Here are a few pet-related perks you now see in the workplace:

1. Under emergency circumstances, if a dog is sick or daycare coverage falters, the dog owner can bring their dog in to work that day.

2. "Furternity" leave: employees receive time off (paid or unpaid) to stay at home with a new kitten or puppy (whether adopted or purchased).

3. Pet health insurance is included in the portfolio of employee benefits.

4. Employees are encouraged to bring their dogs to outdoor company parties, where the inclusion of pets is mentioned in Paperless Post invitations.

5. Dogs are allowed on a leash inside the office once a month or once a week.

6. Behaviorally appropriate dogs are allowed in the office every day, stationed at their owner's desk or cubicle, sometimes evolving into a communal dog for all employees to pamper.

7. Offices provide doggy daycare service.

8. Employers create designated dog runs or play areas at the office.

9. Dogs receive employee badges.

10. The grand prize for employees is daily dog privileges, with morning and afternoon off-leash periods. These office dogs are allowed to run free in the office for an hour or more.

Before Pet Nation, people assumed that a backyard or a crate was sufficient to manage a dog while the owner was at work. Fill the food and water bowls, then lock the door. Fine, take the morning off when your dog goes to the emergency room, but why should a dog be allowed in the office if she is acting up, emotional, or the dog sitter bails? Everything we learned in chapters one and two upended that attitude, as pets leaped onto the pedestal reserved for special friends or immediate family. We don't crate children on a bad day, or consign them to the backyard, so why treat Rover differently? (Cats might hang out at home alone without a fuss, but not a two-year-old Corgi named Hannibal.)

Provided there were no accidents or incidents, an emergency pass for dogs made sense. Many companies have now adopted this practice.

However, like other Pet Nation trends, this small accommodation planted a seed that spread from company to company. Employees argued that their workday improved when Rover was at their side, or they asked to work from home one day a week because they enjoyed Rover's company and "I get so much more work done when I'm with her." The rationale transformed an emergency plea into a human-resource policy, promising improvements in employee morale and performance anchored by a dog's presence. This gradually led to once-a-month privileges for all employees, and then to Doggy Fridays. From emergencies to once a month to once a week, Pet Nation was wagging its tail.

To keep the office from becoming a zoo, companies had no choice but to take pets seriously, formulating official animal rules. Lawyers and human-resource managers rewrote the pet chapter in the employee handbook. Do we only accept dogs, cats, bunnies, gerbils, and turtles? Is a Highland Terrier more worthy than a cockatoo? Common sense governed. If a pet can't sit still and obey her owner (which rules out cats), then she can't come to work, no matter how smart she is. Corporate America settled on dogs, the occasional bunny, and perhaps a small turtle in an appropriate enclosure. But could you bring any size dog to the office? What if the dog wears a muzzle? And why only one dog, when 40 percent of dog owners have more than one—someone will be jealous. A conundrum, but most pet-friendly companies draw the line at one dog per employee.

What about sick dogs, with communicable diseases? Soon, proof of up-to-date vaccinations and regular veterinary examinations were required. Control became a precondition for puppies who weren't potty-trained. The same behavior standard applied to chronic barkers, biters, or aggressors: a canine code of etiquette, like preparing your four-year-old for a preschool admissions interview. Human-resource managers became dog testers, or outsourced the task to animal behaviorists. What if employees are allergic to certain breeds? This means that some dogs are banned from the office, or an area is quarantined. Managing workplace pet policy is not a simple personnel issue, like casual attire on Fridays.

It shouldn't surprise you that we now have national Take Your Dog to Work Day (third Thursday of June). The lure of Pet Nation quietly transformed the vibe of the American workplace. It is the rare design studio today without tattoos, piercings, and pooches at every workstation. BARK, a company with three hundred employees in Columbus, Ohio, mixes dogs and people in every way imaginable: they have doggy beds, water and food bowls, treats, twice-daily "free-range" privileges, and more. Once inside BARK's offices for fifteen minutes, it all seems completely normal and natural: people are chatting or working away, and dogs being dogs . . . they're sleeping.

One might expect a dog-friendly policy to work at a company called BARK, but are dogs at work a benefit or an indulgence? The question of how pets affect employees in the workplace was studied by another Columbus company, Nationwide, and its pet insurance subsidiary. Led by social scientist Kerry O'Hara, Nationwide measured the performance, focus, and attitudes of two thousand full-time employees (fifteen hundred pet owners and five hundred non–pet owners) at companies around the country with more than one hundred employees. The results of the 2017 survey are revealing, particularly their findings with employees who don't own a pet: non–pet owners enjoy working for a pet-friendly company almost as much as pet owners, even millennials. This research has motivated other companies to become pet-friendly, satisfying the need to recruit younger workers.

The Nationwide study concluded:

1. More than 75 percent of non–pet owners report improved physical and mental health if the company is pet-friendly.
2. More coworkers know one another's child's/spouse's/pet's names if an office is pet-friendly (88 percent versus 80 percent).
3. There is a strong correlation between employees having positive

relationships with their coworkers and bosses and an office being pet-friendly (53 percent versus 17 percent).

4. Millennials overwhelmingly favor pet-friendly offices; 58 percent of millennials reported that they would be more satisfied with their work if their organization was more pet-friendly, compared to baby boomers (36 percent).

5. Companies with pet-friendly offices experience significantly higher employee engagement (87 percent versus 56 percent), greater employee retention (80 percent versus 59 percent), and lower rates of absenteeism (85 percent versus 77 percent).

There is something about the presence of dogs in an office—whether it's every day or one day a week—or providing benefits like pet insurance or "furternity" leave, that causes employees to like the company more, and to engage more productively with their coworkers. They even feel better about their supervisors!

The Nationwide survey results are reinforced by a recent Virginia Commonwealth University study of factory employees. This study showed that factory workers feel less stress when a dog is nearby on the shop floor, as measured by saliva samples and the presence of the stress hormone cortisol. Over the course of a day, only workers near a dog had lower cortisol levels at the end of the day.

Surprisingly, at offices allowing employees to bring their dogs every day, only 14 percent of dog owners took advantage of this policy, 23 percent did a few times per week, but 63 percent rarely or never brought their dog to work. This suggests that having even a few dogs in the office has a positive impact on the environment. Why the low uptake? Some pet owners self-police, others say that Rover prefers to stay home (perhaps the owner, too), and some consider bringing a dog to work a logistical challenge. Still, they love a company that gives them a choice. And, 40 percent of employees who choose to work from home want to be with their pets. Pet Nation has a hold on people—to paraphrase Tom

Waits,* "Reality is for people who can't handle pets." As millennials move to the corporate suite, get prepared for more dogs roaming office corridors all over the country.

🐾

THIS SIDEWALK'S GETTING CROWDED

Cities have changed. There are now dozens of dogs of all sizes, shapes, colors, and pedigrees crowding our sidewalks each day, 50 percent more dogs in toto than in the year 2000, in every city, suburb, and town. If you like dogs, it's nirvana; if you don't, or just want to get from point A to point B without tripping over a leash, good luck tuning them out. Certain street corners have become meeting points, where people congregate at noon or in the evening. Owners stop to share stories and wisdom, like mothers with baby strollers. On the way to work, people drop off children at school, dogs at doggy daycare, or both. Dogs *grow up* together, even if they only meet and socialize a few times a month over the course of several years. Dating ploy or luck, people strike up dog-walking romances. If you can't find a doggy daycare site to your liking, get the Rover app and a trained dog sitter will walk your pooch for you and provide hourly updates.

It's no surprise that dogs are popular pets for urban dwellers. Dogs pull people from their houses and apartments out on to the sidewalk, where they meet in passing. They make eye contact. People no longer avoid all passing strangers. They talk to people, if only briefly. They raise their eyes from their phone for a human moment. (See chapter four.)

Brief encounters in busy lives carry emotional weight. People smile

---

* Tom Waits, "Reality is for people who can't face drugs."

and talk about their own dogs, about your dogs, it doesn't matter. Dogs help people connect: on block after block, in cities, in suburbs, in small towns where the dogs are bigger but no less friendly, dogs are knitting society together. People who want a serious canine fix linger at dog runs on the way home from work. Momentarily, the rhythm of city life slows down, people relax their guard, changing their gait: with or without a dog, simply walking down the street has changed.

Like churches or bowling leagues, dogs build social capital and level the playing field: people and dogs meet as equals. There are no language barriers or subtitles at the Great Pet Theater. Dogs appear in surprising places. In New York's Washington Square Park, the annual Dachshund Spring Fiesta in April and *Dachshund Oktoberfest* make people smile. Portland, Oregon, has its Corgi Walk. Now that dogs and cats rule, every city is different, and the same, depending on the mix of breeds.

The scoreboard reads: Pets 1–Human Isolation 0.

Let's Go for a Run

The animal behaviorist Temple Grandin knows more about animals, and dogs, than just about anyone. In her book *Animals Make Us Human*, she fears that, despite the overall improvement in their living conditions, dogs are less free today than they were thirty years ago, less free to run and to play with other dogs:

> *It's obvious dogs like other dogs and enjoy being with their doggie friends. In the past, dogs have always been around other dogs. . . . I worry about the fenced-in lives of dogs today. Family dogs aren't free to come and go the way the dogs I grew up with were. . . . How much time can a dog be left alone and still have good emotional welfare[?] . . . But dogs are too social to be happy staying alone for*

hours on end. . . . This is another bad effect of today's leash laws and fenced yards. It's almost as if dogs have become captive animals instead of companion animals, and the house or fenced yard has become like a really fancy zoo enclosure.

Dog runs and dog parks address this need to run off-leash, to spend time with their doggy friends. Dog parks are great for dogs, dog owners, and even people who don't want anything to do with dogs. Dogs socialize with other dogs, exercise, play, and run, while people enjoy human and canine company, and watch their own dogs interact with other dogs. Many dogs spend daytime hours alone—in crates, in the living room, on a pillow, in a corner of the yard—except for brief, intermittent dog-walker visits. On-leash, dogs are more territorial, inclined to protect their owners; off-leash, they can roam.

Parks isolate dogs, separating them from people in public spaces (parks), relieving some of the pressure on those who don't want dogs underfoot. They change neighborhoods and cities, generally, for the better. In 1979, the first dog park in America opened in Berkeley, California. Today, there are approximately 775 dog parks in the United States, and this estimate could be conservative. Dog parks are a fast-growing part of the American park system.

Dog Parks in the United States, 2015–2018

Year	# of dog parks	Change in # from previous year	Change in % from previous year	Overall increase since 2009
2009	466			
2015	644	26	4.00%	178
2016	681	37	5.40%	215
2017	736	55	7.50%	270
2018	774	38	4.90%	308

There are "dog runs" and "dog parks," similar venues, though dog parks are bigger and have more amenities. A dog run can be as small as thirty by thirty feet (0.0225 acre), while the Elm Creek Park Reserve in Champlin, Minnesota, is twenty-nine acres in size, fully fenced, with off-leash trails that wander through forests and open fields. With more dogs and people living in smaller apartments and homes today, cities that create dog parks and dog runs become destinations, especially for millennials. Here are the eight leading cities, with their concentration of parks.

Dog Parks in the United States, Per 100,000 Residents, 2018

City	Population	# of dog parks	Dog parks per 100,000 residents
Boise, ID	225,405	15	6.7
Portland, OR	637,683	33	5.2
Henderson, NV	290,567	15	5.2
Norfolk, VA	248,958	12	4.9
Las Vegas, NV	642,798	26	4.0
Madison, WI	250,805	10	4.0
Oakland, CA	424,072	16	3.8
San Francisco, CA	871,042	32	3.7

Unfortunately, not all dog parks involve veterinarians, animal behaviorists, and dog-park designers in the planning stage, with the entire community in mind, including non–pet people. The end result: parks that can be noisy, stinky, muddy, too close to residential areas, or a traffic jam. The town of South Windsor, Connecticut, built Bark Park on city land near private homes, without community involvement. Homeowners hear barking dogs and car traffic, which led to a lawsuit against the town for noise nuisance.

In her comprehensive analysis of the subject, *Dog Parks: Benefits and Liabilities*, Laurel Allen cautions that unfortunately experts in dog behavior and dog park design, as opposed to "general park design," are not always involved in the design process.

"By the Way, We Do Have a Cat."

The battle for pet-friendly apartments in American cities is intense, with sore losers on both sides. We should have seen this coming. Millennials grew up in baby boomer families that founded Pet Nation, and it never occurred to them that their beloved pets couldn't move in with them after graduation. While colleges resist the idea that dogs should live on campus (exceptions made, off the record, of course, for the dormitory cat), apartment owners surely would understand and indulge this expectation. The wide disparity in how American cities view pets in apartments is startling; you'll never guess who's the friendliest city of all.

In 2015, my Animal Policy Group studied twenty-five urban markets to find out how welcoming landlords were to pets of any kind, using every available tool for a potential renter to find an apartment. Since we knew that 65 percent of American households own pets, we could expect 65 percent of urban apartments to be pet-friendly, a logical starting point. By "pet-friendly," we meant that a tenant could have at least one cat or one dog, though they might be required to pay for the privilege.

Here's what we discovered:

1. Philadelphia* led the pack with 95 percent of its urban apartments pet-friendly, followed by Fort Lauderdale (82 percent), Charlotte (76 percent), Denver (73 percent), Portland, Oregon (72 percent), Phoenix (68 percent), Las Vegas (66 percent), Seattle (63 percent), Boston (61 percent), and Oklahoma City (60 percent). This group was above or near the target of 65 percent.

---

*The City of Brotherly Love and Sisterly Affection. Is the nickname a clue to Philadelphia's embrace of pets, or the legacy of William Penn's desire for a humane, orderly city?

2. San Jose (55 percent) and Orlando (55 percent) lagged behind.

3. Who surprised us and dropped down the list? San Diego (49 percent), Dallas (44 percent), and Richmond (42 percent).

4. While the rates in those three cities were barely half of the top group, consider the cities at the bottom: Raleigh (38 percent), Columbus (38 percent), Atlanta (33 percent), Boise (33 percent), Salt Lake City (30 percent), Austin (28 percent), Nashville (25 percent), Minneapolis (20 percent), Hartford (15 percent), and poor Madison (11 percent). Apparently the Big Ten conference, with a veterinary school on nearly every campus,* doesn't like dogs and cats as much as we thought.

Pet Nation blankets the country: from old-line East Coast cities like Philadelphia to the Sunbelt (Fort Lauderdale and Phoenix) to the culturally hip Northwest (Portland and Seattle) and socially liberal Denver. Following our 2015 survey, laggards like Columbus and Austin embraced the trend, as apartment owners eager for millennial tenants went all in on pets. College graduates moving to Austin for their first job weren't forced to abandon their pets at a local shelter before signing an apartment lease. The intensity of the millennial embrace of Pet Nation is driving every city with labor shortages toward a new norm: Apartments are pet-friendly unless the landlord has never heard of social media or simply hates cats and dogs. Unfortunately, low-income apartments are not yet joining this trend.

A comprehensive study of market conditions for pet-friendly apartments, including the perspective of pet owners and landlords, was provided by market research company LRW in 2019 for the Human Animal Bond Research Institute (HABRI) and the Michelson Found Animals Foundation. Here are key findings:

---

* Of the thirty veterinary colleges in the United States, eight are located at Big Ten schools, including the University of Wisconsin.

- Twenty-three million out of forty-three million rental units in the United States have a pet in the household.
- 72 percent of renters say that it is difficult to find pet-friendly rental housing.
- The majority of landlords permitting pets have restrictions on the number and type.
- 24 percent of renters with pets have moved because of some circumstance or situation involving their pet, which equals 5.5 million renting households.
- 75 percent of renters (pet owners and non–pet owners) believe that government should make it easier for renters to have pets.
- Removing or easing restrictions on pets in apartments would add 8.2 million pets to Pet Nation.
- Parents will appreciate a final statistic: landlords report that young adults are the source of more complaints from apartment neighbors than pets.

If you ask a developer or apartment association in Austin or Miami if they have any problems with pets, you may receive an odd answer, "No, unless you want to talk about service animals." But who would complain about the amazing Labradors or Retrievers helping blind people navigate American sidewalks, subways, or airports? The answer is: no one. Guide dogs, or Seeing Eye dogs, are true "service animals," whom people uniformly love and respect. They are trained to perform specific tasks and are protected by Title II and III of the Americans with Disabilities Act. It is unlawful for a shop owner or business that serves the public generally to refuse entry to a person with a service animal. What rankles developers and apartment owners are "emotional-support" animals that pet owners take to work, to final exams, traffic court, public buildings, and, ultimately, their apartments, where approximately 20 percent of Americans live.

Emotional-support animals, or ESAs, are animals that provide "emotional support that alleviates one or more symptoms or effects of a person's disability." ESAs have no special privileges to access facilities that have a no-pets policy, but they have become the unwitting pawn in a financial maneuver that some people deploy to save apartment renters or owners money. These animals (mostly dogs) are protected under the Fair Housing Act and the Air Carrier Access Act, with certification from a doctor or therapist documenting a person's need. Most support animals provide a legitimate benefit, enabling people with ADD, depression, or learning disabilities to engage with the outside world. Others are a scheme to save money (a thousand dollars or more) so owners can avoid paying pet deposits or circumvent a ban on resident pets in apartments or condominiums. Understandably, this maneuver frustrates fellow tenants, who either paid a handsome deposit to keep their pet or had to abandon them altogether. The problem is that support letters can be procured online for $75–$100, sometimes for as little as $25. There are no standards, so it's anyone's guess if these issues ever get resolved.

Senator Manny Diaz, a Florida Republican from Hialeah, tried to restrict this practice in South Florida. He commented to the *Tampa Bay Tribune* in March 2019, "We've had a problem where folks have just started to *claim* these things. The most egregious I've seen, and I think we all saw it in South Florida on TV, was a gentleman claiming his alligator was an emotional support animal." (Wally the Gator was at an assisted-living facility in Pennsylvania, not Florida.)

As state legislatures debate the legality of landlords charging security deposits and monthly fees for the privilege of having a pet, the state of Oregon even considered outlawing the practice. It's unclear how such a policy would increase the number of pet-friendly apartments if a landlord isn't allowed to charge a tenant for the havoc a Saint Bernard wreaks on a four-hundred-square-foot studio. It's a sign of Pet Nation's swagger that a state legislature would even consider ordering landlords to accept pets free of charge.

WHO PUT THE "LOCO" IN LOCOMOTION?

Pets. All hell has broken loose inside America's transportation system. If Ella Fitzgerald were to sing her signature song "Can't Help Lovin' Dat Man" today, she would likely change the line "Fish got to swim, *birds* got to fly" to "Fish got to swim, *dogs* got to fly," since it's become common to board a flight and find at least one dog on the plane. Though most are no bigger than carry-on luggage, they can raise a racket if untrained and their travel mate is busy watching *Game of Thrones* on their laptop.

While it is not uncommon in developing countries to share a bus or a train car with chickens, goats, or other small critters, that was rarely the case in twentieth-century America. But since American dogs began flying business class with their own passports, there are more animals everywhere, all the time, on American planes, as cargo or passengers. The civility of mid-century travel, whether on early airplanes or the Twentieth Century Limited, "the Most Famous Train in the World," has evaporated. Here are some of the ways Pet Nation has impacted our transportation system.

Airplanes

Airplane travel has become a free-for-all, with unruly passengers cutting lines to steal your overhead luggage compartment, badgering the flight crew, brawling in the aisles, and doing everything possible to wrangle animals, especially dogs, onto planes. People regularly use the "emotional-support gambit" to secure genuine emotional support from a dog or to avoid paying the $100–$125 animal flight fee so that Mittens can travel to Napa on the family vacation.

IT'S A JUNGLE UP THERE

Online media is filled with harrowing stories of dogs big and small barking like mad for three hours on a flight to Miami, relieving themselves in the aisle somewhere over Ohio, or snoring to beat the band. These anecdotes are almost normal today.

What is abnormal are the people who try to fly with squirrels or peacocks, brandishing their "emotional-support" certificates like immigrants landing at Ellis Island in 1906 with their passports to freedom. The variety of animals that people have tried to bring onto airplanes would be amusing if it didn't underline the larger, *Wild West* problem on American airlines today: ferrets, parrots, small birds, cats of all shapes and sizes, pig, duck, monkey, turkey, miniature horse, marmoset, wolf, and the shy, retiring kangaroo.

In a *Wall Street Journal* article from 2018, titled "On U.S. Planes, the Dogs Are Winning," journalist Scott McCartney detailed the staggering number of pets flying an American planes each day: "Last year [2017]," he wrote, "the number of pets carried by U.S. airlines (usually for a fee in the cabin or cargo hold) increased 11 percent to 784,000, according to Airlines for America, the industry's lobbying organization. The number of service animals increased 24 percent to 281,000, according to A4A. And the number of emotional-support animals leapt 56 percent in that one-year period [2016–2017], to 751,000 . . . The airline now carries about 700 emotional-support animals and service dogs on flights each day [2017], up from 450 a day in 2016. The total number of animal incidents on airplanes—from urination to barking to biting—has increased 84 percent since 2016, says Gil West, Delta's chief operating officer." Though airlines have tried to limit the use of emotional support animals, requiring licensed veterinarian letters and certification from mental-health professionals for each traveling animal, the dogs are, indeed, winning.

It isn't simply the inconvenience of sharing two-person seating with a stranger and a forty-pound animal. People who are allergic to dogs or cats either suffer or avoid flying. Some standards-setting body may intervene, although individual airlines are taking action on their own.* Airlines themselves cannot control the situation and don't want to alienate passengers by restricting pet travel. The fact that more and more hotels at the end of the flight welcome the same dogs that can create chaos on board a plane doesn't help the situation.

Trains

Train travel is simpler and less frantic for pet owners. Fewer people travel long distances on trains with pets, and pet horror stories in the media are rare. There are dozens of national and regional airlines, each with their own pet regulations, while Amtrak is the *only* national railroad line. It has one, easy-to-follow set of rules on a single website. An Amtrak train from Portland, Oregon, to San Francisco has the same rules as an Amtrak train from Baltimore to Miami.

The policy is clear: Only dogs and cats (with up-to-date vaccinations) under twenty pounds, including the carrier, are allowed to travel, and only five pets per train, though service animals are excepted. People with pets travel only in coach, and business class and sleeping cars are off-limits. Pets must be at least eight weeks old and "odorless, harmless, not disruptive, and require no attention during travel," or Amtrak can refuse them passage or remove them from trains or stations.

Steven Eder's 2018 article in the *New York Times*, "Pups Onboard: Why Trains Are a Great Way to Travel with Your Dog(s)," chronicles trips he's taken to Washington, DC, and other cities with his Pugs, Rufus and Hamilton, in mellow contrast to airline travel, and at one-

---

* The American Humane Association, for example, is providing advice and expertise to United Airlines concerning their PetSafe transport program.

quarter of the price: "A few minutes after we sank into our seats, the train whistled out of the station and the conductor made his way down the aisle. It was just like any other trek between Penn Station and Union Station, except one thing. The conductor looked down at our printed ticket and mentally checked off my wife and me before pausing and giving a friendly but perplexed look. 'Rufus and Hamilton,' he read off the sheet. 'You've got four?' At our feet were Rufus and Hamilton, our two black pug dogs. They were nestled into their Sherpa-lined travel bags, quietly being lulled to sleep by the rhythms of the train as we headed from New York to Washington. When we travel, the pugs come along whenever possible because, to us, they are family."

HELLO, ROOM SERVICE, COULD YOU SEND UP SOME TREATS?

In her novel *The Accidental Tourist*, Anne Tyler writes, "I've always thought a hotel ought to offer optional small animals. I mean a cat to sleep on your bed at night, or a dog of some kind to act pleased when you come in. You ever notice how a hotel room feels so lifeless?"

It would appear that this bestselling book about a travel writer who hates to travel is required reading for the hospitality industry. At every stop along the way today, there are people (hotels, Airbnb apartments, travel planners, specialized travel websites) who will accommodate your pet-related whims.

Here is an entirely plausible exchange you could have via BringFido, the largest "pet-friendly dog hotel and travel directory":

Where are you going?

Cairo.

Which one?

There's more than one?

Yes.

Okay, I need a hotel that's dog-friendly, and I'll be traveling with two Schnauzers.

Let's see. You have Cairo: Egypt,* Georgia, Illinois, New York, West Virginia—there are several Cairos. Take your pick.

They all have pet hotels?

Yes.

Okay, it's Cairo, Egypt, and, if possible, put me near the pyramids at Giza for one night.

That's easy. A bed-and-breakfast, thirty-one dollars, for any size dog.

Okay, and then I'll splurge on a fancy hotel in the city for three days.

You have some choices: the Four Seasons, the Fairmont, the Hilton, Le Meridien.

KIMPTON HOTELS—WAGGING TAILS WELCOMED

1. At check-in, they greet your pet by name.
2. Plush bed-loaners.
3. Concierge list of nearby pet-friendly restaurants, parks, shops, and groomers.
4. Door hangers to alert other hotel guests that your beloved pet is in the room.
5. Courtesy bags for walking your dog.
6. No additional charge or deposit required for your pets.
7. No size or weight limit: hello, Great Mastiff, at one hundred sixty pounds. And those amazing jowls.
8. No limit on the number of pets: Queen Elizabeth and her Rowdy of Corgis are always welcome.
9. Nightly wine reception with pets welcome.
10. A director of pet relations at certain locations.

---

* Egypt, like many Middle East countries, a place where dogs historically lived in the streets and were routinely abused.

Fine, the Four Seasons.

Giant Schnauzer or Miniature?

Miniature Schnauzer.

Then it's the Four Seasons Cairo Nile Plaza, five hundred sixty-seven dollars per night, pets under seven kilograms no extra charge.

Perfect. Cleopatra and Caesar are both around twelve pounds, so please book it.

In a few minutes, you've secured hotels (one a leading luxury hotel) that welcome your two beloved Schnauzers in a country five thousand miles away. Like Petfinder, Rover, and Chewy, BringFido solved the pet equation:

1. Select a category with a broad user base, unmet needs for information and services, and money to burn.
2. Research the heck out of the category.
3. Find the answer to every possible question, then aggregate the data into one seamless site, so your guests won't wander away to another site to find a detail you missed.

Choose your continent (no hotels on Antarctica), city, dates, and then the hotel that suits your dog(s): size, age, number, activities. In 2020, there are more than 150,000 dog-welcoming hotels in one hundred countries worldwide; restaurants (57,902 at last count); activities (from Doggywood at Dollywood to the National Mall); events (PetOberfest in Woodbridge, Virginia; Poodle Day, in Carmel, California); and services (whatever Mittens needs while away from home). Why would you ever leave her at home in a kennel again?

Any hotel that isn't pet-friendly today is turning away business. The sidebar detailing the policies and philosophy of the hip national chain Kimpton reveals how far we've come. The phrase "pet-friendly" is the twenty-first-century "Michelin star," the millennial badge of approval. The first sentence of Marriott's pet policy could be an industry mantra:

"Your pets are family, and no vacation would be complete without the whole family. . . . At Marriott International, we love your pets and welcome them, just as we welcome you."

🐾

ARE YOU THIRSTY?

If you drive across America today, you will happen onto a new kind of entertainment venue, a Pet Nation construct, that blends three elements: pets, travel, and beverages. That is correct, places that serve food and drink and welcome dogs or cats with open arms—sorry—paws. Recognizing the differences between the two species, the people who care for them, and the ways people fold pets into their lives, the hospitality industry (food and drink) has evolved formats appropriate to each—specific in character, mood, preferred beverage, location, and ambience—tailored to both the animals and their owners.

Cat Cafés

Koneko, the Japanese word for "kitten," is the name of the first Japanese-style cat café in New York City, which opened on the Lower East Side, in 2015, on National Cat Day, with two indoor cattery spaces and an outdoor catio. The world's first cat café opened in Taipei, in 1998, before the concept spread to Japan and countries around the world. New York has been slow to this trend, with only a handful—Tokyo now has sixty cat cafés. Every major American city has cat cafés, which promote the adoption of at-risk cats, celebrate our furry friends, and allow cats of all sizes and colors to roam about while people relax, sometimes dine, drink tea, and contemplate the next member of their household.

With twenty cats available for adoption, Koneko is typical of this trend. Each week, there are different events that celebrate cats and Japanese culture. One part café, one part rescue network, Koneko is a place to meet cats who need a home of their own; your handsome tabby must, sadly, stay at home. Those are the rules, whether at Koneko or Meow Parlour, a popular tea lounge and cat sanctuary.

Dog Brewpubs

Tea and beer are different "animals." Tea drinkers sit in comfortable Danish chairs and philosophize, speaking in low voices. They settle in. It always seems to be cold outside when the kettle is on, which reinforces the warming, restorative aspect of tea. Tea drinkers sip, beer drinkers chug. Even the sounds of beer consumption are different. Beer drinkers don't stand or sit on ceremony. Rules are off the table; no topic of discussion or joke is off-limits. Nor are dogs when it comes to beer, particularly craft beer. Cats play hard to get, while a dog's tail says, "I'm yours." Dogs are rambunctious, needy. Turn up the volume. They bound into the room, with no need for introductions.

Natural sidekicks, beer and dogs have met up in Austin, Texas, to create a new restaurant format, the dog brewpub. These bars are as forward and boisterous as the cat café is restrained and laid-back. In a city known for partying, where music is part of the backstory, bars and beer gardens have opened their doors to dogs. Unlike the indoor cat café, this is a fluid indoor/outdoor environment, with casual tables set among the trees. Beer and dogs need room to rumble and won't be sitting down for a long, soulful conversation. The ambience is active, celebratory, competitive. It is not cerebral. It wants to and often seems to spin out of control. The Austin Beer Garden and Brewing Co. is dog-friendly, with biscuits and watering stations. "There's plenty of room to sit outside with your dog in the shade thanks to a few beautiful trees in the beer garden."

In Austin, ABGB calls them "Divine Canines," encouraging patrons to support therapy dogs and beer by "Buy(ing) a *Pawsport*! One pour per Pawsport, so check out as many (brew-dog pubs) as you can." A noble undertaking: the sale of beer glasses benefits free therapy dog visits at 195 partner sites in Central Texas. The formula is tight: great local beer, dogs, Texas music, old trees, and a friendly, welcoming audience.

Each animal, dog and cat, has inspired an entertainment niche plus a beverage with wide appeal and a personality appropriate to the species. While many a cat owner enjoys the occasional cold brew, and dog owners sometimes drink green tea, the essence of each species is comfortably at home within their respective cat café and dog brewpub.

PUPPIES BEHIND BARS

No, this is not the title of a *National Enquirer* article or an ASPCA exposé of a puppy mill in central Arkansas. It is the name of a national program, Puppies Behind Bars, that simultaneously improves the lives of at-risk dogs and prison inmates by letting inmates socialize puppies that become guide dogs for the blind. This initiative was grounded in a few logical, congruent insights that hinge on the irresistible power of unconditional love, the canine holy grail. If "a dog is man's best friend," then why couldn't dogs help criminals change their ways?

Criminologists in Bedford, New York, thought it was worth a try. They put an odd (prison inmate and damaged animal) couple into an equation that yielded the fabled "1 + 1 = 3" result: A sad, negative, and depressing locale (prison) became less sad and more vibrant when innocent, furry creatures needing therapy entered the prison cell. Each party trained the other: prisoners socialized euthanasia-bound dogs who'd been abused in puppy mills and dog-fighting rings, and trained them to become service animals or loving companion dogs. The dogs gave unconditional love to the inmates (many the product of broken homes and lost childhoods lacking empathy or kindness), and inspired them to become different, better human beings.

Each learned a trade, the dogs becoming service dogs, sight dogs, ordnance-detection dogs, or companion pets, adopted into new and loving homes, and the prisoners becoming more productive individuals with meaningful lives, including:

- Careers as dog trainers and groomers.
- A detour around crime, a path to a new life.
- Lower rates of recidivism: Why return to your old loveless way of life and risk losing or betraying the love of your best friend, your own dog, who will never desert you, but who will not accompany you into prison if you return to a life of crime?

In an ABC News story about a Jacksonville, Florida–based program called TAILS (Teaching Animals and Inmates Life Skills), Jennifer Wesely, a professor of criminology at the University of North Florida, observed, "The positive behavioral effects of prison animal programs include enhanced empathy, emotional intelligence, communication, patience, self-control and trust." She believes that the human-animal bond can interrupt the prisoners' " 'criminogenic masculinity' traits such as risk-taking, never backing down, and violent behavior." The prisoners in these Florida prisons receive certification as animal trainers.

It isn't all about dogs. Created in 2011, the Larch Cat Adoption Program, formerly Cuddly Catz, brings cats who need rehabilitation to a prison in Yacolt, Washington. The cats learn how to live with inmates, while the inmates care for the cats and kittens, learning new social skills and how to be gentle. Eventually, the cats are adopted out. Working with the Bureau of Land Management (BLM), the Arizona Department of Corrections and Colorado Correctional Industries match prisoners with professional horse trainers to manage and train wild horses controlled by the BLM. The program is called WHIP (the Wild Horse Inmate Program). After training, the horses are adopted by qualified families and farms.

Given the success of these programs, which mutually benefit animals and inmates, it is surprising that more state and federal penal institutions have not followed suit. The national debate on our criminal justice system demonstrates the challenges existing treatment methods face. There are plenty of dogs who need help and an equal number of prisoners who need love. Let's put them together.

THE LAST HOLDOUTS

Despite the advance of Pet Nation, there are still places in America where pets are not allowed—ever, some of the time, or even when people follow the rules. Given the relentless desire of people to be with their pets all the time, the question is how long these entities will be able to withstand legal challenges and keep the little ones, and sometimes not so little ones, outside. (More on this in chapter nine.)

Food Establishments

The Food and Drug Administration's food guide sets policy: with few exceptions, live animals of any kind are not permitted on the premises of a grocery store, a restaurant, or any other food establishment. The prohibition applies to dogs, cats, birds, and other animals. The law is designed to protect the national food supply from contamination from animal feces, or parasites, or any number of other possibilities. There are exceptions, such as law-enforcement dogs with a police officer, or service dogs with their owners. City and state governments can adjust policy. Outdoor cafés (and some casual indoor restaurants) in many cities allow dogs on-leash, especially for take-out purchases. Bakeries and new age grocery stores often say nothing if a patron carries a small dog in her arms.

Retail Stores

As people drift from brick-and-mortar stores to online shopping, multi-tasking, saving drive time, retreating into their smartphones, or examining products in-store before buying online, any strategy that brings people to a shop, not a digital portal, should interest retailers. People today expect to take their dog(s) on Sunday shopping expeditions. Nevertheless, some stores are immune to the charm of four-legged creatures. It all depends on the store:

Home Depot: yes
Walmart, the world's largest retailer: no
Target: no
Best Buy: no
Bed Bath & Beyond: yes

It pays to query. Although IKEA's official policy in America is no pets allowed, they have tested a pet service called "Dog Parking" in their German stores, offering guests a covered outdoor area with Astro-turf, water bowls, and small kennels. Unfortunately, the pets are left unattended, so there is a security risk.

The presence of pets in stores is not a settled issue, as more people build their lives and free time around their companion dogs. If an animal is on-leash, well behaved, quiet, and nonaggressive, the risk of store damage or shopper annoyance is slight, but, ultimately, the retailer sets the policy. More on this dynamic in chapter nine.

State Parks

Dogs are not allowed in California state parks and on many public beaches, "to protect the state's natural resources." State park ranger Ken Low explains, "Dogs will affect wildlife patterns; they leave behind a scent that will deter some animals. And dogs can carry diseases such as parvo that can transfer to coyotes."

Funeral Parlors

Though there are no federal or state laws prohibiting animals from entering mortuaries or funerals, they normally don't attend funerals. But when Senator John McCain lay in state at the Capitol rotunda, his dog Burma lay beside him, as he had during his illness.

Colleges

Only a handful of America's four thousand colleges allow dogs, or pets other than the occasional turtle or betta, to reside on campus. Protected by the Americans with Disabilities Act and Fair Housing Law, service animals and emotional-support animals are allowed, though most colleges will request documentation for an emotional-support animal. As Rice University, a leading university in Houston, gently declares, "Animals that disrupt the educational, research, administrative, or other core operations of the university must be immediately removed from the campus."

Alfred State University, part of the New York State university system, has tested a policy to allow select breeds of dog on campus. The prohibited list of breeds includes the usual tough guys (Alaskan Malamute, Bulldog, Doberman Pinscher, Great Dane, Mastiff, Pit Bull, Rottweiler) and a few head-scratchers—the stylish Papillon, the Audrey Hepburn of small dogs, more fluffy tail and stand-up ears than muscle, and the "ferocious" Toy Poodle, at a towering ten inches tall and weighing in at six pounds.

Though more colleges are tinkering with their pet policy, most do not allow dogs or cats on campus for now. There is no uniform collegiate rationale, but it appears to be a mutt approach, a blend of these elements:

- Fear that lectures will be disrupted.
- Insurance squabbles.
- Damage to the physical plant.
- Health issues for certain students.
- Housing—does your roommate want an English Sheepdog in your twelve-by-twelve dorm room?
- Stability—students are mobile, vagrant, unpredictable in their hours and routines; animals could suffer.
- Expense—what happens if the cat gets sick and the student cannot afford care?
- They're messy—it's hard enough for some students to make their bed once a semester; how will they keep the litter box tidy?

Churches

The Catholic Church only allows animals into churches on the feast day of Saint Francis of Assisi, October 4, when animals receive a blessing. Some evangelical churches practice snake-handling. Other than that, animals and their owners must worship in the great outdoors, from whence they came.

Federal Court Rooms

"Your Honor, I object."
   "*Woof woof.*"
   "Your barking is in contempt."
   "*Meow.*"
   Case closed.

Private Clubs

They set their own rules.

Native American Tribal Councils

While there is no published reason for this policy, stray dogs are a growing problem on reservations.

The list of places that are off-limits is shrinking daily, though it makes sense that any sterile environment, such as hospital emergency, observation, and operating rooms will keep the doors locked, and food establishments will be a continuing contested arena.

HEALTH RISKS AND PUBLIC RESISTANCE

Let's pause and look at the underbelly of Pet Nation's invasion of America. There are two reasons advanced to oppose or to limit the introduction of pets (primarily dogs and cats, but turtles, too) into public or previously pet-free spaces. The first is valid, and I will address it in detail. The second is a complex, volatile set of issues that the 35 percent of American non–pet households sometimes raise, but with little chance of changing the direction or halting the momentum of Pet Nation:

1. Pets carry diseases that can be transmitted to people (zoonotic diseases), and vice versa, from people to pets (reverse zoonotic diseases). Some people have allergies to pets. These are serious medical issues that demand analysis, public policy, and controls.
2. Some people don't like cats or dogs. They echo the sentiments expressed in the section "Why do some people hate dogs?" in chapter one, namely, that some dogs are dangerous, some sidewalks are littered with dog waste, dogs control public spaces, and "dogs are not children" and are expected to be occasionally "inconvenient." Since one of every three people in America does not have a pet, these concerns are real, though in the minority. However, it doesn't mean that they should control public spaces, any more than people who don't like children should ban kids from parks, ballparks, stores, airplanes, and restaurants. Bias has its limits outside the home, where parents try to set the rules of conduct.

Pets can serve as carriers or precursors of nineteen of twenty public-health risks in the United States, including zoonotic diseases caused by viruses, bacteria, parasites, and fungi. Some of these diseases are common and well-known, such as rabies, anthrax, West Nile virus, Rocky Mountain spotted fever, Lyme disease, Ebola virus, and certain strains of bird flu. HIV was initially a zoonotic disease in the late twentieth century, before it began to spread from person to person.

BITE ME

1. America has 325 million people and 90 million dogs. According to a Centers for Disease Control and Prevention (CDC) study, 4.7 million people are bitten each year, one out of every sixty-nine people.
2. Of that total, 81 percent do not require medical attention.
3. From 2002 to 2016, 5,473,893 people were treated in emergency rooms for dog bites. Of that number, 91,244 were hospitalized.
4. In 2015, 28,000 people with dog bites needed reconstructive surgery.
5. Men are bitten slightly more often than women.
6. Children under the age of twelve are the most bitten demographic.
7. Most people are bitten at home.
8. 77 percent of biting dogs are the family dog or a friend's dog.
9. Postal carriers are bitten more than any other profession: 6,400 times in 2018.
10. Breeds that bite the most, in descending order: Chihuahua, Bulldog, Pit Bull, Rottweiler, German Shepherd.
11. The top three breeds in strength of bite, as measured by pounds per square inch (PSI): Kangal, 743 PSI; American Bandogge, 731 PSI; and Cane Corso, 700 PSI.
12. Americans are twice as likely to die of a bee sting as a dog bite.
13. The insurance industry pays out $500 million annually to settle dog-bite claims.

It isn't news that dogs, cats, birds, and turtles come into contact with, and transmit, diseases or infections. They don't live in hermetically sealed laboratories; they run around outdoors in the muck and grime where bacteria thrive, and are not bashful about sniffing here, there, and everywhere. This has consequences for people and pets vis-à-vis the specific environments (and types of people: infants and sick adults) that aren't appropriate for unrestricted pet-people encounters.

The names of these diseases and infections sound ominous, and rightly so. Though rare, methicillin-resistant staphylococcus, caused by contact with dog feces or urine, or feces, bites, or scratches from flea-bitten cats affects babies and the elderly. Puppies and kittens, which are irresistible for most people, are the worst offenders and the hardest to control. While staphylococcus is serious, hookworm and roundworm are more common threats for children, from contact with cat and dog feces. Cat-scratch fever from the Bartonella henselae bacteria affects 40 percent of cats and can cause swelling, fever, aches, and headaches in humans.

The preventive measures for most of these diseases are simple but not foolproof: wash hands, avoid cat scratches (not easy), and cat and dog feces. However, there are other risks with simple (often unavoidable) transmission points: pasteurella from dog or cat licks can cause soft tissue, bone, and joint infections. Campylobacteriosis affects 1.3 million Americans with diarrhea, fever, and myalgia each year. Normally a foodborne infection, it can also be caused by a bacteria found in dogs and cats, especially puppies and kittens.

Rabies is a serious condition but extremely rare in the United States from dog bites. Most rabies bites come from other critters. The CDC reports, "Human rabies cases in the United States are rare, with only 1 to 3 cases reported annually. Twenty-three cases of human rabies have been reported in the United States in the past decade (2008–2017). Eight of these were contracted outside of the U.S. and its territories. The number of human rabies deaths in the United States attributed to rabies has been steadily declining since the 1970s thanks to animal control and vaccination programs, successful outreach programs, and the availability of modern rabies biologics."

Dogs can transmit Bordetella (kennel cough) to humans, especially those with weakened immune systems. Public-health risks are not limited to dogs and cats. Approximately seventy thousand Americans contract salmonellosis each year by touching turtles, snakes, lizards, and other reptiles.

There is one basic rule, which is ignored every day somewhere in America: pets, and dogs in particular, do not belong in food establishments. This upsets pet owners, and they have successfully lobbied for the right to take pets to outdoor or terrace tables. Many bakeries (unsurprisingly, French bakeries) and small New York cafés now allow dogs on-leash to enter the premises while their owner makes a purchase. They are no different than restaurants, but it has become a common sight in America, from big cities to small towns to family entertainment meccas like Disney World. However, no city, county, or state will force restaurants to allow pets inside, particularly if they can reach the kitchen. Though people use the emotional-support gambit to slip small "handbag dogs" (Chihuahuas, Yorkies) into restaurants, this practice should not be allowed.

Only true service dogs belong in food establishments, and even that is a loaded issue. A restaurant cannot refuse service to a person with a service dog. It is illegal at both the state and federal levels to ask a service dog to demonstrate a task.

American restaurant interiors and certain areas of hospitals will remain off-limits to animals. It's hard to see Pet Nation taking the "No Pets Allowed" sign seriously anywhere else.

WHERE DO WE
(DOGS AND CATS) GO NEXT?

If we retrace the dog's path from bedroom, wedding, airplane, market, the office, Congress, back to the hunter-gatherer camps in Central Asia thirty thousand years ago, where man's bond with dogs (and pets) began, it would seem that the public presence of pets in America will continue to expand, pitting public patience and legitimate, common-sense health concerns against the millennial chant: "I must have my dog with me all the time, everywhere, anywhere I go. It's just not fair. Change the policy now or I won't shop here or eat here. Period. Twitter, here I come."

"No Pets Allowed": "We'll see about that. You'll be hearing from my lawyer. Or my advocate's lawyer. Or my Poodle's lawyer. Or the local humane society. It's cold outside and Colette wants a cookie and a comfortable pillow right now! Open the door!"

· 4 ·

THE SECRET TO PET NATION
The Human-Animal Bond

Fads come and go. Whatever happened to pet rocks, Cabbage Patch Dolls, and Beanie Babies? Some trends disappear or fade into historical footnotes, while others gain traction and become a part of daily life. Few people wear bell-bottom jeans anymore, but organic food, once considered trendy, is now ubiquitous. Are pets a fad whose cachet will wane, or did something deeper and more profound take hold over the past few decades, a benign but incurable addiction? I would argue the latter, for the simple reason that pets make people healthier, feel better, and help them successfully navigate life's challenges—from day-to-day problems to life-threatening situations—with less stress and more joy.

The deep appeal of a pet is more than the fuzzy sensation you experience when your Siamese kitten stretches from head to tail, then glides onto your shoulder while you're reading a book in bed. Scientists call our unique relationship with pets the human-animal bond, a subject supported by enough research to fill twenty-nine thousand entries at the Human Animal Bond Research Institute (HABRI) at Purdue University. They define the human-animal bond as "a mutually beneficial and dynamic relationship between people and animals that is influenced by behaviors essential to the health and well-being of both." However, this definition is too clinical to capture the emotional contours of this phenomenon, which is almost primal. Pet Nation happened because many Americans came to understand and enjoy the medical, psychological, and social power of pets. It was a question that research scientists have been studying since the 1960s—do pets enrich the lives of people, families, and communities? Ultimately, they proved that it does, and once people understood that the human-animal bond wasn't merely instinct or folklore, the implications exploded onto the front page of American culture. It turned out that pets may be the best (and most affordable) medicine we have, but we didn't realize it.

The transit to Pet Nation and the universal embrace of the human-animal bond was long, roundabout, and bumpy. To become an equal partner in the bond construct, animals (pets) needed several things, which took years to materialize:

1. **Protection:** relief from physical abuse at all levels of society, at work, on farms, in the street, and even in medical schools where they were dissected for research, sometimes with minimal sedation.
2. **A point of view:** their own vantage point, for people to consider daily life through their eyes; only then could people understand both their plight and the potential benefits to man and animal if their lot were reversed.
3. **Philosophy:** a theoretical framework underlying the dynamics of their interactions with people.
4. **Value-added work:** pets helping people see, hear, and combat illness—a range of medical benefits—demonstrating their sensitivity to people and the power of that affinity.

The Human-Animal Bond:
Milestones

1822: The United Kingdom passes the first serious animal-welfare law.

1866: Henry Bergh founds the American Society for the Prevention of Cruelty to Animals (ASPCA), America's first animal-protection organization.

1949: Konrad Lorenz writes *Man Meets Dog* and creates the discipline of anthrozoology, with his analysis of animal imprinting.

1960–1975: Boris Levinson develops the theory and foundation for the use of pets to treat psychological and physical disorders.

1977: Delta Foundation created, now the national leader in animal-assisted therapy, as Pet Partners, www.petpartners.org.

1980: Friedman study on coronary heart disease survival with pet intervention.

1981: The American Veterinary Medical Association (AVMA) creates task force on the human-animal bond (USA), www.avma.org.

1987: The National Institutes of Health (NIH) holds a conference on "The Health Benefits of Pets."

1990: The Americans with Disabilities Act requires hotels, restaurants, and other businesses to admit service animals.

1983: Leo Bustad is credited with the first use of the term "human-animal bond" recorded in an academic setting at a conference celebrating Lorenz's eightieth birthday.

2011: HABRI is founded.

2013: Lackland Air Force Base unveils the US Military Working Dog Teams National Monument to honor the service of canine soldiers.

Without these psychological, emotional, and scientific advances, a therapy organization like Pet Partners, formerly the Delta Foundation, could never perform three million annual visits in America today, with thirteen thousand registered animal therapy teams "helping patients in recovery, people with intellectual disabilities, seniors living with Alzheimer's, students, veterans with PTSD, and those approaching end of life." Absent scientific validation, the American public would not have the information and trust to make informed decisions about the health benefits of pets.

Until recently, such a program would have been dismissed by critics. Reinforced by the second-class status of animals (and centuries of neglect), skeptics challenged the notion that people experience anything beyond emotional pleasure (nothing to sniff at) from engagement with cats or dogs. When animal scientists began to publish studies that showed the deeper, positive effects of the human-animal bond, scholars questioned the methodology of the science. A good example is an article by Harold Herzog titled "The Impact of Pets on Human Health and Psychological Well-Being: Fact, Fiction, or Hypothesis?" published in *Current Directions in Psychological Science* in 2011. Herzog maintained that human-animal bond research lacked rigor and adequate sample sizes. He argued that research conclusions can reflect experimental bias, the unconscious desire to prove a point, without acknowledging a range of possible explanations or causes beyond human-animal bond factors.

Such critiques are common in academia, and perfectly valid. It is part of the scientific method to question data and sample sizes, or to wonder if a prior relationship between owners and pets undermines the objectivity of the study. Eventually, such arguments must be weighed against a body of evidence. Herzog's arguments would be more persuasive if the human-animal bond claims rested on a handful of studies. However, the quantity and diversity of research programs with similar outcomes overwhelmingly supports the hypothesis that the human-animal bond is real, positive, and profound. Let's explore.

How does one prove that the human-animal bond exists? And how do you conduct scientific, medical, and psychological studies of such a relationship? In the 1970s, Leo Bustad, the former dean of the Washington State University College of Veterinary Medicine and the founder of the People-Pet Partnership, tackled the challenge with his research into animal behavior. Using a multidisciplinary approach, he worked to "develop new and creative ways to realize the potential inherent in people/animal/environmental interactions properly studied and utilized." It was Bustad who coined the phrase "human-animal bond" at a 1983 conference, where he credited Konrad Lorenz, the author of the 1949 book *Man Meets Dog* and the founder of modern ethology (the study of animal behavior), with the birth of the movement. Yet even with the stamp of Lorenz, a Nobel laureate, Bustad's theories about the human-animal bond were slow to take hold, and over decades pigeonholed as "folk wisdom," like your grandmother's homemade flu remedy.

RESEARCH

Today, three organizations lead the way in continuing Bustad's research and raising awareness in the United States and around the world: the IAHAIO (International Association of Human Animal Interaction Organizations); WALTHAM Petcare Science Institute (Mars Petcare's research center); and HABRI (Human Animal Bond Research Institute). IAHAIO is an umbrella organization for groups around the world (primarily Europe and the United States) studying and/or developing programs related to the human-animal bond. It was established because scientists saw promise in the outcomes of engagement between humans and animals, and needed a platform to share plans, data, and discoveries. IAHAIO's insistence on strict scientific protocols and peer review informed the academic and medical communities that human-animal interaction was a fertile field of research, not a topical "filler" for the evening news.

I've worked with Dr. Sandra McCune, human-animal interaction scientific leader at the WALTHAM Centre for Pet Nutrition outside London. WALTHAM has earned an international reputation for advanced studies in nutrition for pets of all kinds, and its support for human-animal bond research. Few people know that Mars, Incorporated, the company that brings us Snickers candy bars and M&M's, is also the world's leading pet food and veterinary provider. WALTHAM is part of Mars. It is meaningful when an organization like Mars recognizes the legitimacy of scientific research in the human-animal bond. With funding from Mars, the National Institutes of Health created a federal research program to study human-animal interaction. Operated through the National Institute of Child Health and Human Development, the program offers scientists research grants to study the impact of animals on child development, in physical and psychological therapeutic treatments, and the effect of animals on public health, including their ability to reduce or to prevent disease.

HABRI is a Washington, DC–based nonprofit organization with an ambitious profile. Its mission involves:

1. Funding academic research into the human-animal bond, to study the scientific foundation of the subject.
2. Gathering all the studies and articles in the world concerning the human-animal bond in one archive, the Purdue University College of Veterinary Medicine. The current count is twenty-nine thousand entries and growing. Through its online database, HABRI enables skeptics and advocates alike to access information, evaluate research, and stay abreast of current treatment discoveries.
3. Expanding practical, real-world applications of human-animal bond research in areas of public policy, veterinary practices,

education, human medicine, and consumer awareness. The research is developed for public use, not academic discourse, including the funding of research projects, such as a 2015 AAT (animal-assisted therapy) study of breast cancer patients during counseling, which recorded:

a. Increasing calm and feelings of anticipation of cancer patients toward participation in counseling.

b. Increasing disclosure of information and engagement by patients with therapists.

c. Increasing communication with health professionals.

d. Cancer patients undergoing chemotherapy who had a weekly, hour-long session of therapy with a dog rated their symptoms of depression and anxiety at half the level of those who did not.

Steven Feldman, the executive director of HABRI and a prolific author and animal advocate, is an evangelist for the physical- and mental-health benefits of animals. "HABRI believes," he has written, "that everyone living with a mental illness should have access to care, services, and support that would benefit their mental health, including positive interaction with companion animals."

Each of these three organizations has focused their research on two key areas:

1. Measuring human behavior or outcomes *with* and *without* the presence of companion animals, particularly with people in challenging situations, such as autism and senior isolation.

2. Scientific analysis of chemical or physiological reactions with humans after engagement with pets, producing either a decrease

in cortisol (the primary stress hormone), or an increase in oxytocin (the beneficial "love hormone").

Establishing a link between these two areas of research helps researchers and clinicians determine how chemical or physiological
changes in the body and brain correlate with positive behavioral or
physical outcomes. When engaged with a dog or cat or horse, does
something happen in the human brain that explains improved health or
pleasure factors, or a stress reduction? If the answer is verifiably yes,
then it removes much of the mystery surrounding the effects of pet contact with human beings. Here is some of the evidence to date.

Autism

No field of human-animal bond research draws greater interest than the
study of an animal's impact on autistic children and their families. Sophie Hall, a pioneer in this field at the University of Leicester Medical
College in the United Kingdom, has focused on the long-term benefits
of autism-assistance dogs for both the individual with autism and the
surrounding family and caregivers. Her research has found that these
dogs can increase child safety and promote outdoor access, communication, and independence, while improving sensory perception and reducing parental stress. The pet effectively lowers the burden on the parents
serving as the sole focus, since it provides an alternative object of attachment for the child. The research is ongoing, though it is complicated by the inconsistency of regulations and standards regarding
autism-assistance dogs.

Yet more evidence is provided by a 2015 study published in *Anthro-
zoos* that found that frequent contact with dogs helps improve the social
skills of autistic children. Dogs navigate their surroundings and social

interactions in an unfiltered, sensory-based way, constantly making pattern-based associations, like adults and children on the autism spectrum do. Consequently, dogs invite positive social interactions for these children, verbally and nonverbally, lowering stress levels.

Dogs are not the only animal helping autistic children today. A 2012 NPR story by Julie Rovner describes the work of the Northern Virginia Therapeutic Riding Program in Clifton, Virginia. "The beauty of the horse is that it can be therapeutic in so many different ways," says Breeanna Bornhorst, executive director of the center. "Some of our riders might benefit from the connection and the relationship—building with the horse and with their environment. Other riders maybe will benefit physically, from the movements, and build that core strength, and body awareness and muscle memory." Rovner recounts speech therapist Cathy Coleman, an instructor in the program, working with nine-year-old Ryan Shank-Rowe, who has autism, and a pony named Happy. During the session, Ryan takes Happy through his paces, riding bareback, while talking with Coleman. According to Coleman, the equine therapy has improved Ryan's speech, language, and personal engagement; Ryan's mother has seen progress in core life issues with her son, such as dressing, following directions, and staying safe, thanks to the horseback riding.

Children with autism often experience extreme stress in new or unknown situations, considered an "anxiogenic stimulus." Research shows that a pet's presence can distract the child, triggering an attention shift, which reduces their anxiety. The child can settle into or address new environments more easily. Thus, a family pet can improve an autistic child's ability to focus, to concentrate, and to learn.

Therapy and Pet Dogs in Hospitals

For centuries, the idea of bringing a dog into a sterile hospital environment was anathema, but, increasingly, nurses and doctors are welcoming dogs into hospitals to relieve patient stress and to improve the overall outcomes for patients and their families. There are myriad examples of this change in attitude, and in practice, throughout the medical world.

The Royal College of Nursing in the United Kingdom has published a universal protocol, setting out guidelines that any health-care facility can follow when working with dogs. They invite professionals and laymen to "expert teas" to "meet one of our four-legged friends and learn about how pets can enhance health and well-being." It took time for New York State—which had always banned dogs from hospitals—to see the wisdom of this approach. But now, through the work of the Good Dog Foundation and others, New York allows therapy dogs into hospitals to work with cancer patients.

The Mayo Clinic's Caring Canines Program, a formal, animal-assisted initiative, was launched in 2011. Registered dogs and their owners make "meet and greet" visits in hospital and clinic waiting areas. Before deployment, dogs are tested and registered by the nationwide therapy group Pet Partners. The Mayo Clinic program utilizes therapy dogs in several situations at their campuses in Phoenix and Scottsdale, such as dental procedures with children and radiation treatments for cancer treatments. They have found that therapy dogs are helpful for residents of long-term-care facilities, particularly people suffering from dementia, cardiovascular disease, PTSD, and anxiety.

Doctors at both Mass General (Boston) and Johns Hopkins (Baltimore) bring therapy dogs into their intensive-care units to cheer up patients, humanizing and softening the ICU experience. Research confirms that dogs lower the stress of family members in waiting rooms, a universal challenge. Some animals-in-hospital programs have expanded to allow people to bring family pets into a child patient's room, since a personal pet can have more impact than a trained therapy dog. A study in Barcelona, Spain, found that animal-assisted therapy can lower stress levels in schizophrenia patients within a conventional rehabilitation setting.

Therapy dogs play a role in hospital emergency departments, reducing a patient's general anxiety level and their desire for pain medication, no small achievement in an America ravaged by opioid addiction. Sometimes, both the animal and the health-care professional profit from the interaction. Danielle Geronimo, a paramedic in Richmond, Virginia, had an idea: Why not pair shelter dogs who need loving homes with paramedics during their shifts, when they need to relax and be calm? Paramedic work in cities is mentally taxing and, at times, physically dangerous. Paramedics are exposed to serious injury and crime each day. So the Richmond SPCA established a program called Pets for Paramedics to improve the lives of both the paramedics and dogs in need. The SPCA brings pets to the Richmond Ambulance Authority headquarters each month so that staff can interact with shelter dogs who need homes. The paramedics get a break, return to work refreshed, and the dogs often find new homes.

The evidence is compelling and documented: animal-assisted therapy with dogs produces objective health changes in people of all ages, from children to seniors, with reductions in measures of cardiovascular stress, improvements in neurophysiological stress markers (e.g., cortisol), increases in endorphins and oxytocin, and the enhancement of immune factors.

Keeping Allergies at Bay

A 2017 Canadian study at the University of Alberta explored the benefits of placing cats and dogs in a household to expose children to a wider range of microbes and bacteria than they normally encounter. The practice results in fewer cases of pediatric allergies. What's the science? "It used to be that we were exposed to lots of dust and feces . . . and 'good friend' bacteria," says Kim Kelly, a postdoctoral fellow at the University of Arizona's Human-Animal Interaction Research Initiative. "As we evolved to living indoors, we became underexposed to [microbes], and we hypothesize that predisposes us to a host of health issues." Pets come in contact with some rough stuff, to put it bluntly, so kids exposed to pets are better armed to respond to allergies.

Seniors Need to Eat Better

In 1996, a Colorado State University study discovered a positive correlation between a senior interacting with a pet and the pet's need to eat on a regular schedule. This pet-feeding interaction stimulates the senior to eat, too. It's logical: The instinct to feed the cat or dog, or, in this study, fish, prompted the senior herself to eat. Linsey Knerl reported on this phenomenon when writing for *Delaware News Online,* in March 2019, observing: "Older adults can struggle with maintaining weight and keeping interest in food. That's why many senior living centers and communities have incorporated fish tanks and aquariums into their dining room décor." As we explore in chapter eight, an element of fish keeping is the simple pleasure of watching their movements back and forth in an aquarium. By watching fish, seniors have been recorded as eating more food and having better weight-gain outcomes than those who don't have access to these aquatic beauties. Studies with a variety of pets demonstrate that individuals with limited capacity or interest in interaction with other humans will respond positively to engagement with pets who need regular feeding.

Dogs and Diabetes

According to the Centers for Disease Control and Prevention, more than one hundred million Americans are living with either diabetes or prediabetes, a condition which, if untreated, can become full-blown diabetes within five years. More than thirty million Americans have diabetes and eighty-four million have prediabetes. Which leads to an article by Maria Cohut, a writer for *Medical News Today*, who documented a 2018 study from the University of Bristol in Great Britain that was published in the journal *PLOS One*. It showed that therapy dogs can be trained to detect sudden drops in the blood glucose level of a diabetic patient: a hypoglycemia episode. With their heightened sense of smell, dogs smell the patient's breath and register the onset of the episode, a kind of early warning system. These dogs had an accuracy rating of 83 percent in alerting the diabetic patient to a pending hypoglycemic episode—in time to administer life-saving glucose tablets, fruit, or fruit juice with the needed carbohydrates. This research highlights a dog's ability to recognize the medical need of a person in their household, and the potential of such a therapy to address broader medical problems.

The litany of pet-assisted disease-detection programs continues. A 2004 study, published in the *British Journal of Medicine*, followed six dogs trained to detect bladder cancer in patient urine samples. While their 41 percent success rate wasn't perfect, it exceeded the 14 percent "coincidence rate" of human researchers. Dogs can now spot cancers, including skin, prostate, lung, breast, and colorectal cancers. Researchers at the Pine Street Foundation in California trained dogs to sniff out both breast and lung cancer from breath samples from the patients. They achieved an 88 percent success rate with breast cancer and a 97 percent rate with lung cancer. In 2011, at Kyushu University in Japan, dogs detected colorectal cancer by sniffing breath samples, with 98 percent accuracy, which surpassed results from traditional diagnostic tests.

Less Cortisol, More Oxytocin

In the past decade, medical research has confirmed a chemical foundation for the human-animal bond: engagement with pets decreases the release of cortisol and increases the release of oxytocin in children. This reduces stress for children in both day-to-day and behaviorally challenging situations. By increasing a child's ability to manage anxiety and new environments, it promotes social interaction. Physician Kristen Fuller from the Center for Discovery explains, "Hugging a dog or cat releases oxytocin and dopamine, hormones that reduce stress, lower blood pressure and heart rates, and increase happiness. . . . Touch can inhibit certain regions of the brain from responding to threat cues that would normally produce fear." Rebecca Johnson is a nurse who heads the Research Center on Human/Animal Interaction at the University of Missouri College of Veterinary Medicine. She states that oxytocin has value beyond stress reduction: "Oxytocin has some powerful effects for us in the body's ability to be in a state of readiness to heal, and also to grow new cells, so it predisposes us to an environment in our own bodies where we can be healthier."

Veterans with PTSD and Service Dogs

In 2018, Dr. Maggie O'Haire at Purdue University conducted innovative research on the link between service dogs and combat veterans suffering from PTSD. She found that veterans with service dogs have lower cortisol levels in the morning than those on the waiting list without service dogs. As they wake each day (often reliving their memories of war), veterans with PTSD typically experience rising cortisol levels. O'Haire's research has revealed that a service dog will lower a veteran's level of anger and anxiety and help them sleep better. "It's not a cure, because we can't expect to get a dog and cure autism or PTSD," O'Haire said. "But for some people, it is helping in a way that is unique. We have data that shows it can make a difference. A common thing I hear from veterans with service dogs is, 'I can actually leave my house now,'" a major step for housebound veterans whose reentry into civilian life is often traumatic. CNN journalist Elizabeth Landau tells the story of Valor, a half Labrador half Great Dane, helping retired sergeant Charles Hernandez in the Bronx, New York, manage seizures and anxiety attacks, and avoid day-to-day conflicts, with her sustained and supportive physical presence. As Sergeant Hernandez says, "I'm alive again. What keeps me going is my dog." A testament to both the power of the human-animal bond and the redeeming value of service pets.

Pets in the Classroom

HABRI released the *Pets in the Classroom Study*, conducted by the American Humane research team and funded jointly by HABRI and the Pet Care Trust. The manuscript has been published online in the *Human-Animal Interaction Bulletin*, a publication of the American Psychological Association. The study assessed social, behavioral, and academic effects of the presence of small classroom animals, such as gerbils, hamsters, turtles, and more, for 591 third- and fourth-grade students across the United States over the 2016–2017 school year. The research indicates that pets in the classroom may help improve academic performance and social skills in children:

- Significantly greater increases in overall social skills (including communication, cooperation, assertion, responsibility, empathy, engagement, and self-control).
- Improved social skills and academic reading competence.
- Significant decreases in internalizing behaviors (e.g., withdrawal) and hyperactivity/inattention among their students.
- Clear increases in pro–social behaviors among their children compared to parents with children in classrooms without pets.

Presurgerical Stress Relief to Reduce Sedation Levels

One promising HABRI-funded study considers the effect of animal-assisted intervention on preoperative anxiety and sedation dosage of children. The University of Tennessee College of Veterinary Medicine is learning that interaction with a therapy dog before surgery—placing a child's pet in the hospital room for a few hours before the child enters the operating room—can significantly reduce their anxiety level, allowing them a lower dose of sedation medication for surgery.

How Do Doctors View the Human-Animal Bond?

A 2014 HABRI survey of doctors, with a sample size of one thousand, found that 69 percent have worked with pets in a hospital, medical center, or a medical practice to improve patient therapy or treatment. The data is telling—witness the percentage of doctors reporting animal-assisted patient improvement in the following areas:

- Physical condition (88 percent)
- Mental health condition (97 percent)

- Mood or outlook during treatment (98 percent)
- Relationships with medical staff during treatment (76 percent)

Fully 97 percent of the doctors believe that owning a pet delivers quantifiable health benefits, and 60 percent of them have recommended pet ownership to their patients. The psychiatric and chemical foundations of the human-animal bond are becoming part of American medical protocols.

The human-animal bond isn't only saving people's health, it's also saving health-care dollars. A study by George Mason University's Terry Clower and Tonya Neaves conservatively estimates that pet ownership produces $11 billion in savings for the health-care system. Savings primarily come from fewer visits to the doctor due to improved health, and cardiovascular gains from weight loss by exercising with a dog.

Before considering the "consequences" of the human-animal bond, we should dispel the myth that cats cannot bond with owners like dogs do. Many dog connoisseurs believe this is true, because of behavioral differences between the two species, but, in 2019, three researchers put this canard to rest. Kristyn Vitale, Alexandra Behnke, and Monique Udell published their findings in *Current Biology*, "Attachment bonds between domestic cats and humans."

While researched more often than cats, dogs apparently form attachments like cats. In this study, kittens and cats were recruited to go through a secure base test, which measures the bond between dogs or other animals and their caregivers. Cats and their owners were put in unfamiliar environments together for two minutes. The owners exited the area for two minutes, then rejoined their pets. After they returned, the cats' actions were measured and sorted into attachments. Attachments were described as "secure" or "insecure" and were determined if the cat saw their owner as a calming stimulus. If secure, the cat would greet their owner and then continue to explore, while insecure cats would clutch their owners.

"This idea that cats don't really care about people or respond to them isn't holding up," Dr. Vitale said. Roughly 35 percent of cats in the study displayed insecure attachments. This matches the numbers when the same experiment is performed with dogs, or infants. After these tests, the researchers took half the kittens and enrolled them in social-ization courses. After this training, they were tested again, and the results remained constant. This suggests that cats develop their bond-forming capabilities in infancy, and could be tied to their relationship with their parents, as it is with babies. Cat and dog behaviors in these studies were nearly identical.

SOCIAL CAPITAL OF PETS

The social capital of pets is the human-animal bond writ large. Let's be clear, the community-building quality of pets doesn't flow directly from the wellness that individual pet owners experience with their dog or cat. Social capital is not the sum of the goodwill of one hundred pet owners holding hands around a public square, singing songs from *Beauty and the Beast*. As we discussed in the previous chapter, pets—particularly dogs—take us into public spaces and create a new and different social environment in which people who would never otherwise meet, or make the effort to meet, do so, regularly and predictably, if only for a few minutes. That's social capital, and it raises the power quotient of Pet Nation dramatically. We've learned this from studies of three large American cities: San Diego; Nashville; and Portland, Oregon; though the seminal study came a decade earlier, in 2002, from Perth, on the western edge of Australia.

Let's start with the definition of "social capital," best explained in an article presenting the American study of San Diego, Nashville, and Portland previously mentioned: "Putnam's (2001) definition of social capital is one of the most widely used, defining it as the *'connections among individuals, social networks* and the norms of reciprocity and trustworthiness that arise from them' . . . the *'glue'* that holds society together (Lang & Hornburg, 1998) or the *raw material of civil society* that is created from everyday interactions between people (Onyx & Bullen, 1997)" (emphasis added).

Social capital is what makes a neighborhood, town, or city *work*. These are the places where people want to live, the cities and towns they return to after college, where they choose to raise families and to spend their lives. For example, Philadelphia brownstones have front stoops where people linger at the end of the day, chatting with neighbors, watching children play or dog walkers wander by. Over time, this architectural feature unites a neighborhood, block by block, which builds social capital.

The Perth study of 339 randomly chosen residents of three suburbs compared pet owners and non–pet owners, studying these factors: individual health, mental wellness, community involvement, and emotional outlook. It represents a comprehensive look at the social dimensions of pet ownership, the largest study of its kind to date, addressing the question of whether pet ownership improves community engagement and satisfaction among neighbors.

The results were clear: pet ownership makes a meaningful difference in the social life of any town or city—not in every category, perhaps, but in key areas of daily life. Since 1980, considerable study had been applied to the individual dimensions of human-animal-bond research, yet few academics had considered the social capital of pets. In 2007, I was fortunate to meet with Lisa Wood, the lead Perth researcher from the University of Western Australia's School of Population and Global Health. A Mars team visited with her a few years after her publication, and the collective response from our American colleagues was "stunned." My meeting with Lisa Wood prompted a professional epiphany. It was at that moment, sitting at a conference table in Portland,

Oregon, that the emergence of a pet-driven culture, the essence of Pet Nation, began to make sense to me. Pets weren't merely fun or entertaining; they changed lives, they improved people and transformed the neighborhoods they lived in. Not in small ways, but exponentially. Here are key findings from the Perth study:

- Pet ownership at 59 percent of households resembled the United States, and pet owners were significantly more likely than non–pet owners to report that they were in "good" or "very good" health.
- Significantly fewer pet owners reported being lonely than non–pet owners.
- 74.5 percent of pet owners reported "rarely" or "never" finding it hard to get to know people, compared with 62.6 percent of non–pet owners.
- 89.5 percent of pet owners felt that people generally said hello when walking in the neighborhood versus 79.1 percent of non–pet owners.
- After adjusting for age, sex, education, and children, pet owners were 57 percent more likely to be civically engaged than non–pet owners.
- Among dog owners, more than half of them had met people within their suburb as a result of their dog, and more than 80 percent had talked to other dog owners when walking their dog.

In a country like the United States, with a 50 percent divorce rate, where twenty-year-olds go online to try to meet people, these are persuasive statistics. Lonely? Depressed? Want to meet people? Why not adopt a mutt from your local shelter?

What happened when the study was replicated in balmy San Diego, culturally hip Portland, and the rising star of the Bible Belt, Nashville? In each city, the results replicated the original Perth research (as well as a resurvey of Perth residents) on several factors, while making an even stronger case for the social capital of pets. This research added the dimension of comparing pet owners who walk their dog with: (1) other pet owners; (2) dog owners who don't walk their pet; and (3) non–pet owners. It isn't surprising that the highest awareness of social capital came from people who walk their dogs, and this was true in all four cities (including Perth). Yet, in each city, there was a marked difference between pet owners (walkers or not) and people who don't have pets.

The American study (including researchers Lisa Wood and Sandra McCune of WALTHAM) also explored four theories about why pet owners exhibit greater social capital than non–pet owners:

- In studies, pets of all kinds have been shown to create, or are linked to, *trust*. The presence of pets enhances the perception of trustworthiness in others, which is central to building community capital.
- The hormone oxytocin boosts people's trust of others, and interaction with pets increases the production of oxytocin in people.
- Pets are icebreakers, curbing social inhibitions among strangers. Picture two people pausing to talk about their dogs as they walk along a city sidewalk. This rarely, if ever, happens when people walk alone, avoiding eye contact with strangers.
- Dog walkers have enhanced the perception of safety in neighborhoods, for all residents, especially women and the elderly. Safety is a premium value in building social capital or trust.

Has any single study definitively established the validity of all these points? No, but the growing volume of research, and the congruence between the studies, supports the conclusion that pets make people and communities better, a lesson for city planners and job seekers alike, considering the movement of Americans from one city to another.

HOW SHOULD PET NATION HARVEST THIS EVIDENCE OF GOODWILL AND BETTER HEALTH?

Is it enough to enjoy the science, and for 65 percent of Americans to congratulate themselves on having the good sense to enjoy cats and dogs? Or should we explore what Pet Nation could mean for government policies designed to improve human health, lower the cost of medical care, and strengthen the social fabric of towns and cities throughout the United States? I'm involved in pet politics around the country daily, so let's dig in.

The benefits are difficult to ignore. It's a fact that pets make individuals and communities better. You could say that drugs or alcohol make people feel better, too. But those are only temporary. Pets don't come with side effects, hangovers, bad trips, driving accidents, broken homes, or addictions. It's true that pets do carry some negative consequences: dog bites (a statistically insignificant and declining number of bites annually, as a percentage of the population); furniture damage; or waste on public sidewalks. But these conditions are all manageable (often the fault of distracted or careless pet owners) and carry no serious social or long-term costs. I think it's safe to say that pets do many good things at little cost. Now, what are the implications of that statement?

Get ready: we need more people to have pets, and more people who already have pets should own more pets. Why stop at 65 percent of households with pets in America? Why not 100 percent? Why stop at 185 million cats and dogs for 325 million people? Why not 325 million cats and dogs, or more? Consider the evidence, or look around you, and ask yourself if any other societal change can make so many people happy and so many communities better places to live in the United States than the increased presence of pets? If I'm right, then we should develop governmental, social, and business priorities to maximize the ownership and care of pets. I challenge any reader to tell me what alternative would accomplish more, at less cost, than encouraging—in every possible way—all Americans to enjoy the human-animal bond.

That changes things, doesn't it? Let's consider the mosaic of Pet Nation and turn Herbert Hoover's 1928 "a chicken in every pot" into "a pet in every house and apartment," with every adult in our country. I'm not suggesting that we pass a law requiring people to own a dog or cat, but we could have policies that encourage ownership, so that every community and household enjoys what pet owners know to be true: Pets make things better.

If Pet Nation is real and sustainable, then it has gravitas, consequences, and monumental potential. Why, it's bigger than *Sgt. Pepper's*, Air Jordans, and Italian gelato on the first hot day of summer combined, with the power to change the world in a small but meaningful way. All it takes is four paws, a tail (most of the time), or wings, and a loving home. I've lobbied politicians and decision-makers for many years on pet issues. Fifteen years ago, congressmen and legislators would nod and agree that pets are fun, and then show me a picture of their dog or cat. But they didn't, or couldn't, see the consequences. They didn't understand that pets have real-world benefits. That was before Pet Nation took hold, and studies were completed, research published, and the news and social media discovered that no story attracts more readers than a pet story. It doesn't matter what topic, just show a picture and tell a story about something that a cat or dog did for someone in the community, and readers can't get enough. It's not a temporary buzz, it's a tonic for the entire country, at a time when we could use one.

What kind of government policies could we enact?

1. Cities and counties should legislate that all apartments be pet-friendly, meaning that a tenant can have at least one pet, along with rules and safeguards to keep life comfortable for other tenants. This is a struggle we'll discuss in chapter six, but it is possible, and evidence proves that pet owners are willing to pay more for this privilege and will stay in their apartments longer. Apartment developers shouldn't object, and they can always keep sections of a residential complex pet-free, satisfying everyone.

2. American employers, take notice that your employees or team members love pets and you'll keep them longer, at higher levels of productivity, if they can bring their pets to work some of the time, or work from home one day a week. If you want to hire and keep millennials and Generation Zs happy, this is the best decision you'll ever make.

3. Securing federal recognition of pet ownership as a wellness program might seem daunting, at first glance—but it is feasible. Our federal government encourages a variety of behaviors to promote human wellness and better health: It creates anti-smoking initiatives and exercise programs, encourages annual checkups, good nutrition, less junk food and soda. It educates people about the risks of driving drunk or using drugs, among many examples. These are all good ideas, which benefit from direct federal funding, tax credits, or tax deductions (alongside human health-care expenses). So why not add pet ownership and veterinary care to the list? Is there any reason not to do this, other than that it's never been done? We could provide Americans with a tax credit for acquiring a pet, and a deduction or other health insurance credit for basic veterinary care. If pets promote good health and can help prevent costly surgery by im-

proving daily wellness, as the evidence shows, then more pets *could* reduce the nation's health-care bill.

4. Motivate communities to build more dog parks. Make it easy for Americans to walk to a dog park. Pet owners will likely pitch in to help pay for it, perhaps even volunteer to build the park and fences to keep dogs inside.

5. Encourage stores and retail centers to welcome pets and to provide amenities, to make it frictionless for pets and shoppers to cohabit. It's all about making things comfortable.

6. Find every possible way to bring pets into the classroom. Kids love them, we know from studies that they learn better, are less stressed, and behave better around pets. What teacher or parent wouldn't appreciate those improvements?

7. Adopt travel (airline) policies that are fair, practical, uniform, and enforceable so that pets and traveling families aren't separated any longer than necessary, and non–pet owners aren't subjected to canine overload and emotional-support abuse. We've made some progress toward that goal, but it is still far simpler to travel with pets on Amtrak than on any American airline.

8. Institute a pet registry, state by state, as I discuss in our final chapter. Besides providing an instant communication tool regarding diseases, vaccines, and public health, registries in Europe have allowed people to know precisely how many pets, and types of pets, they have at any given time.

9. Strategically, the government (federal, state, and local) should make it easy to say yes to pets and hard to say no.

All of these ideas can be achieved with less money than our government wastes in a single day. Would community life across America be different? Definitely. Better? I would say so.

Come on, you might say: Is this truly a science, or simply a scheme to promote pet ownership? Granted, the human-animal-bond construct has commercial value for the pet industry. However, the high number of high-quality, peer-reviewed studies in multiple medical and psychological fields from leading scientific institutions like Johns Hopkins offers overwhelming—many would say irrefutable—proof that the human-animal bond is mutually beneficial to pets and people, and of substantial value to society. With the American health-care system in a state of perpetual turmoil and financial strain, pets could be a small but dependable part of a solution. And a whole lot more fun than property taxes.

· 5 ·

DOG SHORTAGES
AND CANINE FREEDOM TRAINS

Dogs and cats come and go. During their stay—ten to fifteen years if we're fortunate, twenty years or more if we have a Siamese cat—they affect us in myriad ways. Powerful creatures, they change our lives, while we change theirs.

For pets, there are three primary scenarios, with corresponding emotional effects:

1. Pets enter our lives, stay for a meaningful period of time, and eventually pass away: the longer they stay, the more intense and lasting the benefits to the people who care for them, and to the animals themselves.

2. They enter our lives, but only briefly, before they run away, get lost, or are stolen. The uncertainty of such a loss, not knowing their fate—where and how they end up—is devastating. Sometimes, the shorter the stay, the deeper the emotional impact.

3. The star-crossed pets are the ones who do not find a loving home through rescue, adoption, or purchase. They languish for weeks or months, waiting for the kennel door to open, ready to leap into the arms of a welcoming family or individual. But it doesn't happen. We know how this drama ends—with dogs crammed into cages in pet shelters, desperate for homes that don't materialize. Eventually, these neglected animals are put to sleep, and a human being is denied a pet.

Fortunately, the third scenario is increasingly rare today, occurring only 5 percent of the time. If that number seems low to you, you're not alone. I routinely get quizzical looks at conferences when I share this fact with audiences. "But there are shelters everywhere," people say, "and they always seem to be filled with dogs. And you're saying only a small percentage of these dogs are euthanized? How is this possible?" It might seem like a magic trick, but it isn't. Instead, the solution is a surprising mix of mathematics and emotion (the key to this chapter), and a testament to the ingenuity of the American people and their passion for pets.

In my pet advocacy practice, it took me several years to fully comprehend the laws of canine supply and demand. Where do our dogs come from? How do we get them? How many are lost each year? And, do we have enough of them in America? I'll share some facts and figures with you to demonstrate what I've learned about these questions, but first I'll tell you a story about a single dog, in my childhood, and how he shaped my initial feelings on this subject.

It all started with Prince—not Prince the musician from Paisley Park, Minnesota, with his blistering guitar solos and soulful lyrics—but Prince the stray Collie who wandered into the front yard of my family's white frame house by the railroad tracks in McMinnville, Oregon, in 1956. I was three years old and he was the first dog I'd ever known: hazel eyes, thick white coat, a golden ruff, perhaps forty pounds, hungry and friendly. This was often how people in small-town America acquired dogs in the fifties, casually, without drama or planning. A dog strolled into the yard and your parents said, "Yes, you can keep him," or "No, we can't afford a dog." That was a parental decree a child couldn't challenge. Adopting a dog followed a simple rule: no collar, no questions (this was long before microchip implants). We were lucky that summer day in 1956. The bond between us was immediate, and though I had three siblings, I considered Prince *my* dog. Since I was only three years old, we could play and roughhouse together all day long, while the others were at school.

One day, Prince growled at the neighborhood milkman on his early-morning rounds, and the man broke a glass bottle over my dog's head, cutting him badly. The next day, our dad found Prince a safe home at "a farm outside town," where he wouldn't be "in harm's way." Or so we were told. My brothers and sister and I learned the truth some twenty-five years later. Dad had actually taken Prince to the local veterinarian, who gave him a lethal injection of the euthanasia drug pentobarbital. Prince went to sleep forever, after only two years with us. It was tough to hear this admission years later from Dad, and my sorrow for Prince was profound, but as a child I was powerless to prevent the dog's death or to find a friendly, four-legged replacement. Though my parents both grew up on Nebraska farms with plenty of animals, the economics of maintaining a dog in a household with four children, later five, plus the hard rule that he must live outside, ruled out a substitute Collie.

In the fifties, dogs were an accessory to the American home, like a bicycle or a stepladder, consigned to a doghouse in the backyard, and kept if they stayed out of the way. They were not automatically replaced if they died. Supply and demand was unpredictable and tentative.

Cats, too, were a part of my life growing up. There were two kinds of cats in our neighborhood: feral cats that ran wild and caught plump, two-pound rats from the granary over the back fence, and pedigreed cats, like the three Persians that enjoyed a pampered existence with our neighbor Dorothy. Then, one day, a handsome black kitty with one white toe (I never forgot that feature) poked his head up through a loose floorboard in the mudroom. I named him Bosco; he hung around with me for a year, before wandering away, like many American pets before they became a national obsession. Pets were a tangent to our lives, not a necessity.

We aren't short of cat lovers in America. If you go by the numbers, we have slightly more pet cats than dogs—ninety-five million—and both animals are equally celebrated on social media. However, dogs are the face of Pet Nation in public venues by a wide margin. The relationships people have with dogs and cats are fundamentally distinct, and they manifest themselves differently. We spend less money on cats, particularly with veterinarians, and rarely take them out in public. Cats are private, opaque, and independent. Temple Grandin has observed that cats are "hard to read because their facial expressions do not betray emotion the way dogs do." The old saying "Dogs have owners, cats have staff" is true. And they enter our lives in different ways.

Over the years, I began to recognize slowly, accidentally, almost by osmosis, the ways pets enter our lives, and the beneficial effect they can have on a family. The emotional windfall for people was obvious, but for most Americans the process of acquiring a pet was still serendipitous, not carefully planned. Today, understanding the multiple (and sometimes confounding) parts of the question "Where do American dogs come from?" is a fundamental part of my working life.

Fast-forward to 2010. I was working full-time on animal policy, shuttling between Portland and Washington, DC. I began to see glimmers of Pet Nation in my daughters' lives. I made an eleven-hour round trip from Portland to Boise—the new American family road trip—to find the perfect puppy for my youngest, Annelise, netting a "short, fast, smart, funny" Corgi named Holmes. Jillian was now almost a self-taught veterinarian, it seemed, passionately raising her Boxer, Dena, with that breed's special medical challenges. Caitlin had volunteered at shelters since she was ten, and her go-to escape from law school was the downtown Seattle Animal Shelter.* She described traffic jams on the block when the shelter posted pictures of a litter of puppies. By midday Sunday, the dog kennels were nearly empty, and it was clear that things were changing.

I had been conditioned by the national media to believe that our shelters were overflowing with dogs. However, Caitlin's shelter experience opened my eyes. If a well-managed, local shelter in Seattle (the same was true at Oregon Humane Society in Portland) runs out of adoptable stock every week, was it an anomaly, or did shelters around the country face the same challenge? Three years later, after working on various pet-policy issues, I came to a startling conclusion: America has a dog shortage! I was astonished. If you think that all American shelters are filled with dogs that will never find homes, you're not alone. But you are wrong. America doesn't have enough dogs to meet demand, and the situation is getting worse. It is perhaps the single biggest problem for would-be dog owners in America. In this chapter, I will explain how this happened and why most people think the opposite is true. I'll also tease out the implications of this conundrum for American pet owners and breeders. Fortunately, there is a way to fix this problem, if we choose to do so.

Going to the Dogs (but Cats Count, Too): 2020

The shelter-dog adoption process today is much more streamlined. Every week, no later than Thursday, shelters post photos of dogs for adoption. By Monday morning, the cages are empty except for dogs with medical or behavioral issues. Yes, there are more elaborate methods of finding the perfect dog. You could import a Sicilian Mastiff from

---

* The same Seattle shelter that provided kittens for the wedding of Iz and Colleen in chapter one.

a specialty breeder in Ukraine, as my brother's groomer did; or, like my colleague, rescue a Labrador puppy from Arkansas online, which, two weeks later, tumbled out of a Volkswagen van packed with dogs at a roadside delivery stop in Connecticut. All procurement methods are now fed by the voraciously viral phenomenon of digital media.

Visit the Dumb Friends League in Denver, one of America's leading animal shelters, and you'll understand some of the differences between the two species. Since 1910, this shelter has offered an impressive array of services: adoption (for dogs, cats, and horses); spay and neuter procedures; pet surrender; community education; and youth camps. If any shelter can place animals safely in loving homes, the Dumb Friends League can, with one of the highest placement rates for homeless pets in the country. In fiscal year 2018, 18,271 pets and 304 horses were adopted, reunited, or transferred to placement partners or animal control and welfare agencies from its single location.

Adoptable dogs are in short supply at the Dumb Friends League. The average length of stay is only eleven days, which includes the time required for medical treatment. In August 2019, Dumb Friends League CEO Apryl Steele told me that "only twenty to thirty dogs remain after most weekends, and those require medical care or behaviorally aren't ready to be adopted." But take a tour of the shelter and you will see plenty of *cats*. The numbers each year are declining, but they still outnumber dogs. That doesn't mean that Denver cat owners are abandoning their kitties at the Quebec Street facility in droves. It's because cats who have never been spayed or neutered still run wild in America. Shelters like the Dumb Friends League try mightily to steer families toward cats, with some success, but it's a challenge keeping up with the numbers.

It is a constant problem for shelter managers: despite their efforts, shelters remain *shelters* for stray *cats*, who'd make delightful pets, versus low-inventory, quick-turning *retail shops* for *dogs*, except those that cannot be adopted. The average price differential between adopting out a dog or a cat (somewhere between $150 and $350 at many urban shelters) is a function of supply and demand.

Which brings us back to dogs.

For a decade, you've watched animal-welfare ads on television showing forlorn, malnourished dogs packed into shelters across the United States. You can now lower the volume during those commercials. America's dog shortage is a serious problem—there is a deficit of two million dogs per year, and growing. Ironically, a major reason for the public misconception about a surplus is the tens of millions of dollars that the ASPCA and the Humane Society of the United States (HSUS) spend each year on direct mail adoption initiatives and those heart-wrenching TV commercials. Remember the funereal ads with Sarah McLachlan singing "Angel," as the camera pans over cage after cage of dogs hungry for a home? "Every hour an animal is abused or beaten," the ASPCA ads intone, seeking $228 a year from each viewer, in part to address a dog surplus that no longer exists. Together, HSUS and the ASPCA raise more than $350 million each year through ads and other campaigns, to shape public opinion and to advocate for animal-welfare issues relating to pets and farm animals.

The initial ad campaigns were a good idea. Fifteen years ago, when the campaign was launched, shelters were filled with dogs, and more than ten million dogs were euthanized annually. Thanks to country-wide spay-and-neuter programs, shelters now euthanize only 770,000 dogs each year, a 95 percent decrease. Most of the euthanasia cases have chronic behavioral or health conditions. Some credit must go to famed game-show host Bob Barker, who built the *Price Is Right* franchise from 1972 to 2007. A passionate animal rights advocate, Barker ended every show with the exhortation, "This is Bob Barker reminding you to help control the pet population. Have your pet spayed or neutered." Little did we know that our noble goal of slowing America's euthanasia trend would succeed so dramatically. We have improved the health of our dog population, but unwittingly depleted a precious resource: puppies.

Large shelters such as the North Shore Animal League on Long Island or the Nevada Humane Society in Reno have volunteers calling shelters around the country daily, searching for dogs to adopt and place. Is the public aware of this situation? Not yet. How many people have failed to find the right dog and then given up or adopted a cat? We don't know, because Pet Nation is only now waking up to this new reality.

I could fill this book with accounts of people desperate to find a new dog at a shelter, only to be told by an apologetic volunteer, "We ran out of dogs yesterday . . . hopefully we'll have some more next weekend, but get here early!" In New York City's Union Square, a white van full of dogs just arrived from the South is the highlight of an adopt-a-thon on Saturdays—and half the dogs are spoken for even before the van arrives. By day's end, the cages are empty, and the van is back on the road to collect more dogs for the following weekend.

Faced with these challenges, do would-be pet owners give up, start googling breeders, or call Craigslist leads (without background checks)? The answer is *yes* to all of the above and more, because Americans, and millennials in particular, are determined to find the right dog, regardless of cost or difficulty. It doesn't help that 250 American cities and three states have banned the retail sale of dogs. It's a crisis we didn't know we had. So what do we do about it?

The Pet-Count Challenge

I am a policy adviser to the Pet Leadership Council, a group of senior executives across the pet industry, from veterinary associations and animal-welfare organizations to pharmaceutical companies, from pet stores to pet-food suppliers. Our mission is to promote humane pet-care services and access to family-friendly pets. In October 2014, the group's chairman invited me to make a presentation at a meeting in Scottsdale, Arizona. For months, I'd been developing a theory, and I decided this was my chance to test the industry's reaction. I loaded my slides with three points I thought would intrigue council members:

1. We can make educated guesses but actually don't have a clue about how many dogs are in America.
2. We don't know where our dogs come from.
3. We're guessing when it comes to the number of dogs America needs.

I knew this because my staff had spent six months rummaging through every pet website and Google link to track down data and had found nothing conclusive. Americans are obsessed with pets, and we enjoy a booming pet industry, yet no one on the nonprofit or for-profit side knew if our dog supply was adequate, or whether the existing procurement system was sustainable. It was puzzling. Several factors were responsible for the industry's collective myopia: the rapid zero-to-sixty growth of Pet Nation since 1998; the lack of protocols to share what little data existed; the patchwork of sources delivering dogs to the marketplace; and the glut of effective, but questionable, television advertising.

For twenty years, shelters large and small had been running effective spay-and-neuter campaigns, funded by pet companies and millions of compassionate donors. Yet we still didn't know the size or provenance of our dog population. We had built a massive and profitable network of providers and suppliers to service our pets, but no one knew if we had enough of them. Is there another $95 billion consumer industry that cannot answer these basic questions? The sporting-goods industry, for instance, is similar in size. In 2018, do you think Dick's Sporting Goods buyers knew how many basketballs they would need in 2019, and where they would come from? Or do you think they crossed their fingers and prayed that delivery trucks would show up with the correct number of balls at exactly the right time of year?

A significant dog shortage has social and economic implications. If the demand for dogs continues to exceed the supply, dogs will become a luxury good. Veterinary visits and pet-product sales will then decline due to a puppy shortage. Jobs will be lost. Roughly 1.3 million Americans are employed in servicing Pet Nation, and a supply problem threatens every link in the chain, including would-be pet owners, breeders, shelter volunteers, pet-food manufacturers, toy vendors, veterinary hospitals, veterinary clinicians, national retailers, neighborhood pet shops, dog groomers, research scientists, pet therapists, and dog walkers, some of whom earn $200,000 per year. A 25 percent shortage of new dogs would harm people and businesses. Pets provide little benefit to society if only the rich can afford them, as it was in the Victorian era when companion dogs first became fashionable.

The emotional and financial consequences for Pet Nation would be grave. And when you consider the medical and sociological studies highlighted in chapter four that demonstrate the countless ways that pets help people and communities, such a shortage would be even more shortsighted.

Show Me the Numbers

My presentation to the Pet Leadership Council sparked a discussion on the magnitude of the problem. Was this a temporary trend, short-term and curable, or a systemic problem that had been percolating for years? Should the pet industry prepare to lay off 20 percent of staff? To make decisions, we needed dependable population data and an accurate national growth rate.

The Pet Leadership Council asked our team to find these answers with the help of professional survey and research organizations. Could we conduct a thorough, first-ever study of all animal shelters in America, to determine how many dogs land in shelters annually, and what happens to those dogs after they arrive? Various animal welfare and veterinary organizations had tried to gather this information, but the results were fragmentary and scattershot. Unlike Sweden or the Czech Republic, which have national dog registries, the United States has no such system. Nor does our government require shelters to report data to state or federal agencies. Run by volunteers, most shelters are skeletal operations with limited resources and equipment. We don't have reliable dog or cat ownership data, or a comprehensive national pet census.

For decades, we had all trusted the anecdotal evidence—myself, industry leaders, retailers, pet enthusiasts: "There are too many dogs in American shelters. Too many dogs are euthanized each year. Shelters mainly handle local strays. Breeders are producing the breeds and volume of dogs we need." The Pet Leadership Council directed us to do some research, and the data told a different story.

In early 2015, I enlisted the help of a veteran pollster, Bob Moore of Moore Information, and his analytics team in Portland, Oregon, to conduct a rigorous national phone survey of fifteen hundred households (the same sample size as a national presidential campaign poll). Their brief was to determine how many dogs were in American homes and where they came from. Once we knew these two chunks of data, by region, we could explore solutions. The study took nearly a year, but we got our numbers. They were a surprise.

How Many Dogs Does America Have?

The Moore data revealed that dog ownership was broadly distributed in the United States, by region and by income. It also provided the first two pieces of the population puzzle: (1) the number of households with dogs; and (2) the number of dogs per household. Extrapolating this information to the number of US households, in 2015, gave us a national estimate of eighty-eight million dogs, generally more than the pet industry expected. Digging deeper into the survey, we learned that:

- **Nearly half of all households with dogs had more than one dog.** Dogs are social creatures with a pack mentality and can suffer psychological damage if left home alone for long periods. In writing her book *The Hidden Life of Dogs*, anthropologist Elizabeth Marshall Thomas followed a pack of dogs around a neighborhood, studied them, and concluded that dogs who live in the company of other dogs "know they are understood" and are more "calm and pragmatic." Of the 44 percent of American households with a dog, 26 percent had two dogs, 10 percent had three dogs, and 7 percent had four or more. Raising two dogs together from a young age is a good way to socialize them—not only in their behavior with other dogs, but with people. This data supports the thesis that dogs can play a central role in family life and raise its overall level of happiness.

Number of Dogs in Household

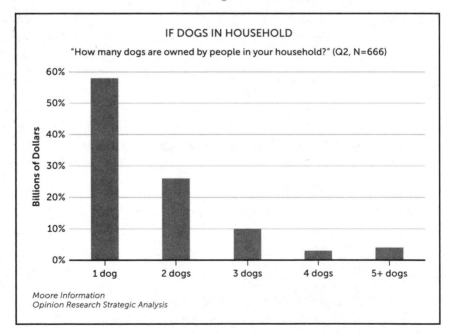

IF DOGS IN HOUSEHOLD

"How many dogs are owned by people in your household?" (Q2, N=666)

Moore Information
Opinion Research Strategic Analysis

- **Red states have more dogs than blue states.** The Northeast and the West Coast (both at 39 percent) lagged behind the rest of the country in dog ownership versus households in the Midwest (46 percent) and Rocky Mountain states (52 percent). Does the higher concentration of farms in the Midwest, which can accommodate dogs more easily than city apartments, distort the regional data? Do blue states skew *cat* because of urban density and the prevalence of apartments? Is there a correlation between pet ownership and the voting habits of Americans?

Dog Ownership: Key Subgroups–1

	Yes	NA	No	Net yes
All Residents	44%	1%	55%	-11%
Region				
Pacific	39%	—	61%	-22%
Mountain/Plains	52%	—	48%	+4%
North Central	46%	—	54%	-8%
South	44%	1%	56%	-12%
Northeast	39%	2%	59%	-20%
Gender				
Men	43%	1%	56%	-13%
Women	46%	*	54%	-8%
Age				
18–34	45%	1%	54%	-9%
35–44	44$	—	56%	-12%
45–54	55%	—	45%	+10%
55–64	45%	1%	54%	-9%
65+	37%	1%	62%	-25%

Moore Information
Opinion Research Strategic Analysis
*Less than one-half of 1 percent

- **Dogs are *not* a luxury item only for high-income Americans.** Income variation had relatively little effect on ownership, with the largest group—at 56 percent ownership—falling into the $50,000 to $99,000 income range, considered America's middle class. It is logical that the explosion of dogs in Pet Nation is driven by the country's largest demographic, but it's worth noting that the lowest income group—earning less than $30,000 a year, at 43 percent ownership—is only three percentage points behind the highest income group (earning $100,000 plus a year), representing 46 percent ownership.

Dog Ownership: Key Subgroups–2

	Yes	NA	No	Net yes
All Residents	44%	1%	55%	-11%
Ethnicity				
Caucasians	49%	*	51%	-2%
Total non-Caucasians	37%	1%	62%	-25%
African Americans	32%	2%	66%	-34%
Hispanics	42%	—	58%	-16%
Others	36%	*	64%	-28%
Kids under 18 in household?				
Yes	53%	1%	47%	+6%
No	41%	1%	58%	-17%
Income				
Less than $30K	43%	*	57%	-14%
$30K–49K	41%	1%	59%	-18%
$50K–99K	56%	—	44%	+12%
$100K or more	46%	*	53%	-7%

Moore Information
Opinion Research Strategic Analysis
*Less than one-half of 1 percent

Knowing how many dogs we had in America, we could determine how many *more* we needed each year. Based on an average canine life span of eleven years (American Veterinary Medical Association longevity averages, including all breeds and sizes), we calculated that it would take approximately 8.3 million dogs to replenish the dog population each year, while factoring in the human population growth rate (since not all pet owners immediately replace their lost or deceased dog). This calculation led to two questions: (1) Does the supply of dogs from disparate sources add up to 8.3 million; and (2) where do our dogs come from?

SHELTERS AND CANINE FREEDOM TRAINS

From Moore Information data, we knew how many dogs we had (eighty-eight million), and we could calculate how many we needed (8.3 million annually). But we didn't know what percentage of the 8.3 million target figure shelters could provide. If 50 percent or less, then we had to make some hard choices about the future of commercial breeding, the only scalable American-made solution. Ultimately, we need puppies. Some do end up in shelters, but where do we find the balance? If the supply is inadequate, do we counsel American pet owners that the only way to replace their favorite dog when she passes away is to pay a hefty premium for a new one?

To answer these questions, I traveled to Starkville, Mississippi, in the fall of 2015, in the heart of cotton country, the home of Mississippi State University. Though well-known for college baseball stars and raucous cowbells at SEC football games, Mississippi State is also a leading research university with a student body the same size as the town of 25,000. Mississippi State was founded in 1862 as a land-grant university for "agricultural, horticultural, and mechanical studies," and "other scientific activities . . ." That was why I was visiting its excellent veterinary college. There, I met a talented pair of scientists, shelter veterinarian Kimberly Woodruff and epidemiologist David Smith.

The Mississippi State College of Veterinary Medicine has earned a national reputation in shelter medicine, a worthy field of study in a state whose rural communities are starved for resources. Mississippi shelters have an abundance of stray dogs but little funding to manage or care for them. With the Bulldogs as the university mascot, Mississippi State seemed like the perfect place to begin a dog survey.

As an epidemiologist, Dr. Smith could extract the information we needed from a representative national sampling of shelters. Dr. Woodruff was more hands-on, running an innovative shelter medicine program for veterinary students who drive mobile surgery units around rural Mississippi (where many dogs run wild), and help shelters by spaying and neutering thousands of dogs each year. Outfitted with three surgery beds per rig, it is an impressive program, bringing expert veterinary services directly to local shelters. Without Dr. Woodruff's pioneering work, the shelters could not spay or neuter the dogs, and the local dog population would remain out of control. Proud of the program's accomplishments, Dr. Woodruff explains, "We teach students how to be real veterinarians by serving communities without resources but full of volunteers eager to make a difference. I've lived in west Tennessee and Mississippi most of my life, and it still impresses me what we are able to accomplish with a handful of students."

And what happens to those fine Mississippi pups after being spayed or neutered? I soon learned what makes the American shelter/adoption wheel turn. The dogs travel north in air-conditioned vans to shelters in Minneapolis, Chicago, and other Northern cities, to be adopted out to families. That's right, "canine freedom trains" run from south to north all across America: Mississippi to Minnesota, Tennessee to New York, Alabama to New Jersey, Los Angeles to Portland. When you visit a Boston or Newark or San Francisco shelter, you rarely see local strays. This is an efficient, well-ordered network, a marketplace in which underfunded and understaffed Southern shelters are motivated to spay and neuter, shipping quality dogs to Northern shelters to satisfy local demand.

Southern donor shelters collaborate with their Northern counterparts to ensure medical and behavioral quality before the dogs head north. The receiving shelters specify the kinds of dogs they want, or don't want (often Chihuahuas and Pit Bulls). These "migrant" dogs represent most breeds, but the lion's share are mixed breeds (a.k.a. "mutts"). They range in age from six-week-old puppies to fourteen-year-old Retrievers with arthritic hips. Northern demand seems never-ending, and it's heartening to see how many families passionately want dogs, no matter the breed, age, or physical condition of the animal.

Though this sourcing matrix might seem improvised or stopgap, it works. Certain geographic regions (South, Southwest, lower Midwest) are slower to adopt spay-and-neuter practices common elsewhere, and a high volume of their dogs land in shelters. Other regions (the Northeast, upper Midwest, the Pacific Northwest, Northern California) need dogs for families and will pay for spayed or neutered dogs, plus transport. The caravans save the dogs from euthanasia. Shelters in the lower half of the country gain income and peace of mind that their dogs find good homes, while Northern shelters satisfy demand and earn income from adoption fees. Everyone wins.

This is the topsy-turvy world of animal shelters that we commissioned the Mississippi State team to study. We asked them to conduct a comprehensive national survey of all shelters in America (more than seven thousand in total) to answer five questions:

1. How many dogs enter shelters in one year?
2. How many dogs are adopted out?
3. How many dogs are transferred to other shelters or rescue groups?
4. How many dogs are returned to owners?
5. How many dogs are euthanized?

Once we knew these figures, we could build a model to determine where Americans could find new dogs. With a catch-and-release method used by wildlife researchers to estimate the number of animals in a specific region, Dr. Woodruff and Dr. Smith answered our questions. Here are the findings in 2015 for the 7,076 shelters in the United States that my team had identified.

Number of Dogs

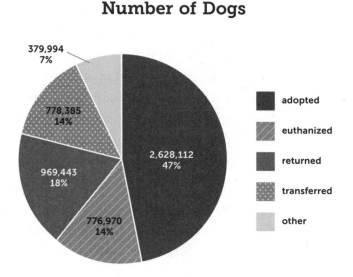

Of the 8.3 million dogs needed each year, shelters adopt out 2.6 million. That is slightly more than 25 percent of the target 8.3 million, but it leaves a gap of 5.7 million dogs that shelters cannot supply. We know from separate industry sources that local breeders, American Kennel Club (AKC) breeders, the Internet, and large-scale breeders add another 3.4 million dogs to the pool, taking us to 6 million. That's still 2.3 million dogs short. Shelters are only part of the solution, which leaves commercial breeders, foreign dogs, or other undefined sources to fill the breach.

Several years ago, my friend Alexis was working on her computer in New York, browsing the available animals at online shelters. Her eyes fell on a photo of an emaciated English Springer Spaniel with matted hair and chewing gum stuck to his tail. He was slightly cross-eyed but had wonderful chestnut-colored markings. Without telling her husband, she hurried to the 110th Street kill shelter to give him a closer look. He had been microchipped (with no response from his owner), and though the English Springer Spaniel rescue group was on its way to inspect him, his fate was uncertain. Alexis adopted Bailey on the spot.

This anecdote reminds readers that the dog marketplace isn't dominated by large commercial breeders. Pets come from multiple ad hoc sources, which makes the acquisition process more difficult to analyze, predict, and quantify.

Where Shelter Dogs Go

The Mississippi State shelter study discovered that during the year (2015):

1. 5.5 million dogs entered shelters.
2. 2.6 million dogs were adopted.
3. 970,000 dogs were returned to owners.
4. 778,000 dogs were transferred to other shelters or rescue groups.
5. 777,000 dogs were euthanized.

Professors Woodruff and Smith presented their analysis at the North American Veterinary Community conference in Orlando, Florida, on February 7, 2017. The next day, this research became national news— *The Washington Post* ran a lead story with the headline: "Does America

Have Enough Dogs for All the People Who Want One?" For the first time ever, the mainstream media had covered this issue, and it drew attention from policymakers to industry experts to existing and would-be pet owners.

For years, internal pressures had routinely forced shelters to euthanize dogs to make room for the next pack. Budget, staff, and space limitations were the constricting factors. Some no-kill shelters never euthanize, even when dogs are too sick or behaviorally challenged to be adopted. However, those shelters are the minority, and they usually limit their dog intake or have more space than many nonprofit shelters. Once the dog-loving public learned about adoption alternatives, particularly in Northern metropolitan markets, the situation began to change. As supply caught up with demand, euthanasia rates declined.

Though ten million dogs were euthanized annually in the eighties and nineties, we euthanized only 777,000 in 2015 and transferred approximately that same number to other shelters or rescues. This wholesale shift is still difficult for many people and animal advocates to believe, but our spay-and-neuter campaigns have been wildly effective. Perhaps too effective.

Americans now face a dilemma we couldn't have imagined twenty years ago when three of every four dogs in shelters were put down each year because no one adopted them and shelters ran out of space or resources. Though Americans need 8.3 million dogs each year, shelters can only supply 2.6 million. Americans want dogs now, and Pet Nation has a dog shortage to address.

THE BATTLE ROYALE
OVER COMMERCIAL BREEDING
AND PUPPY MILLS

The *Washington Post* story that brought these findings to the general public was written by Kim Kavin. She is the author of an excellent book, *The Dog Merchants*, which explores the mysteries and economics of puppy production in America. In her book, she divides dog breeders into two categories: commercial (big) and hobby (small). Commercial breeders raise puppies in large-scale operations; hobby breeders are much smaller, producing one to three litters each year at home. Hobby breeders are not inspected by federal agents. They produce pet dogs and show dogs, so their dogs are more expensive than accidental breeders and commercial breeders. Responsible hobby breeders generally produce no more than three to four litters with a single female before she retires as a pet. Veterinary science differs on how many litters a healthy female should produce in lifetime, but commercial breeders often cap this at six.

As with any profession, size is not a predictable measure of quality. Small law firms beat the international heavyweights more often than you think. In *The Dog Merchants*, Kim Kavin quotes Elizabeth Brinkley, a small-scale breeder and legislative liaison. "I've been in kennels with a hundred dogs," Brinkley said, "and they're fantastic and I've been in hobby breeder kennels that I wouldn't let my dogs near. It's not about numbers. It's about care . . . without commercial breeders, there wouldn't be enough of the popular purebred and cross-bred puppies . . . to satisfy consumer demand." Ms. Brinkley understood that commercial breeders are essential if we want to provide the quantity of puppies needed. Not every observer agrees with her, as we shall see.

In 2006, HSUS launched a tactical offensive against puppy mills, a wickedly effective epithet they applied to all commercial dog breeders. In a public relations and political broadside comprising advertising, direct mail, lobbying, and articles in the mainstream media, HSUS accused commercial breeders of animal abuse and slipshod care. The name "puppy mills" stuck, and large breeders have been on the defensive ever since. Once a profession or individual is branded "abusive" or "profiteering," it is difficult to shake the image. Though an obvious solution to our dog shortage is to increase commercial production, the puppy mill stand-off undermines that idea.

Commercial breeders keep to themselves, in part because of political pressure from activist groups. They operate out of the spotlight in rural areas of America, such as Arkansas and Missouri. Their facilities are often located behind tall hedgerows, making public viewing difficult, if not impossible. Though opponents claim that they "must have something to hide," commercial breeders argue that it's done to protect the dogs from threats outside their premises. They maintain that dog breeding is no different than raising cattle or chickens, albeit with unique humane standards and practices. Many are carefully run operations, with regular access to professional veterinarians, AKC registration, DNA testing, mandatory microchip implants, hygienic facilities, and plenty of room for their dogs to exercise. Unfortunately, the HSUS campaign indiscriminately threw every commercial breeder under the puppy mill bus.

Breeders and the two large activist groups, HSUS and ASPCA, have an ongoing adversarial relationship. If there is one area of common ground, it's that each group considers the other to be mercenary. Breeders say that HSUS and ASPCA demonize them to promote fundraising campaigns to aid shelter dogs, and that these organizations falsely claim that 25 percent of shelter dogs are pure breeds. (An Arizona State University study estimates that it is only 5 percent.)

HSUS and ASPCA, on the other hand, argue that breeders operate purely for financial gain, to the detriment of dog health and behavior. They claim that most commercial breeding operations are unsafe and unsanitary for animals, with minimal veterinary care and small, confining cages. They contend that it is unethical to operate large-scale breeding facilities for dogs, like cattle yards or chicken farms. They assert that no one should be allowed to breed more than a handful of female dogs ("bitches" is the technical term), regardless of the conditions and level of care.

AMISH BREEDERS

A fascinating but little-known chapter in the puppy mill story is the role of the Amish. The Amish are traditionalist Christian fellowships living in isolated rural communities sprinkled across Pennsylvania, Ohio, Indiana, and other Midwestern states, like the one in the Harrison Ford film *Witness*. They emigrated to America in the early eighteenth century and are known for simple living, plain dress, and aversion to modern technology. They are successful farmers, drive horse-drawn carriages instead of cars, and use animals in their farmwork, so breeding dogs is a natural business for them.

Amish dog breeders are some of the largest and most powerful breeders in America. Activists claim that 20 percent of all puppy mills in the United States are Amish-run. One opposition group called Bailing Out Benji has been especially vigilant in its research. It focused on one county within each of the three aforementioned states, whose concentration of puppy mills warranted state or federal government citations.

Bailing Out Benji contends that 98 percent of the offenders have Amish surnames, which doesn't prove that all Amish breeders run puppy mills. It's probably no coincidence that Amish leaders in southern Indiana have reached out to Purdue University's Center for Animal Welfare Science, in a public manner, to help improve Amish breeding standards, institute best practices across all Amish farms, particularly with respect to dog socialization and exercise, and educate the public that Amish breeders aren't bad.

But how do we increase the number of puppies in the United States if commercial breeders can't earn a living? If conditions are clean, safe, and humane, with compassionate, modern veterinary care and room for exercise, the size of a facility shouldn't matter. Is it necessarily different than cattle ranching? If humane breeding standards are established *and* rigorously enforced (undercutting the activist attacks), then why wouldn't pet owners welcome healthy dogs from large-scale breeders?

HSUS claims that the United States has at least ten thousand puppy mills, including what they call the Horrible Hundred, a collection of breeding operations concentrated in the four worst-offending states: Missouri, Ohio, Iowa, and Pennsylvania. They have exposed shocking examples of neglect that frequently air on the evening news. One example is the breeder in Randolph County, Arkansas, who, in 2015, was charged with abusing forty-six dogs, mainly Great Pyrenees, by giving them limited access to food or water, no outdoor exercise privileges, and no protection from the cold ("icicles on their whiskers"). The facility also had crates of female dogs stacked one atop the other, and piles of feces and urine on the floor that dogs couldn't avoid. This falls squarely within the HSUS definition of a puppy mill: "A dog breeding operation, offering dogs for monetary compensation, in which the physical, psychological and/or behavioral needs of all or some of the dogs are not being consistently fulfilled due to inadequate housing, shelter, staffing, nutrition, socialization, sanitation, exercise, veterinary care and/or inappropriate breeding."

No one defends puppy mills, but when an alleged puppy mill operator doesn't allow the press or third-party groups inside facilities to verify conditions, they invite suspicion of animal cruelty. Transparency and a system of enforceable oversight are vital to ensure ethical treatment of the animals. At the same time, it doesn't necessarily follow that a large breeding operation is deplorable (or, by definition, more poorly run than a small breeding facility). Good, responsible breeders should be able to breed as many dogs as they can manage at a verifiably high level of care.

There has been some progress recently in the puppy mill saga. A few states, including Ohio, have begun to regulate breeders with enforceable standards to address egregious behavior. This has shuttered some breeders, but both sides concede that there is still a long way to go. There are many ways for unethical breeders to market puppies, the Internet being the most difficult to track. Regulations with enforcement tools and "good" breeder buy-in (like the coffee industry's fair-trade initiative, which changed consumer behavior) could solve this problem, but, to date, no state has achieved an effective balance of standards with inspection.

ANIMAL WELFARE ACT

"USDA Animal Care, a unit within the Animal and Plant Health Inspection Service, administers the Animal Welfare Act (AWA). This federal law establishes requirements concerning the transportation, sale, and handling of certain animals and includes restrictions on the importation of live dogs for purposes of resale, prohibitions on animal fighting ventures, and provisions intended to prevent the theft of personal pets. Regulations established under the AWA set standards for the humane care and treatment for certain animals that are exhibited to the public, sold for use as pets, used in research, or transported commercially. Facilities using regulated animals for regulated purposes must provide their animals with adequate housing, sanitation, nutrition, water and veterinary care, and they must protect their animals from extreme weather and temperatures."

—*USDA website*

USDA inspectors are required to conduct routine, unannounced inspections of all facilities licensed or registered under the AWA. Inspectors are classified as veterinary medical officers (VMOs) or animal care inspectors (ACIs). All VMOs have graduated from a veterinary medical college, and many have been private-practice veterinarians prior to joining USDA Animal Care. Inspectors pursue regulatory enforcement actions or closure if a facility does not meet standards or correct violations on a timely basis, if they choose to do so.

A related conflict involves pet stores. Activist groups have convinced 250 cities, twenty-two counties, and the states of California, Maryland, and Ohio that most pet stores sell puppies from puppy mills. Their solution has been to stop the retail sale of puppies altogether, believing that this will eliminate puppy mills. Pet stores counter with evidence that their puppies do not come from puppy mills and that activists have painted the picture with an unfairly broad brush. Many city councils have sided with the activists and now limit pet stores to selling dogs from shelters. Given the scarcity of shelter dogs, this isn't a realistic population approach, nor will it satisfy demand for purebred puppies. If substandard breeders can successfully sell puppies on the Internet, pet stores aren't the problem. Unfortunately, no person or government agency knows where most Internet dog sales originate, or which Internet breeders are humane.

A major regulatory challenge involves our federal government, specifically, the Department of Agriculture's Center for Animal Welfare division. It regulates animal breeders, including anyone selling dogs across state lines ("interstate commerce"), and the importation of dogs for retail sale. HSUS, ASPCA, and other activist groups have battled the USDA for years over allegedly weak standards and the lax enforcement of laws (only a few operations have been closed or refused licenses by the USDA, see sidebar). A controversial USDA decision in 2017, prompted by a lawsuit, to keep the names of federally regulated dealers confidential and to remove thousands of documents detailing animal-welfare violations from the USDA website has inflamed the fight. These documents included the inspection reports for every commercial animal facility in the United States for decades.

The USDA cited privacy concerns, applying their logic to both private and public companies. However, many experts don't believe that this legal argument should apply to public companies. Dan Ashe, head of the Association of Zoos and Aquariums and the former director of the US Fish and Wildlife Service, commented that the USDA's removal of records is "not in the interest of credible, legitimate animal care facilities. It erodes public confidence, because when people see something like that, they're inclined to think that the government is trying to shield something from their view."

As in many areas of public life, the federal government has the tools but appears to lack the will and/or the resources to address this problem. There is no end in sight to this drama.

Dial Back Spay-and-Neuter Programs

Juvenile dogs are treated better today than at any time in canine history, so is it time to slow down the rate of spays and neuters? It may be heresy to disagree with Bob Barker, but we have to ask the question in *Pet Nation*. If we don't have enough puppies, then America has a dog shortage—it is basic arithmetic. Would it make sense to scale back spays and neuters, and encourage more puppies to be born in the United States? It sounds simple, but the politics are complex, and finding the mechanism or resolve to rein in an extraordinarily successful, twenty-year spay/neuter juggernaut fueled by a constant flow of emotional TV advertising will not be easy.

Four arguments challenge the widespread view that all puppies must be spayed or neutered, and they are raised by serious thought leaders:

1. We no longer have a dog-surplus crisis; instead, we face a chronic shortage. That's been the focus of this chapter, and it forces the question of why we continue to spay and neuter at the furious pace of the last two decades. If the overarching rationale for spay-and-neuter campaigns no longer exists, due to dramatic changes and reduction in euthanasia rates over the past twenty years, then why wouldn't Pet Nation reconsider the matter?

2. Researchers have produced credible findings that spay and neuter procedures, particularly neuters of large dogs, pose major health risks due to the loss of access to hormones. These discoveries should be addressed, as they undermine the folk wisdom that spays and neuters are "good for dogs." Here's a short list to date of serious health risks:

   a. Increased risks of joint disease, cancer, and obesity (Dr. Benjamin Hart, UC Davis study)

   b. Hip dysplasia, knee ligament damage, mast cell tumors, cancer of blood cell walls, lymphatic cancer (Dr. Benjamin Hart, UC Davis Golden Retriever study)

   c. Obesity prevalence (Dr. Missy Simpson, Morris Animal Foundation)

3. A spay or neuter changes a dog's behavior, and not always for the better. Doesn't Pet Nation have a moral obligation to evaluate these behavioral factors before maintaining our policy of automatically spaying or neutering every young puppy?

4. Sweden and Norway are sophisticated societies with long histories of advanced animal welfare and a high percentage of dog owners. Spays and neuters are the exception there, not the rule. Alexandra Horowitz's excellent commentary in a 2019 article in the *New York Times*, "Dogs Are Not Here for Our Convenience," explores this issue and observes that Scandinavian pet owners manage sexually intact dogs—in public and private—with seemingly few problems, challenging the notion that America will run amok with humping dogs and canine sexual encounters if we relax our national policy of mandatory spay and neuters of puppies. Keep in mind that two-thirds of states have laws on the books requiring that shelter dogs be "altered" before adoption.

The spay/neuter process is so automatic that abstaining is a cultural taboo, and dogs who are not fixed may not be allowed to board in doggy daycares or play in dog parks. While this was not the original intent of ASPCA in launching a nationwide campaign, it has become ASPCA's official creed. Dr. Horowitz highlights that neutering is convenient, and this explains much of its popularity. Pet owners do not want to deal with non-fixed animals and are offended by humping behavior, which is natural for a dog. Horowitz put it bluntly: "We are implying that dogs should be asexual, in body and mind."

Alternative procedures such as tubal ligation or injectable sterilant are available but uncommon in the United States. Another challenge is political pressure to lower the minimum age of spaying or neutering puppies to four months, which is now a common shelter practice. Many studies in recent years suggest that there are hidden health costs to spaying or neutering your pets if they are too young. The American Veterinary Medical Association (AVMA) says in a guide for veterinarians, "There is no single recommendation that would be appropriate for all dogs." Shelter policies do not show any signs of changing in the near future, but the maturation of Pet Nation and a growing shortage of dogs causes your author to predict that the debate is only beginning.

The challenge is to establish the right formula or balance of spay/neuter efforts and humane commercial breeding operations. If we aggressively spay and neuter every puppy we can find, and shut down commercial breeding, then America is left with no choice but to rely upon unregulated foreign breeders or accept that puppies will become a luxury good.

LAND-GRANT UNIVERSITIES GET INTO THE GAME: COWS, HORSES, PUPPIES, KITTENS?

Another way to tackle our dwindling supply of dogs is to take advantage of one of the United States' greatest public resources—our land-grant universities.* In 1862, Vermont congressman Justin Morrill introduced a bill to provide grants to states for the establishment of colleges specializing in agriculture and the mechanical arts. Iowa was the first state to establish a land-grant university, and we now have seventy-six such institutions, including Ohio State, Purdue, and Mississippi State, which conducted our national shelter survey. These universities have animal science programs that research the breeding of many species, from cows and chickens to llamas and *beavers*. The breeding of beavers—hardly an American obsession—is being studied in American universities, so why not study the 185 million cats and dogs living in American homes, applying the same skills and experience that animate Dr. Woodruff and Dr. Smith at Mississippi State?

If Americans decry the conditions at commercial dog-breeding farms, why not motivate land-grant universities (with a century of expertise in animal science) to help? They could develop standards for humane breeding, a subject only Purdue is exploring at the moment. They could teach laypeople to breed dogs safely and profitably, something no school is currently doing. And they could work with commercial breeders to improve the conditions and success rate of their breeding operations. Such a collaboration could improve the reputation of commercial breeders and benefit land-grant colleges. University extension

---

* A little-known legislative achievement of Abraham Lincoln.

agents and 4-H clubs could also teach people to be good breeders. If two of three dog owners consider their dog their "best friend," then dog breeding should be an honorable profession. We don't hide cattle or sheep farms from the general public, so let's open dog-breeding facilities to the public. It's time to trim the hedgerows at commercial breeders.

Professional breeders are now exploring a standards-based approach, led by the commercial firm PuppySpot. Thus far, these efforts don't extend to any land-grant universities beyond Purdue. They should consider a campaign to open breeding farms for public and educational viewing. If the public could visit breeders, where they would see and understand humane ways to raise puppies and to care for their mothers, then more people would consider studying dog breeding at respected land-grant colleges. Considering that Americans spend $11 billion annually to acquire dogs, there is a financial logic in responsible, professional dog breeding.

Learn a Lesson from Zoos

American zoos could teach the pet-breeding industry a strategic lesson in transparency. Zoos once looked and felt like jails—concrete cells with metal bars. The Portland Zoo I visited as a child had "inmates," from lions to tigers to bears to monkeys. Zoos had an image problem, and animal liberation groups attacked them regularly. Eventually, they woke up. They improved their animal habitats, opened their doors to children, parents, and educators, and welcomed the media behind the scenes, showing veterinarians delivering baby pandas. They took educational outreach and conservation projects into local communities. Zoos said, "Come on in. We have nothing to hide," and, today, are thriving attractions, a favorite field trip for elementary students and adults. The Tisch Children's Zoo in Central Park, a New York City landmark, has over one million visitors each year. Dog breeders could do the same, with land-grant universities leading the way.

DISNEY WORLD

Disney World has a long-standing commitment to humane animal care, through Animal Kingdom and other programs. Sensing the public's curiosity about animal care, it placed a glass viewing wall in front of its veterinary clinic, allowing guests to watch veterinarians treat wild animals. Colorado State University dean Mark Stetter, formerly chief veterinarian at Disney World, said: "Nothing we did was so powerful as those glass walls to let guests know how seriously we took the care of our animals, from the tiniest bird's wing to a hippopotamus needing heart surgery."

YOUR PASSPORT, PLEASE

We live in a globalized world, with high levels of human migration between countries. But foreign pets cross borders, too, in many different ways. When people move to the United States, for instance, they often bring along their pets. Some people import exotic pets to sell, like the snakes and reptiles you find in Florida pet stores. (Fifteen-feet Burmese pythons occasionally end up in suburban swimming pools or the Everglades, where they are now an established breeding population.) Commercial breeders ship a relatively small number of dogs through legal entry points to rescue groups and pet retailers. Some dogs straggle across the border on their own four legs, or are smuggled in without documentation or customs clearance from Mexico, Ireland, the Philippines, and Eastern Europe. Though it is illegal to import puppies under the age of four months, people do so.

We don't know exactly how many illegal dogs arrive here each year. US Customs keeps track of dogs entering America legally, and the official number is normally in the twenty thousand to thirty thousand range. These are often the pets of students or people on extended work or travel visas, and not packs of dogs for commercial sale. In 2008, US Customs recorded 28,000 official entries, but they estimated that another *280,000* dogs entered illegally. Since the goal of illegal entry is to elude capture, estimates of the number of dogs entering the United States illegally (and the identity of the smuggling parties) differ widely.

However, on August 26, 2019, the US Department of Agriculture adopted the Centers for Disease Control and Prevention's estimate that "approximately 1.06 million dogs enter the United States each year, including 700,000 arriving at airports and 360,000 arriving at land border ports of entry within Canada and Mexico." The announcement confirmed that less than 1 percent of these dogs are properly screened for medical conditions and diseases.

The illegal importation of dogs is a serious problem. These dogs can carry a disease and safety risk. In 2017, Denver veterinarians discussed with me a spike in the number of new dogs carrying diseases of foreign origin, such as parvo. The press has reported several incidents of unhealthy dogs spreading disease to existing shelter dogs. A highly publicized public investigation of importation through the Los Angeles airport uncovered quantities of unvaccinated puppies arriving with fake records. Public-health veterinarians examined the dogs and determined that they were six to eight weeks old.

As long as American breeders cannot meet demand, foreign sources will bring puppies across our border any way they can, and they will skirt the law to do so. One solution might be to ease importation restrictions so that we can funnel all incoming dogs (or as many as possible) through legal entry points where they could receive legitimate inspection and be properly registered. This would reduce the number of illegal dogs entering the country and the attendant risks. Currently, no government or nonprofit group is investing time or resources to address this problem.

Do illegal foreign dogs reduce our annual dog shortage? The lack of data makes it impossible to know, but the CDC estimates in 2019 suggest that perhaps half the shortage already is being met through foreign sources. Critics argue that rescue groups pursue dogs from foreign sources to boost their revenue. If this claim is accurate, the practice endangers public safety, leading to cases of rabies and other diseases. The rescue groups respond that they are saving the lives of dogs at risk, while meeting consumer demand for specific breeds in the United States. A news investigation in 2017 led to the temporary suspension of one group for rescuing imports from Puerto Rico. In a statement, the president of National Animal Interest Alliance (NAIA) Patti Strand wrote: "There is a lot of money in this new kind of rescue. These groups move dogs from just about any place that they can get them." Strand emphasized the risks to American communities from dogs carrying canine brucellosis, rabies, and other vector-borne diseases.

We could initiate discussions with the governments of countries sending dogs to America, to establish standards for the humane breeding of puppies, proper veterinary care, and record-keeping. The suspect nations include Guatemala, Honduras, Mexico, Turkey, Colombia, the Philippines, Romania, and several Central Asian countries. These would not be easy conversations, considering the questionable state of their current animal welfare practices. It is hard enough to establish standards here in the United States. If our borders remain porous, without surveillance and disease prevention, the foreign importation of dogs will continue to resemble the Wild West.

Where Does This Leave Things?

We have a dog shortage, and if we don't address it, dogs will become a luxury item. This is a complex problem, and it will require a combination of approaches to solve it. The most efficient way to get more dogs is to breed more dogs, and the most effective way to breed more dogs is through large, commercial dog breeding. But commercial dog breeding is hamstrung by political and public relations issues, many of the industry's own making. If Americans trusted a certification process that demonstrated that dogs are treated well, bred humanely, receive regular veterinary care, and are inspected transparently, then commercial breeders could thrive.

We've seen the success of such initiatives before in the retail coffee industry, which was once condemned for the quality of its product, environmental practices, and the treatment of farmworkers abroad. The industry successfully changed its reputation with a certification program for the country of origin for coffee beans. Retail chains and growers cooperated because it made good business sense. American consumers were more than happy to pay more (a significant premium)* to know that their coffee was ethically sourced.

Requiring and enforcing a certification program for breeders might make dogs more expensive at first. Would Americans pay more for healthier, well-bred puppies? They do now, and they will, so an initial pricing bump should not be an issue. Shelters could play a valuable role in this effort to produce more puppies and generate more income in the process. If American breeders produce enough puppies to meet demand, the price of both foreign imports and domestic retail prices should eventually decline, satisfying complementary consumer desires: more good dogs at even lower prices. Land-grant universities could accelerate this process. The USDA's Animal Welfare service might even participate, since one of their stated priorities is to regulate the safe and healthy production of animals, no matter the species.

The solution to the dog shortage is relatively simple in concept, but the political environment surrounding it is charged and the number

---

*In 1971, the year Starbucks was founded, the average cost of a cup of coffee in America was $0.35. Today, a Starbucks grande latte costs $3.65 at its 28,018 locations. A Dunkin' Donuts medium-size plain cup of coffee is $1.89 at its 12,000 stores.

of moving parts daunting. Perhaps it's no surprise that your lawyer/lobbyist author suggests that political compromise and legislation could be the solution. We need to: (1) strike a fair deal on certification among all interests (private, public, and nonprofits); (2) enforce strict breeding standards based upon such an agreement; (3) improve border control; (4) let the market take care of the rest; and (5) insist upon transparency. Breeders, distributors, pet-shop owners, shelters, and Internet vendors must be open about their practices. Otherwise, animal activists like ASPCA and HSUS and the public will never be satisfied, and rightly so. A "Humanely Bred" tag for every new dog could be a safety label that Americans come to trust, and pave the way to that magic 8.3 million number.

· 6 ·

THE GOOD, THE BAD, AND THE UGLY
Legal and Political Fights Are Just Beginning

In 2019, more than five thousand pieces of legislation affecting animals were filed in America—surely a sign that pets in the United States have come of age. Like it or not, the national political conversation now includes Poodles, Persians,* and pedigrees. The first two decades of Pet Nation started scores of political wildfires across the country, and many are still smoldering. I'm in the middle of most of them.

Seven questions underlie the political or moral battles of Pet Nation. We will consider each through the lens of pets, pet owners, the government, lawyers, and advocacy groups across the country. Together, they constitute the often maddening but unavoidable "furball" where people, economics, and the law intersect—with cats and dogs center stage.

Why do we treat cats and dogs as property and not independent beings? Shouldn't they be allowed to roam free?

---

* The four-legged fluffy cats with a round face and short muzzle that come from Mesopotamia, not Iran's Revolutionary Guards.

This subject touches on philosophy, common law, the cost of veterinary care, and the essence of Pet Nation, specifically the idea that, for most Americans, pets are part of the family. There are two parts to this issue. The first is a common-law doctrine that does not allow pet owners to collect emotional or noneconomic damages from any person (or organization) who injures or kills their pet, because pets are considered property under the common law. Pets are injured or killed every day, due to the negligence of people or organizations. What rights do the bereaved owners have? Precious little, as you will see. The second part of this issue is PETA's (People for the Ethical Treatment of Animals) argument that pet ownership is akin to slavery and should be abolished, *setting all pets free.*

NONECONOMIC DAMAGES

Here's what happens in American courts today if your pet is negligently injured or accidentally killed by a veterinarian, faulty medication, tainted food, or a disgruntled neighbor. You can recover the cost of medical care, replacing your particular type of pet, and the training for the new animal. That's about it. These types of cases rarely involve enough money to interest personal injury lawyers, who work for 33 percent of the damages awarded and only get paid if they win or settle the lawsuit. While 33 percent of a multimillion-dollar medical malpractice verdict is motivating, one-third of a $2,500 veterinary verdict is not. That might sound harsh, but it is real life, and there's more to the story.

American courts apply the same unforgiving standard to the negligent injury or death of your best friend, parents, girlfriend or boyfriend, partner, grandparents, brother or sister, or favorite aunt or uncle. This part of the law is called torts, and, for centuries, legislatures and judges have held that the tort system cannot tolerate big-dollar damage awards for every special person in everyone's life. Emotional or noneconomic damages are only allowed when it involves your spouse or child. That's it, that's all.

The line is narrowly drawn, but many people, including legal scholars, have argued for a broader interpretation of this statute. They contend that pets should enjoy the same status as spouses and children. People have uniquely intimate relationships with their pets, and spend hours each day feeding, walking, and caring for them. Why should your loss of a fifteen-year-old cat (at the careless hands of another) be treated any differently than the loss of a fifteen-year-old son? Especially for anyone who does not have children, and for whom the moral equivalence is clear? Others argue, why draw the line there? Why not include every important person in your world? That's where things get sticky.

For readers who avoided law school or have never seen an episode of *Law & Order*, a plaintiff is "a person who brings a case against another in a court of law." Three recent cases highlight the challenges and emotions embedded in this issue.

Strickland v. Medlen, 353 S.W.3d 576 (TX)

The plaintiffs (the Medlens) owned a dog named Avery who escaped from their backyard and then was recovered by animal control in Fort Worth, Texas. Before the Medlens were able to pick up Avery at the shelter, an animal control worker, Carla Strickland, erred and placed Avery on the euthanasia list. Avery was put down. The Medlens sued Strickland for causing Avery's death and sought damages for Avery's "intrinsic value." The trial court dismissed the suit, ruling that Texas law barred such damages. The Court of Appeals reversed, becoming the first Texas court to hold that a dog owner may recover "loss of companionship" or sentimental damages.

Verdict: The Texas Supreme Court reversed that surprising decision, holding that, under established legal doctrine, recovery in pet-death cases is limited to "loss of value, not loss of relationship." Only the Texas Legislature could change this rule of law, and it hasn't, and there's little chance that it will. Legislatures resist the same arguments for all "special relationships" for which people might seek emotional damages if someone is negligently injured or killed. No interest group has taken up this fight, or rebutted the counterargument that the inevitable rise in the cost of veterinary care will limit low-income access to pets.

Barking Hound Village, LLC v. Monyak, 794 S.E.2d 664 (GA)

In 2012, the Monyaks boarded Lola, their eight-and-a-half-year-old Dachshund mix, at a kennel owned by Barking Hound Village, LLC for ten days. At the same time, the plaintiffs (the Monyaks) also boarded their thirteen-year-old mixed-breed Labrador Retriever Callie, who was taking an anti-inflammatory medication for arthritis pain. The plaintiffs gave the medication to the kennel employees, along with directions that it be administered to Callie. Three days after retrieving their dogs from the kennel, Lola was diagnosed with acute renal failure. Despite receiving veterinary care, including dialysis, during a nine-month period, Lola died in March 2013.

The plaintiffs sued Barking Hound Village for damages, arguing that Lola was administered toxic doses of the medication prescribed for Callie, a dog three times her weight. The plaintiffs asserted various claims of negligence and sued for noneconomic damages, plus $67,000 in veterinary and other expenses incurred in treating Lola. The Court of Appeals concluded that the proper measure of damages for the loss of a pet is the actual value of the dog to its owners rather than the dog's fair market value. (This was a novel theory in Georgia and other states.)

Verdict: The Georgia Supreme Court reversed that decision and held that the damages recoverable by the owners of an animal negligently killed by another are determined by the animal's *fair market value* at the time of the loss, plus interest, *not the owner's perception of value*. The Monyaks did, however, recover their expenses.

Goodby v. Vetpharm, Inc., 974 A.2d 1269 (VT)

The plaintiff's two cats were treated for hypertension at Lamoille Valley Veterinary Services. The plaintiffs then followed their veterinarian's proposed treatment plan and purchased a refill of the medication in early December 2002. According to the plaintiffs, the refill batch of amlodipine triggered a series of events leading to the death of both cats. The plaintiffs claimed that the refill medication manufactured by Vetpharm contained at least twenty times the labeled dose of the drug, causing severe toxicity in their cats.

The case challenged whether noneconomic damages are available when a companion animal dies due to negligent acts of veterinarians and/or a pharmaceutical company, and whether a claim for negligent infliction of emotional distress is allowed for the death of a pet.

Verdict: The Vermont Supreme Court held against the cat owners on both issues, again pointing to the state legislature as the only body able to change the law, which it hasn't. Pet owners can recover replacement costs, expenses, and training services against veterinarians, manufacturers, or pet-food companies (as happened during national pet-food recalls), but not noneconomic or emotional damages.

The strongest argument against any changes to our current pet law is economics. Allowing people to collect noneconomic or emotional damages for the loss of pets would impose extraordinary costs on the pet health-care and social system. Could the United States, a country with 185 million dogs and cats, afford these extra costs? What would they be? The first is much more expensive professional liability insurance for veterinarians. In human medicine, annual malpractice insurance premiums for some specialties exceed $200,000, because of the threat of emotional damages and the potential size of judgments. Veterinarians currently have extremely low insurance premiums, because of their protection against noneconomic damages. They also earn less than medical doctors, and if their annual premiums bounce from $750 to $75,000, the price of a checkup for your Westie will bounce as well.

Even before trial judgments, the threat of large legal settlements adds costs to human health care, as providers insulate themselves from lawsuits by practicing defensive medicine. Malpractice defense lawyers have checklists of every procedure or test that doctors should perform to protect themselves at trial. When the plaintiff's lawyer asks a doctor if she "did everything possible" to treat the patient, she is prepared. It takes only one slip-up, or omission, to trigger a huge judgment. This also means that medical practices and hospitals are "forced" (their language) to buy the latest technology, to protect themselves against the plaintiff's lawyer. This equipment is expensive and increases the cost of health care. These financial pressures, which distort the cost of human care, do not exist in veterinary medicine to any meaningful degree.

This leads to an argument that expensive damage awards could limit access to medical coverage for pets of Americans of lesser means. How would access to veterinary care change? As the cost of practicing veterinary medicine increases, the cost of veterinary services increases for their clients, and every $100, $500, or $1,000 increment causes another pet owner to delay regular veterinary care for their pet or expensive surgery, or to postpone getting a pet altogether. Why would we make pet ownership less affordable? Shouldn't we be spreading the benefits of this unique bond? Is a multimillion damage award for one pet owner's loss worth this trade-off? Maintaining access to affordable veterinary care for all Americans, regardless of income, is paramount.

Another argument against noneconomic or sentimental damages is distasteful (my apologies in advance) but inevitable. Pets live a relatively short life compared to people, this reasoning goes, and you can replace a Shar-Pei or a Manx more easily than a beloved child. Therefore, even though it doesn't mean that you forget the pet you loved and lost, there is still a ready recovery mechanism absent in human tragedies. If the human-animal bond works its magic with your new kitty, then the loss ultimately isn't as dire or permanent. This is tough medicine, to be sure—which some people practice, replacing their pet immediately after a loss—but it is reality.

Every year, two or three state legislatures, and often an appellate court, face challenges to the rule against noneconomic damages. Recent battlegrounds include California, Texas, Georgia, Maryland, Connecticut, Massachusetts, Ohio, Vermont, and Oregon—a nice mix of red and blue states. Pet owners haven't rallied at the state capitols supporting change, nor have trial lawyers spent millions of dollars fighting for reforms, as they have with alcohol, tobacco, asbestos, and opioids. The issue typically surfaces when a legislator's next-door neighbor loses a pet due to a third party's negligence, then is outraged to learn how little money she would recover in a lawsuit.

Still, when I lecture on animal welfare policies at veterinary colleges, I draw gasps when I tell students that, in lawsuits, pets are treated like "chairs." Twenty minutes later, after we work through the cost equation, yawns or quiet resignation replace shock. One state, Tennessee, has passed a law allowing for noneconomic damages, with a limit of $5,000, but veterinarians were exempted from liability.

PETA

The United States legal system recognizes pets as property. The opposing view is brought to us courtesy of PETA (People for the Ethical Treatment of Animals). PETA is a flamboyant, media-savvy animal rights organization, founded in 1980, with aggressive strategies and tactics against perceived "violators" of animal rights. With four hundred employees and annual revenue of $54 million in 2018 (according to the PETA website), PETA is a formidable force. On the ideological continuum from left to right, PETA stands proudly on the distant left.

PETA argues that animals should be treated like persons. Since slavery was abolished during the Civil War, it has been illegal to own persons in the United States. Following PETA's logic, if animals resemble "persons," it is, therefore, wrong for people to "own" them. Case closed. It is time to set pets free. PETA argues that pets then will no longer be oppressed by American pet owners (we should all enjoy such oppression), dogs will not be bred for people, and the world will be a better place. Interestingly, PETA doesn't promote this position in the public media. They've demonstrated that they know how to raise awareness for a cause, as they did with their provocative anti-fur campaign "I'd Rather Go Naked," in which actors and supermodels posed naked. Why haven't they pushed for greater public awareness of their strong animal rights stance? I suspect that PETA's accountants and board of directors know what promoting an outright ban on pets would do to fundraising.

Instead, PETA carefully tucks their root philosophy inside their website:

> *We at PETA very much love the animal companions who share our homes, but we believe that it would have been in the animals' best interests if the institution of "pet keeping"—i.e., breeding animals to be kept and regarded as "pets"—never existed. The international pastime of domesticating animals has created an overpopulation crisis; as a result, millions of unwanted animals are destroyed every year as "surplus."*
>
> *This selfish desire to possess animals and receive love from them causes immeasurable suffering, which results from manipulating their breeding, selling or giving them away casually, and depriving them of the opportunity to engage in their natural behavior. They are*

restricted to human homes, where they must obey commands and can only eat, drink, and even urinate when humans allow them to.

Because domesticated animals retain many of their basic in-stincts and drives but are not able to survive on their own in the wild, dogs, cats, or birds, whose strongest desire is to be free, must be confined to houses, yards, or cages for their own safety.

Cats and dogs might quibble with PETA's vision. After twenty years of Pet Nation, American pets have a good thing going, and I suspect they know it. Wandering alone, hungry and frightened, through fields and mountain ravines doesn't sound like fun for a four-pound York-shire Terrier. If PETA's liberation "movie" came to life, coyotes would happily escort every kitten and puppy back to nature. Picture the "Dog Tested, Dog Approved" Subarus (from chapter two) depositing the Barkleys (three Golden Retrievers and one Lab, two of America's favor-ite dog breeds) at the edge of the forest, as their owners yell "FREE-DOM!" like Mel Gibson in *Braveheart*.

The United States no longer is "overpopulated" with pets, and PETA's worldview of suffering pets in homes also collides with evidence that pets enjoy their relationship with their owners. Scientific research confirms the value that pets receive from engagement with their "op-pressors." A 2011 study in Skara, Sweden, "found that dogs' oxytocin levels, the hormone that promotes attachment between individuals and stimulates interactive social behavior, significantly increased three min-utes after they begin interaction with their owners. Cortisol levels also decreased, after fifteen- and thirty-minute intervals, and their heart rate decreased after fifty-five minutes. A 2000 study in Pretoria, South Af-rica, revealed that dogs interacting with their respective owners (versus a stranger) had higher levels of oxytocin. PETA's medieval vision ig-nores the fact that the relationship between people and pets is mutually beneficial. Though they might think that Stockholm syndrome is at work here, no research supports such a theory.

Ultimately, to change the mind of 85 million American households that own pets, PETA must make the case that it would be better for cats and dogs if there were a dramatic decrease in their populations, with pets bred accidentally by the few animals that escape hungry predators. Only then will our brutal oppression of pets inside our warm and comfortable homes, atop our beds, on their Marimekko pillows, with cupboards stocked with fancy diet-calibrated pet food, end. Rover and Mittens will be free to spend their days hunting for food in the wilderness while dodging wolves and coyotes. Sign 'em up!

Nevertheless, the real-world application of PETA's theory has led to court cases seeking to establish the "personhood" of animals, often horses, gorillas, and chimpanzees. The major cases summarized below—all from New York or the West Coast, PETA's fundraising sweet spots—are colorful and fascinating, and provide a taste of the logic behind their cause.

Justice v. Gwendolyn Vercher, Case No. 18CV17601 (OR)

The Animal Legal Defense Fund sued the owner of an eight-year-old horse named Justice who allegedly had neglected him, and in this unusual case, the suit was filed on behalf of the horse.

Verdict: The court held that an animal, including the equine plaintiff, lacked the legal capacity to sue. This decision is a straightforward refusal to grant legal rights or personal status to a horse. Individuals or interest groups with standing may sue to protect an animal, but the horse as an animal is not recognized by any court as a legal person with the ability to file suit.

Matter of Nonhuman Rights Project, Inc. v. Lavery (NY)

According to a habeas corpus petition as summarized by the Court, the adult chimpanzees had been confined by their owners to small cages in a warehouse and a cement storefront in a crowded residential area, respectively. The case fell on the issue of whether habeas corpus can be used to seek a transfer to "an institution separate and different in nature from the facility to which petitioner had been committed." Habeas corpus is a centuries-old legal maneuver to allow someone in jail or prison to be brought before a judge to challenge their incarceration.

Verdict: The Appellate Division concluded that chimpanzees are not persons because they lack the "capacity or ability . . . to bear legal duties, or to be held legally accountable for their actions" (*Matter of Nonhuman Rights Project, Inc. v. Lavery*, 152 A.D.3d 73, 78 [1st Dept 2017]; see also *People ex rel. Nonhuman Rights Project, Inc. v. Lavery*, 124 A.D.3d 148, 152 [3d Dept 2014], *lv denied* 26 N.Y.3d 902 [2015]).

Nonhuman Rights Project, Inc. v. Presti (NY)

The court declined to answer the question of the personhood of the chimpanzee, instead focusing on the fact that the claim being made would not entitle the chimpanzee to immediate release. Of note, the court's opinion did not dismiss the possibility of one day accepting the argument that animals are entitled to personhood in some cases.

Nonhuman Rights Project, Inc. v. Stanley (NY)

Petitioner sought a writ of habeas corpus for Hercules and Leo, two young adult male chimpanzees who had been held at the SUNY Stony Brook campus since November 2010 and used as research subjects in studies on the locomotion of chimpanzees and other primates. According to the Nonhuman Rights Project, the sole issue was whether Hercules and Leo may be legally detained at all. Based on the belief that chimpanzees are autonomous and self-determining beings entitled to such fundamental rights as bodily liberty and equality, petitioner sought a determination that Hercules and Leo are being unlawfully deprived of their liberty.

Verdict: The court held that it is bound by precedent on the issue of animal personhood and found that animals are not persons under the law. Any decision to abandon precedent should be answered by the New York legislature. Animal research at American universities and corporations is heavily regulated, and limited in many cases to mice or pigs, because of their unique value to the human application of medications or procedures. Most primate research is the subject of intense protest from animal rights groups and has moved offshore.

Cetacean Community v. Bush, 386 F.3d 1169 (9th Cir. 2004)

Whales, dolphins, and porpoises allege that the navy has violated, or will violate, the Endangered Species Act (ESA), 16 U.S.C. §§ 1531-1544, the Marine Mammal Protection Act (MMPA), 16 U.S.C. §§ 1371-1421h, and the National Environmental Policy Act (NEPA), 16 U.S.C. §§ 4321-4347. The court held that the world's whales, dolphins, and porpoises, through their self-appointed lawyer, had standing under Article III, but they lacked statutory authority. The court wrestled with the idea that an animal could be deemed a person in a lawsuit under circumstances explicitly recognized by Congress, but that wasn't the case here. The ESA contains a definition of a "person" who is authorized to enforce the statute, which means an individual, corporation, partnership, trust, association, or another private entity; or any officer, employee, agent, department, or instrumentality of the federal government, or any state, municipality, or political subdivision of a state, or of any foreign government; any state, municipality, or political subdivision of a state; or any other entity subject to the jurisdiction of the United States.

Verdict: Whales, dolphins, and porpoises don't fit any of these categories.

Naruto v. Slater, No. 16-15469 (9th Cir. 2018)

The Ninth Circuit Court (America's West Coast federal appeals court) upheld the district court's dismissal of copyright infringement claims brought by a crested macaque monkey, related to selfies the monkey took on an unattended camera owned by wildlife photographer David Slater. Naruto took several photos of himself on the camera. In 2014, a publisher, Blurb, published *Wildlife Personalities,* using both the monkey selfies and the photographer's own photos. Slater recognized Naruto as the taker of the monkey photographs in the book. PETA filed suit as next friend to Naruto, alleging copyright infringement. The panel held that the complaint included facts sufficient to establish Article III federal standing to sue, because it alleged that Naruto was the author and owner of the photographs and had suffered concrete and particularized economic harms. The monkey's Article III (federal constitutional) standing was not dependent on PETA. However, Naruto lacked statutory standing because the Copyright Act did not expressly authorize animals to file copyright infringement suits.

Verdict: The court granted defendants' request for attorneys' fees on appeal, which likely will deter similar lawsuits. Like *Presti,* this case forced the court to wrestle with the federal impact of a growing animal welfare and animal-abuse-prevention movement, which opens the door to the creation of legal rights for individual animals. This, however, wasn't the case to pry open that door.

Tilikum v. Sea World Parks & Entertainment (S.D. Cal. 2012)

The suit alleges that the orcas are being held in captivity as slaves in violation of the Thirteenth Amendment because they are: (1) held physically and psychologically captive; (2) without means of escape; (3) separated from their homes and families; (4) unable to engage in natural behaviors and determine their own course of action or way of life; (5) subjugated to the will and desires of Sea World; (6) confined in unnatural, stressful, and inadequate conditions; and (7) subject to artificial insemination or sperm collection for the purposes of involuntary breeding.

Verdict: The case was dismissed. The Thirteenth Amendment grants no relief, as it can only be interpreted in the historical context of the uniquely human concepts of "slavery" and "involuntary servitude."

Another topic involving the legal identity of pets gained traction in California from 2000 to 2008, leading seventeen cities (nine from California), one state (Rhode Island), and two California counties to pass laws equating the legal "owner" of a pet with a new term, the legal "guardian" of a pet. Most of the cities and counties, plus Rhode Island, are politically liberal (i.e., Boulder, Berkeley, West Hollywood, San Francisco, Woodstock, Amherst) except for a few traditional Republican or bipartisan surprises, such as Saint Louis, Missouri; Sherwood, Arkansas; and Bloomington, Indiana.

At the time, there was the expectation that "guardianship" would sweep the nation. But the idea sharply divided the pet community between animal rights groups and everyone else comfortable with the premise that people own pets. It's been more than a decade since any jurisdiction has considered this idea, and the flame appears to have flickered out. Why does this name change even matter? Guardianship has a special legal definition in all fifty states, effectively granting the state the right to step in and take legal control of a person(s), including the removal of children from their parents. Guardianships are typically granted by the court when a person cannot manage their personal or financial affairs on their own (for example, an elderly parent gives $100,000 cash to a predatory, "boiler room" lottery company), or when parents cannot care for their children.

Many supporters of the stillborn guardianship movement wanted to see this legislation proliferate to protect pets, though some simply sought the semantic satisfaction of a friendlier term than pet "owner," or quietly hoped that the concept of pet ownership could be dropped from our lexicon. Critics foresaw pet owners defending themselves before a state agency or judge about their cat- or dog-rearing practices— "You do not have the right to feed your German Shorthaired Pointer raw, uncooked chicken every day." It could have become a cause célèbre for Pet Nation, but there's barely a whisper about the "guardian" movement now. Evidence suggests that nothing has changed in those nineteen cities and counties, or the state of Rhode Island.

Where Did You Get Your Pet?

The sourcing of pets in America has been a source of legal conflict for many years, in multiple jurisdictions. It is an issue that continues to vex animal advocates and breeders alike. Here's a brief summary of what's happened regarding pet ownership over the past twenty years:

- Millions of dogs were entering shelters each year, so people were urged to adopt a shelter dog instead of buying a purebred, to help prevent mass euthanasia.
- Northern and Southern shelters woke up and launched spay-and-neuter campaigns that spread like brushfire across the country.
- Northern shelters began to earn significant revenue from the adoptions of dogs originating in the South, lower Midwest, and Southwest shelters or animal control facilities.
- An organized marketing campaign was unleashed across the United States with a single theme: "Adopt, don't shop." Americans were told that they have a "moral duty" to adopt a dog from a shelter or humane society, rather than purchase a purebred or mixed-breed dog from a "commercial" source.

This "moral imperative" fit neatly into a larger political narrative: shelter dogs are good; breeder dogs are bad. You read in chapter five that, in the eyes of many people and advocacy groups, all breeders are synonymous with puppy mills. This moral creed was buttressed by growing criticism of certain AKC breeds prone to specific physical challenges caused by selective breeding. These breeds often appear in televised "best in show" competitions.

Millennial pet owners who want a particular breed of dog, whether a purebred, like a French Bulldog, or a mixed breed, like the popular Labradoodle, are now challenging this paradigm. These dog owners demand a choice (for their own reasons), so the moral premise of "shelters or else" doesn't sit well with them. As consumers learn more about how breeds interact with families, the moral pull of adoption wanes. Awareness of the national dog shortage is growing, and most shelters are limited in their overall supply.

Nevertheless, years of broadcasting an anti-breeder message have had an impact, and many owners of shelter dogs wear their ownership like a badge of honor. The badge has the additional effect of stigmatizing pure-bred owners, because: (1) all breeders are *bad*; or (2) the purchase of a breeder dog implies that a shelter dog was euthanized instead of adopted.

This issue will divide Pet Nation for years, as there will always be shelters somewhere (the South, lower Midwest, Southwest) with too many dogs that haven't booked passage on the canine freedom train (see chapter five).

Should We Ever Declaw a Cat?

No issue better captures the moral, economic, and political tensions within Pet Nation than the declawing of cats. This surgical procedure is barely fifty years old, but pressures are mounting to ban the practice outright throughout the United States, as has already happened in most of the Western world. Organizations on both sides of the issue are engaged in this battle.

Cats came to America in the seventeenth and eighteenth centuries aboard ships, as workers with one job: to kill rats and mice. They weren't the trophy pets of admirals or captains, but a private workforce commissioned to protect food and cargo and were allowed anywhere on ship, inside or out, to do their job. As America was settled, this continued on the streets of cities in the East and Midwest. Some families had pet cats, and high-maintenance Persians lived opulently, but rats and mice posed a public-health risk and no force eradicated them like cats. Public protection of cats, however, wasn't motivated by cat fanciers but by politicians who courted voters with promises to remove rats and mice from their pest-ridden neighborhoods.

As public sanitation practices improved, cats were laid off the job, so to speak, and became "strays," roaming city streets and backyards, and were soon out of control. Formerly local heroes, cats were then euthanized in massive numbers in major cities. Fortunately, urban Americans began to appreciate the joy of having cats in their homes as playmates or companions (besides catching the occasional mouse), and twentieth-century America witnessed the rise of the domestic cat. I haven't yet mentioned "declawing" in this history tour, since it wasn't practiced, taught in veterinary schools, or discussed in veterinary textbooks until the 1950s.

The medical term for declawing is *onychectomy*: The practice involves removing the growth center of the nails within a specific area of the first bone of the finger. If the entire growth center is not removed, the nail will grow back in, often in a deformed and painful manner. The entire first bone (classified as the "third," visible in the diagram) at the end of the finger must be severed. Along with the third bone comes nerves, tendons, ligaments, and the joint capsule. A more graphic technical phrase for the procedure is "partial paw amputation," rarely used in public discourse or with pet owners.

Declawing became common as indoor cats became popular and the scratching instincts of cats became a behavioral issue, prompting visits to the veterinarian. According to *Feline Behavior: A Guide for Veterinarians*, cats begin to scratch by the time they are thirty-five days old. Thus, as kittens are adopted or purchased, they learn to scratch, to remove old nail sheaths, assert dominance, mark areas with the scent glands on their paws, visually mark property, stretch, and just plain feel good.

The origin of the declawing procedure is unclear. A professional search of veterinary textbooks in the first half of the twentieth century found no mention of declawing. Forty-eight studies from 1973–2002 discuss various aspects of declawing. Accounts of early clinical trials are painful reading, with Japanese doctors testing techniques on newborn kittens without anesthesia. An early reference manual was Ann Nagle's *A Technique for Feline Onychectomy* (1976). In 2005, Nancy Peterson and Katherine Grier published an excellent history of declawing, which includes the authors' discovery of class notes on feline surgery from Iowa State University, in 1955, with a reference to declawing.

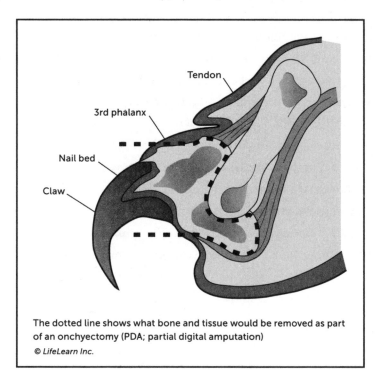

The dotted line shows what bone and tissue would be removed as part of an onchyectomy (PDA; partial digital amputation)
© LifeLearn Inc.

By the seventies, declawing was accepted veterinary practice throughout the United States. Anesthesia methods and pain management for the cats continued to improve, and nearly all professional organizations considered declawing appropriate if an indoor cat's clawing behavior was chronic. Though data is limited, it is clear that declawing revenue was meaningful for veterinarians. A 2001 study estimated that over 25 percent of all indoor cats in America (19.4 million cats) were declawed. This represents approximately $3 billion in industry revenue. Declawing revenue increased as veterinarians coupled declawing with spray and neuter surgery.

Then the nineties arrived. Animal welfare organizations pounced on the issue, veterinarians began to debate the issue publicly, studies revealed problems for cats after operation, and the ground shifted. The Pet Nation era has become a battleground between two camps.

"Leave It Up to the Veterinarian"

The established position is anchored by a simple view: Declawing should be a decision made by a veterinarian, considering all the circumstances, and it is sometimes necessary to avoid euthanizing the cat when the owners otherwise will relinquish the cat or have her put down. Most veterinarians over fifty years of age favor declawing if the only realistic alternative is euthanasia. The AVMA, the Cat Fanciers' Association, and most veterinary associations maintain this position. The only change is AVMA's recent emphasis that declawing should be a procedure of last resort. This argument attracts support for two reasons: (1) it emphasizes that the decision maker must be a trained veterinary medical doctor; and (2) declawing sometimes is the only way for an indoor cat to avoid euthanasia.

"Declawing Is Cruel and Unnecessary"

Opponents trumpet an equally simple view: declawing is painful and cruel, and there is no evidence that euthanasia cannot be avoided unless an indoor cat is declawed. Critics of declawing weigh the alternatives and always argue that a more humane alternative is available other than partial paw amputation. A ban on declawing—unless the medical needs of the cat dictate otherwise (but not avoiding euthanasia)—has moved to the forefront of pet politics, and is the law in these jurisdictions: New York, West Hollywood, Berkeley, Beverly Hills, Burbank, Culver City, Los Angeles, San Francisco, Santa Monica, Denver, and Rhode Island (the state prohibits a landlord from requiring that a tenant's cat be declawed). The movement accelerated when California banned the declawing of exotic animals (usually for film-making purposes), which led even the AVMA to oppose declawing of exotic cats, in 2004.

New York's passage of a declawing ban in July 2019 ironically pitted the state veterinary association against the New York City bar association. The lawyers (and animal welfare advocates) won, and Governor Cuomo signed the bill into law on July 22. Supporters of a ban relied heavily on evidence that the city of Los Angeles showed no increase in the relinquishment of cats to shelters after it banned declawing in 2009. A study by Kass et al. (2001) also showed that 18 percent of pets presented for euthanasia were given up for behavioral reasons, and destructiveness (tearing furniture apart) involved only 14 percent of that population, or 2 percent overall.

The New York law changes the landscape, because the fourth largest state in the country (and media capital of the world) has implemented a ban. The campaign is on, and I expect ten to fifteen states to consider legislation to emulate New York each year until the practice disappears. The veterinary establishment will not retreat simply because New York approved a ban, though they will feel increasing pressure to do so, and anti-declawing groups now have momentum.

The outcome may hinge on the political power of millennials. Younger veterinarians do not support declawing, and millennial pet owners are the largest and fastest-growing group of pet owners in America. Baby boomers who were trained to declaw as an accepted medical procedure and performed the procedure throughout their careers are retiring at the rate of two thousand veterinarians per year. In the next decade, declawing will become politically and culturally unacceptable, a relic of veterinary days past.

How Was Your Dog Bred?

Puppies require two parents, which means that each puppy was "bred" in some manner (accidentally or intentionally). In a 2015 national survey conducted by Moore Information for the Pet Leadership Council, we asked dog owners where their dog came from as a puppy, and the answers were surprising:

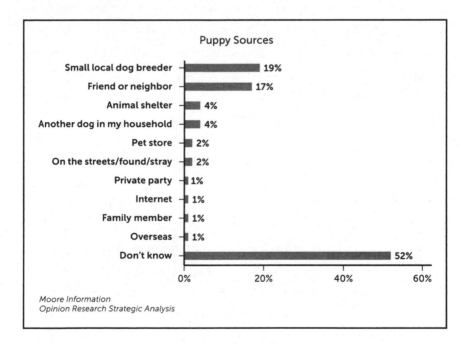

Data shows that 52 percent of dog owners had no idea how or where their dog was bred, and another 10 percent knew only the distribution channel but not the point of origin. Only 6 percent claimed the shelter or rescue dog badge of honor. This data squares with my anecdotal observation that shelter/rescue warriors are urban residents, political by nature, but haven't had a profound impact yet on the general public. Surveys during the past ten years all have established that 25 percent of household dogs are purchased from shelters. On most weekends, they adopt out all of their adoptable dogs by noon on Sunday. This is a function of demand and supply, and less a moral or political statement. It is clear that Americans, especially millennials, get their dogs wherever they can find them.

Still, campaigns across the country to outlaw the retail sale of pets in stores are winning, in favor of shelter adoptions, thus raising the bar for commercial breeders. The net effect could be surprising and positive: Quality breeders will survive (conforming to widely accepted standards) and the Internet (instead of brick-and-mortar retail stores) will continue to serve as a filtering, "best practices" acquisition channel for American pet consumers, as in other product categories. Shelters will continue to play a role, but not for political reasons. That will suit most shelters just fine.

Who Makes Money from Pets, and How Much Do They Make?

Like most issues in the United States, money drives politics in Pet Nation, and in interesting ways. We'll begin with advocacy or lobbying. The hands-down winners are the two large nonprofits, ASPCA and HSUS, who each raise approximately $175 million each year and spend most of this war chest on lobbying, advertising on issues of interest concerning pets and farm animals, infrastructure, and salaries. TV ads and social media are powerful tools for both organizations, and for many years images of woebegone dogs in shelters were nightly fare on cable channels. HSUS, in particular, has had a tricky relationship with shelters and local humane organizations in America, because many donors mistakenly believe that HSUS donations filter down to local groups (because of the naming overlap), and that is not the case. HSUS does not operate or fund shelters or local humane/rescue groups.

ASPCA and HSUS both focus on animal abuse, a worthy cause in its own right, but one that does not affect much of Pet Nation today. Dog breeding and the retail sale of puppies are galvanizing issues for them, and their combined financial might dwarfs that of their opponents. Much of the pet marketplace is small-scale, fractured, and not engaged in the political arena, unlike most American political clashes. With most issues that ASPCA and HSUS lobby, veterinarians remain on the sidelines, alongside the pet pharmaceutical and food companies, since the politics don't impact pet health care directly.

As we discussed in chapter five, the positions that ASPCA and HSUS advocate will make it harder to meet the demand for pets in the future. What's unclear is if the ASPCA and HSUS will ever be willing to negotiate with breeders or industry interests to address the shortage, or to reach a compromise. This must happen with commercial dog breeding, or there won't be a solution to the dog shortage. The question of large-scale commercial breeding will not be "won" or settled by one side or the other in the public media. Money is at the heart of the "dogfight," as with noneconomic damages discussed earlier in the chapter.

Money is also the fulcrum in America's veterinarian shortage, for two reasons. First, historically, it has been expensive to open and to operate a veterinary school, which explains why there are only thirty in the United States for 185 million cats and dogs, versus 185 medical schools for 325 million people. And incoming classes are small, ranging from 50 to 164 students. Veterinary schools and their university boards have been reluctant to expand the size of the student body, due to financial concerns and resistance from local veterinarians, who fear increased competition. Second, on average, veterinarians earn far less than human doctors, even though their undergraduate academic requirements are identical, which reduces demand for admission to veterinary school.

Money is at the core of a dispute between big-box retailers and online pharmacies on the one hand and veterinary practices on the other, a conflict that has festered since 2010. Big-box retailers and online pharmacies have their eyes (and wallets) on the pet medications sold by veterinarians in their daily practices. In 2010, Walmart and other retailers drafted and introduced legislation into Congress called "Fairness to Pet Owners." The idea sounds innocuous but was designed to allow the federal government to exert control over individual veterinary practices through the mechanism of the Federal Trade Commission (FTC). The plan was cleverly designed to force veterinarians to funnel pet owners to big-box retailers and online pharmacies for their purchase of medications, diverting revenue from the veterinarian.

I partnered with the American Veterinary Medical Association and state veterinary associations throughout the United States to defeat this bill, and, in nine years, it has not received a hearing. I've always understood that politicians like veterinarians, and appreciate that veterinarians are popular in their communities (i.e., with voters). This could explain why pet owners and Congress have not warmed up to this legislation, in addition to the fact that clients can always get a prescription from their veterinarian if they prefer. Curiously, much of the limited support for the bill comes from Utah, which has led to much speculation but nothing conclusive. What is obvious is that consumers have and want a variety of choices to find pet medications—online, retail, and through their local veterinarian, and these choices continue to expand.

An interesting twist in this battle is that traditional pharmacy schools do not train pharmacists to handle medications for all the pet species and the different breeds within each species. Cats and dogs are not simply "small people." In the FTC hearing, veterinarians emphasized a point that pet owners know all too well: It isn't easy to get a cat or dog to swallow medications, especially cats, who are rarely fooled by the insertion of pills into their food. Veterinarians and their staff teach pet owners how to do this, and large-chain pharmacy clerks apparently missed that class.

Money was the reason the Nevada State Board of Pharmacy tried to stop veterinarians from shipping pet medications directly to clients.

Certain boards of pharmacy don't like the idea of veterinarians earning money from the legitimate sale of medications to their clients, though they tolerate large pharmacy chains and online retailers doing the same. One company, Portland, Oregon–based Vetsource, challenged and defeated the pharmacy board, with help from the board of veterinary medicine. However, it was an expensive legal effort, and many Nevada pet owners waited two years for the dispute to be decided before again enjoying the convenience of filling their prescriptions online.

Is There a Connection Between Human Abuse and Animal Abuse?

This idea is logical, and disturbing. Violent criminals often launch their careers by abusing animals, as if they've undergone some perverse kind of "apprenticeship." Many studies, such as one conducted at Northeastern University, have established that adults convicted of violent crimes, particularly against women, have previously abused animals as youths or adults. Childhood animal abuse is recognized today as a criterion for the clinical category of *Antisocial Personality Disorder* in the *ICD-10*, which is the *International Statistical Classification of Diseases and Related Health Problems* (tenth edition) created by the World Health Organization, or we could cite the *Diagnostic and Statistical Manual of Mental Disorders (DSM-III-R)* (American Psychiatric Association, 1987), which added cruelty to animals as a diagnostic criterion for *Conduct Disorder*, "a persistent pattern of conduct in which the basic rights of others and major age-appropriate societal norms or rules are violated." Studies of women in domestic violence shelters in Utah confirm that between 68 percent to 75 percent of men who harmed them had also abused pets. Another study of violent adult male criminals at the University of Tennessee, in 2014, found that 41 percent had abused animals, compared to 1.5 percent of the noncriminal male population.

A disturbing pattern is often seen in a man abusing both a woman and her pet as part of the same offense. A brutal example occurred in Saint Paul, Minnesota, in 2006, where neighbors watched a man snap the necks of ten puppies in front of his girlfriend and then threaten to "do to you what I done to the dogs." I could fill this chapter with accounts of gruesome crimes, often involving a woman's child being forced to watch a man kill or torture a family pet. This has led to a national campaign to build animal shelters alongside domestic violence shelters, so that women are not afraid to leave their house or apartment where they are being violated, for fear that their pet will be left behind to suffer.

"Up to 65 percent of domestic violence victims remain in abusive homes out of fear for their pet's safety, and even more women residing in domestic violence shelters reported that a pet was harmed by their abuser," Urban Resources Institute president and CEO Nathaniel Fields said. In 2018, Congress passed the PAWS Act, with HABRI playing a key role, to support shelters throughout the United States. This provision of the Farm Bill establishes grants for domestic violence shelters to create programs to provide emergency and short-term shelter and housing assistance for domestic violence victims with pets, service animals, emotional-support animals, or horses. Grants may also be used to provide support services to enable someone fleeing domestic violence to locate safe housing with their pet.

"No one should have to make the choice between finding safety and staying in a violent situation to protect their pet," said Congresswoman Katherine Clark (D-MA). "This law empowers survivors with the resources to leave a dangerous situation while being able to continue to care for their pet. I'm grateful for the partnerships we've formed between organizations working to end both domestic violence and animal abuse. Together, we will help save lives."

More work remains to be done. Only three states (Colorado, Nevada, New Hampshire) recognize animal abuse as a circumstance enabling a court to enter a protective order against an individual threatening domestic violence. However, thirty-two states do allow pets to be covered in protective orders against violent offenders. The map below shows the policy of each state; one wonders what must happen for the other eighteen states to wake up and do the right thing. All of the laggard states are rural except Pennsylvania, Georgia, and Missouri.

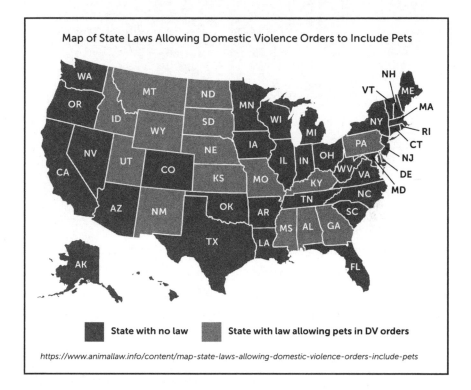

Map of State Laws Allowing Domestic Violence Orders to Include Pets

State with no law   State with law allowing pets in DV orders

https://www.animallaw.info/content/map-state-laws-allowing-domestic-violence-orders-include-pets

In some states (but not most), veterinarians are required to report animal abuse to animal abuse authorities, if they suspect a patient of such behavior. It varies from state to state:

- Reporting is mandatory in seventeen states.
- No action is required in twenty-five states.
- Reporting is encouraged, but not required, in eight states. Legal immunity is given to veterinarians in these states who report suspected abuse and are then sued by their clients.

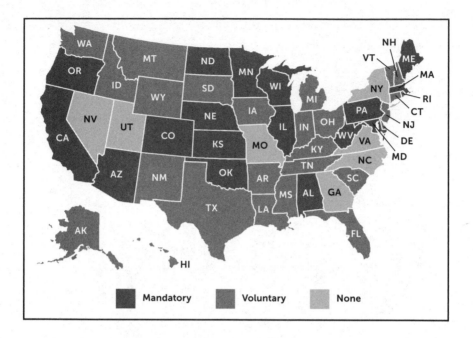

This prompts the question: Why do twenty-five states require or tolerate no action at all, including large states like Texas, Florida, Ohio, Michigan, and Washington? It's hard to believe that a state takes animal abuse seriously when it won't require veterinarians to report animal abuse to authorities, whether it's a violent kick, a cut, starvation, or striking by fist or object. Forty-seven states require human medical professionals to report suspicions of domestic abuse to authorities, so Pet Nation still has work to do.

Great Britain took one step further by linking animal abuse to domestic violence:

1. Veterinarians are encouraged to report to criminal authorities for domestic violence a pet owner suspected of animal abuse. This makes the link between animal abuse and potential domestic violence explicit and official. It is not assumed that the veterinarian has any knowledge or suspicion of domestic violence in the pet owner's household, only that if there is evi-

dence of animal abuse, then human abuse could be occurring as well.

2. Veterinarians have legal immunity from any lawsuit by their client for their reporting. It's easy to imagine a client suing a veterinarian when he discovers that she reported him to the police for potential domestic violence based upon the physical condition of a dog or cat.

No American state has considered such a law.

The other measure of how seriously a state views animal abuse is the length of the recommended prison sentence or jail time for an offender. The green and yellow states below take a lighter view of animal abuse crimes, when compared to the rest of Pet Nation, for reasons hard to comprehend.

Opioid use and abuse are epidemic across the United States. Human medicine and pharmaceuticals are at the heart of the story, but pets unfortunately have been dragged into the spotlight. An occasional headline runs in the news, or a cautionary article appears in a veterinary journal, but individual cases of opioid abuse in pet health clinics demonstrate how vulnerable Pet Nation is to repeat abuse by opioid addicts who are desperate to obtain drugs routinely used each day in veterinary practices.

Federal data shows that opioid prescriptions from the University of Pennsylvania's School of Veterinary Medicine rose 41 percent between 2007 and 2017, even though the annual number of visits increased only 13 percent. Between 2014 and 2017, Pennsylvania vets prescribed 688,340 hydrocodone (Hycodan) tablets, 14,100 codeine tablets, 23,110 fentanyl patches, 171,100 tablets of hydromorphone (Dilaudid), and 7,600 doses of oxycodone (Oxycontin), while opioid abuse and overdoses all over the country were rampant.

The Food and Drug Administration (FDA) created new guidance specific to veterinarians to help increase understanding of state and federal regulations, including how to tell if a prescription is being abused

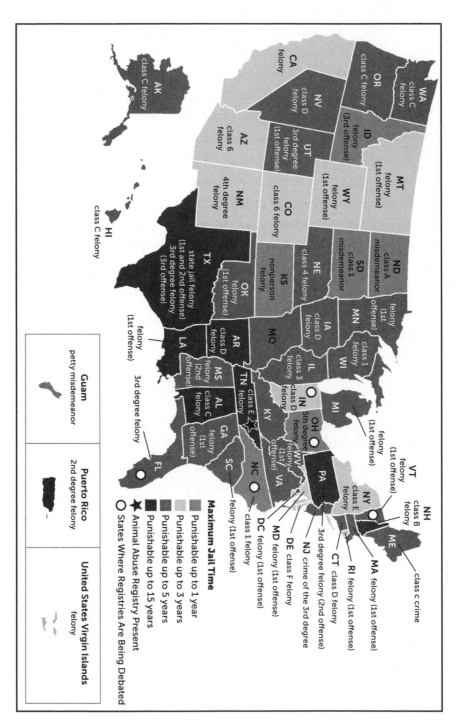

AK
class C felony

CA
felony

OR
class C felony

WA
class C
felony

NV
class D
felony

ID
felony
(3rd offense)

MT
felony
(1st offense)

AZ
class 6
felony

UT
3rd degree
felony
(1st offense)

WY
felony
(1st offense)

HI
class C felony

NM
4th degree
felony

CO
class 6 felony

KS
nonperson
felony

NE
class 4 felony

SD
class 1
misdemeanor

ND
class A
misdemeanor

felony
(1st
offense)

MN
class 1
felony

TX
state jail felony
(1st and 2nd offense)
3rd degree felony
(3rd offense)

OK
felony
(1st offense)

MO

IA
class D
felony

WI

LA
felony
(1st offense)

AR
class D
felony

TN
class E
felony

IL
class 3
felony

MI

VT
felony
(1st offense)

NH
class B
felony

MS
felony
(2nd
offense)

AL
class C
felony

KY
class D
felony
(1st
offense)

IN
5th degree
felony

OH
felony
(1st offense)

WV
felony
(1st
offense)

PA
class E
felony

NY
class E
felony

ME
class c crime

GA
class D
felony
(1st
offense)

FL

SC
felony (1st offense)

NC
felony (1st offense)

VA

Maximum Jail Time

⬤ Punishable up to 15 years
⬤ Punishable up to 5 years
⬤ Punishable up to 3 years
⬤ Punishable up to 1 year
★ Animal Abuse Registry Present
◯ States Where Registries Are Being Debated

DC felony (1st offense)
MD felony (1st offense)
DE class F felony
NJ crime of the 3rd degree
CT class D felony
RI felony (1st offense)
MA felony (1st offense)

3rd degree felony

Guam
petty misdemeanor

Puerto Rico
2nd degree felony

United States Virgin Islands
felony

by a pet owner. According to a recent study in the *American Journal of Public Health*, 13 percent of veterinarians polled were aware of cases where pets were made to appear ill or injured so that a staff member or pet owner could obtain an opioid prescription, and 12 percent had uncovered opioid use or diversion by veterinary staff. Nevertheless, only 62 percent of veterinarians believed that they have a role to play in preventing opioid abuse.

Here are examples of the ways animals are being abused by opioid addicts.

A woman in Kentucky cut her Golden Retriever with a razor and took him to the same vet three times for pain meds. The doctor became suspicious because the cuts "looked like clean cuts instead of the jaggedness that you might see in most animal injuries," and the woman asked for a medication by name.

An Ohio man taught his dog to cough on cue in an effort to obtain hydrocodone prescriptions.

A Connecticut man was charged with animal cruelty, illegally obtaining drugs, and "doctor shopping" after he took two injured dogs to multiple vets to obtain pain pills for himself.

Another concern for veterinarians is the risk of accidental opioid overdose of pets themselves. In a bizarre but true story from New Hampshire, a three-month-old puppy named Zoey ingested an opioid while on a walk with her owner around her neighborhood. Zoey was rushed to the hospital and given naloxone to revive her. The hospital owner, pleased with the outcome, noted that the incident indicates the extent of the opioid crisis.

How Many Pets Do You Have?

Everyone knows about someone in their neighborhood, city, or county who truly loves animals and owns more than their share. The common term is "hoarder," and it often leads to criminal investigations, with the cats or dogs being removed by authorities. Though less an issue in rural communities, hoarding is a growing problem in suburban communities and cities, where neighbors can feel the impact. Recently, a woman in an upscale Ohio apartment complex was found with seventy-seven cats in a two-bedroom unit. The entire unit had to be torn down and rebuilt after authorities learned of the hoarder from a new tenant next door. One cannot help but wonder, "Why didn't the previous tenant notice seventy-seven cats next door?"

The Hoarding of Animals Research Consortium (HARC) website identifies the following characteristics of most hoarders, first listed by Gary Patronek in *Public Health Reports* 114.1 (1999): 81:

Accumulation of numerous animals, which has overwhelmed that person's ability to provide even minimal standards of nutrition, sanitation, and veterinary care.

Failure to acknowledge the deteriorating condition of the animals (including disease, starvation, and even death) and the household environment (severe overcrowding, unsanitary conditions).

Failure to recognize the negative effect of the collection on their own health and well-being, and that of other household members.

Only two states, Illinois and Hawaii, classify hoarding as a felony, with the latter drawing the line at fifteen cats or dogs, or a combination of both, before taking action. Hoarders habitually claim that they love pets and are only trying to take care of them. But something changes when three kittens on a single bed morph into seventy-seven in a two-bedroom apartment.

Consider these recent examples:

• Nearly one thousand animals were found dead in a Montclair, California, warehouse in 2017. With them were two thousand live chickens, parakeets, and other birds, including some exotic species, and dozens of fish. The Inland Humane Society assisted in the rescue of the surviving animals and provided these details. The warehousing of animals at this scale apparently happened quickly, not over a matter of years.

• A couple in Monmouth County, New Jersey, in 2016, had more than 270 dogs in their home. Most of the dogs were found in decent health, but the house itself was in terrible condition. The stench was overwhelming, with holes in the walls where dogs had been living. However, prosecutors could not charge the couple with animal cruelty because the dogs were not in bad health.

• With nearly seven hundred cats, the Haven Acres Cat Sanctuary near Gainesville, Florida, was the largest case of cat hoarding in American history. In 2018, 697 cats were seized with the assistance of the HSUS, and the owners pled no contest to forty-seven counts of animal cruelty. Yet they received no jail time and were sentenced to only fifteen years of probation along with fines. They were prohibited from owning or rescuing any more cats, but one wonders how many cats a hoarder must acquire in Florida before spending some time behind bars.

• In 2016, 108 cats were seized from a small home in northwest Texas, where an entire room was converted into a litter box and cat food was strewn across the floor. The 108 cats were confined to an eight-hundred-square-foot space. The hoarder had been issued twenty citations over the years for improper care of an animal and non-vaccination of her cats for rabies, but had not stopped until the final legal action.

Inconsistencies in the laws and outcomes explains why hoarding is still practiced among us.

SUMMARY VERDICT

With pets, like so many political or legal issues, what looks logical on the surface doesn't always withstand scrutiny when the issues are dissected. The human-animal bond, or the everyday love of a pet owner for her kitty, needn't lead to full-blown legal rights in court for animals. Any more than setting a ten-month-old puppy "free" in a field to play with ground squirrels and cottontail bunnies is a good idea, when a hawk, bobcat, coyote, or wild boar might show up for lunch at any moment. The dramatic expansion of pets in America during Pet Nation, and their ubiquity, have expanded protection for animals, but there are limits to what our society can bear. At least for now.

· 7 ·

PET HEALTH CARE WILL
NEVER BE THE SAME AGAIN

**French Bulldog Survives Six-Story Fall
with Help from BluePearl Veterinarians**

On August 9, 2019, a French Bulldog named Winston fell six stories from the roof of a Manhattan apartment building, crashing through the sunroof of a car parked below. Winston survived and was rushed to BluePearl veterinary hospital on West Fifty-Fifth Street, generating coverage on CNN. Miraculously, he didn't break a single bone. To treat some bruising to his lungs, BluePearl placed him in an oxygen chamber for thirty-six hours. Dr. Harry Weatherson, emergency and critical care resident at BluePearl, thinks the dog's breed might have had something to do with his unbelievable outcome. "He is quite muscular and quite stout. And the fact that he fell through a car sunroof, I think that definitely cushioned his fall to some degree. Six stories is quite substantial, so he is a very lucky dog, indeed."

Before Pet Nation, a lone French Bulldog would not have made it onto the evening news, and BluePearl would not have been there to save him. Pet health care took its time to learn the rhythms and pace of Pet

Nation. Why was there a lag between the sweeping social changes brought about by this revolution and advances in pet medicine? The fascinating journey from the backyard to the examining room is a story that's never been explored.

In the second half of the twentieth century, veterinary care had three defining characteristics: (1) veterinary clinics were scarce and often located in less desirable parts of American towns and cities; (2) people took their dogs (when necessary) and cats (rarely) to the veterinarian to: (a) get vaccines; (b) fix injuries (often from car accidents), or (c) be "put down";* and (3) veterinary specialists were rare, usually found at veterinary colleges. Pet owners were not exposed to the concept of high-end medical procedures to prolong a dog's or cat's life, or to provide them advanced care throughout their life.

In other words, for most pets, health care amounted to getting an annual rabies vaccine,** fixing a broken leg, and then, when your dog struggled to walk at the end of her life, putting her to sleep. That was it. Wellness care for pets trailed far behind the late twentieth-century focus on preventive care for people. While annual physicals and regular dental checkups became staples of the human health-care regimen, they only recently became templates for veterinary care in America.

One obstacle was the absence of scientific research on the value of wellness care in improving or extending the life of a pet. Despite the logic that cats and dogs would profit from regular care and treatment (with shorter life spans than humans but similar organs), no peer-review research existed to support this, and veterinary schools didn't teach this concept. An older generation of small animal veterinarians was reluctant to offend clients by "selling" the idea of annual or, even, biannual visits.

---

* The term, "to put down," as in "to euthanize an animal," is derived from the thirteenth-century phrase, "to put down a rebellion."

** Rabies vaccines are good for one year or three years, depending on the animal's age and rabies vaccine history, and state and municipal laws.

The expansion of the pet industry, with myriad choices for food, bedding, breeds, and amenities woke up pet owners to the potential value of proactive, not reactive, veterinary care. If nutritious food improves pet health, then why wouldn't regular health care have a positive impact on the quality and length of their lives, too? If the pet-food offering—ingredients, variety, customization—stretched beyond grocery stores to pet stores like PetSmart and Petco, as well as smaller, local specialty stores, then why not increase the range of medical providers? The marriage of the retailer PetSmart with a Portland, Oregon, veterinarian, in 1994, ratcheted up pet health care from first to fifth gear in what seemed like sixty seconds.

DR. CAMPBELL AND BANFIELD PET HOSPITAL

Scott Campbell grew up in an itinerant doctor's family on a ranch in the southeast corner of Oregon, where livestock outnumber people by ten to one and the largest town, Burns, has a population of 2,806. Scott is a good friend, and his veterinary creation is a client of my Animal Policy Group, so this account is firsthand and close-up. He dreamed of becoming a farrier,* not an international veterinary entrepreneur. Once Scott considered opportunities beyond becoming the world's best farrier, he graduated from Oregon State University and earned a veterinary degree from Washington State University, just up the road in Pullman, on the Idaho border.

In less than ten years, this would-be farrier turned the world of pet health care inside out and upside down. First, he launched a 130-location

---

*Farrier: A person who shoes horses for a living (and has a high tolerance for pain).

national veterinary practice called Banfield Pet Hospitals. His main innovation was to locate these practices inside PetSmart retail stores. Banfield's shareholders included Mars, Inc. and PetSmart, and the practice grew to more than seven hundred locations before he sold it to Mars and PetSmart, in 2007. Mars subsequently acquired PetSmart's interest and has expanded Banfield to over eleven hundred locations, building the company into the largest veterinary group in the world, which now includes BluePearl, VCA, Antech, and European practices.

Banfield's success was due to innovative business and medical practices. Not only did Scott place Banfield inside PetSmart retail stores, but he introduced the idea of consumer-friendly hours, including weekends, from 7:00 a.m. to 7:00 p.m. This allowed pet owners to drop off their dogs and cats in the morning and pick them up after work, or to tend to veterinary needs on Saturday or Sunday. Banfield also introduced wellness plans as the central feature of its pet-care plan, with a menu of services and diagnostics, anchored by twice-a-year visits to the veterinarian. By charging a fixed monthly fee, wellness plans took the guesswork out of veterinary bills.

Scott introduced the use of electronic record-keeping. From inception, Banfield used digital records, perfected by a team led by another Washington State veterinarian, Kerri Marshall. This practice was so innovative that the Mayo Clinic sent a technology team to Portland to understand how he'd done it. That's how revolutionary Banfield's practice was. Today, with more than three million pets cared for in its hospitals each year, Banfield has the largest custom-built practice management and electronic veterinary health record system in the world, containing twenty years of medical history and more than twenty-seven million unique pet files.

The rise of Pet Nation, the competitive challenge from Banfield, and the emergence of millennial pet owners has transformed the quiet pet health-care industry in the twenty-first century. Dr. Jen Welser, an ophthalmologist, was in the front row after finishing veterinary school in the mid-nineties, and both observed and led the development of specialty practices emulating human medicine. She is chief medical officer for Mars Veterinary Health, overseeing veterinary care at an array of general practice and specialty hospitals:

> *When I started, specialty medicine was tucked away inside of veterinary school teaching hospitals, and barely visible to pet owners or general practitioners. I didn't imagine a career as a private small-animal ophthalmologist. I've practiced in New York City and California, and was fortunate to be on the ground floor as specialists and primary care doctors built true partnerships like we see in human medicine. This gave pet owners confidence in the total package of care being provided to their cat or dog. Now we see this all over the country and it's exciting. Pet owners today want the same quality of care as they receive for themselves, and we can offer it.*

Pet owners came to appreciate the value of preventive care and embraced specialty hospitals offering advanced care and surgical expertise. In an August 2019 survey of one thousand pet owners by consumer finance adviser LendEDU, 46 percent of the participants said they spend as much monthly on their pet's health care as they do on themselves. These factors changed everything in the world of pet care, and are the story of this chapter.

HOW IS PET HEALTH CARE ORGANIZED?

There are twenty-five thousand to thirty thousand pet health-care clinics or hospitals in the United States. The terms "clinic" and "hospital" are used interchangeably in veterinary medicine, unlike in human medicine. In human health care, a "clinic" is almost always smaller than a "hospital." Clinics offer same-day services but not overnight stays, while hospitals provide both. Clients of human clinics rarely stay overnight, and the same is true at most veterinary clinics and hospitals. Some specialty veterinary clinics and hospitals do keep dogs and cats overnight, but not at the scale of human hospitals.

Through 2015, virtually all veterinary practices were owned by one or two veterinarians practicing at a single location, except for the rare veterinarians who assembled groups of small practices. Each practice would have two to four veterinarians, plus a staff of six to ten assistants and veterinary technicians. As a corporately owned practice, Banfield and a handful of other consolidators, VCA, National Veterinary Associates (NVA), and BluePearl, were different from the smaller practices. Corporations that purchased individual practices usually maintained the original names of the clinics or hospitals, while implementing group accounting, purchasing, human-resource management, and other services.

Five years on, there are fifty-five corporate veterinary groups in America, and between 15 percent and 20 percent of all pet veterinarians practice in corporately owned clinics or hospitals. Much of this growth was fueled by private-equity groups and investors outside veterinary medicine, eager to profit from the Pet Nation wave. The growing consumer appetite for high-quality, human-scale pet health care has increased the overall access of pet owners to twenty-first-century health care. It has also improved the lives of veterinarians. The boom has lifted starting salaries and expanded opportunities for veterinarians to enter specialty practices. Many baby boomer veterinarians have been able to retire comfortably. Has this satisfied the national demand for pet care in a country with 185 million cats and dogs? Not at all. There is still substantial room for growth: applications for veterinary schools continue to rise, and accreditors are now reviewing plans for new veterinary schools.

Not all veterinarians have welcomed the arrival of corporate practices, but no movement has challenged them, nor have pet owners complained. Millennials and Generation Z want *more* care delivered conveniently (via smartphones and other digital tools) and on demand. Older veterinary models are eroding or being recast in every town, suburb, and city across America. Pet health care is catching up to Pet Nation.

HOW ARE HEALTH PROFESSIONALS TRAINED IN PET NATION?

To understand what has happened with veterinary education in the United States, it helps to look at human health care and medical schools. The headline is: "Both Systems Struggle with Doctor Shortages, but Veterinary Higher Education is Reluctant to Expand, Unlike Human Medicine." According to a 2019 study by economist and former dean of the University of Florida College of Veterinary Medicine, Dr. James Lloyd, the United States has a shortage of three thousand veterinarians. Two large-corporate-practice executives told me recently that they could hire one thousand veterinarians immediately, *if* they were available. Dr. Matthew Salois, an economist at the American Veterinary Medical Association, has estimated that veterinary sector employment is at 98 percent, with unemployment at 2 percent—most economists consider unemployment at 6 percent to be "full employment."

There are 185 medical schools in the United States (for 325 million people), but only thirty veterinary schools (for 185 million cats and dogs, plus food animals, horses, and don't forget parakeets). That's six medical schools for each veterinary school. When medical schools couldn't meet the American demand for doctors in the seventies and eighties, osteopathic medical schools opened around the country, including some with class sizes exceeding three hundred students. Then, as the doctor shortage persisted, physician assistant programs expanded, followed by nurse practitioner programs. People now receive treatment from four different providers: medical doctors (MDs), doctors of osteopathic medicine (DOs), physician assistants (PAs), and nurse practitioners (NPs). Yet we still don't have enough health-care professionals.

HISTORY

The first veterinarians were Neolithic, living in 3400 BC, at the end of the Stone Age. They performed a procedure called "trepanation," drilling a hole in a cow's skull to treat intracranial disease. During the Twelfth Dynasty, ancient Egyptians simultaneously made medicine for people and for animals and performed veterinary procedures, primarily on horses, which had a high economic value.

The world's first veterinary school was founded in Lyon, France, in 1760, following an outbreak of the cow plague, which decimated the French cattle population. The Royal College of Veterinary Surgeons was established in London by royal charter, in 1844. America's first veterinary colleges opened in the early nineteenth century, in Boston, New York, and Philadelphia. Knowledge was moving from the barnyard to the classroom.

Contrast those statistics with veterinary medicine: only twenty-five American schools existed until 1978, when two more opened. Twenty years later, another school was added, then there was a fifteen-year wait until the twenty-ninth and thirtieth schools* were approved. Pet health care doesn't have the equivalent of DOs, PAs, or NPs. It's obvious that veterinary medicine provides fewer treatment alternatives for its patients and proportionately fewer doctors than human health care, and there is a critical need for more pet health-care professionals. As millennials demand increasingly more pet care (happy to spend as much on their Cockapoos as on themselves), and the high percentage of pet owners who currently *don't* access regular care decide to seek veterinary care (potentially 40 percent of 85 million American households, or

---

*Lincoln Memorial University at the Cumberland Gap, where Tennessee, Virginia, and Kentucky meet.

thirty-four million households), the veterinary shortage will become even more strained and acute.

As Pet Nation has evolved, so has the composition of those providing pet health care. The most visible change in veterinary medicine during the span of Pet Nation is its wholesale transformation from a male to a female profession. The gender makeup of the veterinary profession has flip-flopped 180 degrees. A male-dominated profession in the seventies and eighties, with classes nearly 90 percent male, American veterinary graduates are now 80 percent female. And the male percentages continue to decline. American professional education is correcting the gender imbalance in all fields of study, increasing opportunities for women, none more aggressively than veterinary education. Why more men aren't entering the profession is concerning, though, especially as economic opportunities for veterinarians expand across the United States and abroad.

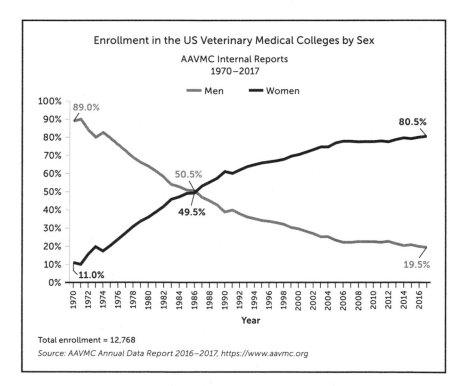

Enrollment in the US Veterinary Medical Colleges by Sex

AAVMC Internal Reports
1970–2017

━━ Men   ━━ Women

Total enrollment = 12,768

Source: AAVMC Annual Data Report 2016–2017, https://www.aavmc.org

In other ways, the demographics of the veterinary profession have not changed much at all. Veterinarians are the least diverse profession by ethnicity in America, despite more than a decade of effort to reverse the trend, although the situation is improving:

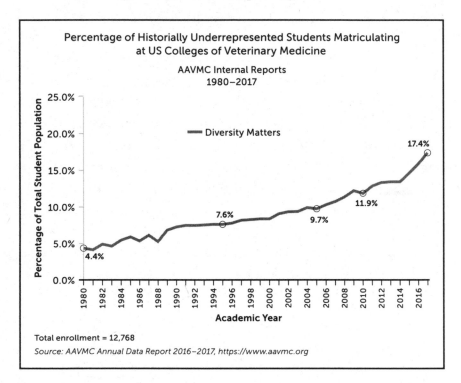

Percentage of Historically Underrepresented Students Matriculating at US Colleges of Veterinary Medicine

AAVMC Internal Reports
1980–2017

Total enrollment = 12,768

Source: AAVMC Annual Data Report 2016–2017, https://www.aavmc.org

Hispanic Americans own dogs at the same rate as other American households (43 percent), yet they represent only 5 percent of the veterinary profession (far short of Hispanic's 18 percent share of the total American population in 2018, per the United States Census Bureau). It appears that there is no correlation between dog ownership in an ethnic group and their participation in veterinary medicine. African Americans own dogs at a lower percentage than other American ethnic groups, which could account for reduced African American interest in the veterinary profession (2.5 percent of veterinarians, but 12 percent of total US population). But the Latino data suggests that there is no correlation. Either way, this is a problem that needs attention.

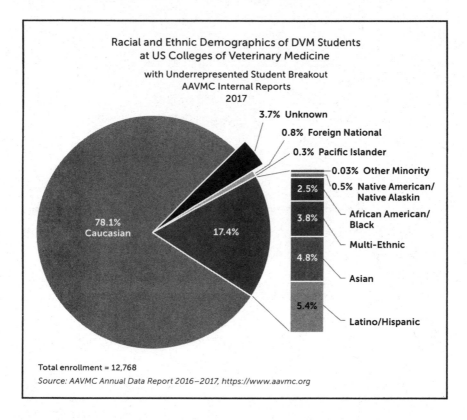

Racial and Ethnic Demographics of DVM Students at US Colleges of Veterinary Medicine

with Underrepresented Student Breakout
AAVMC Internal Reports
2017

3.7% Unknown

0.8% Foreign National

0.3% Pacific Islander

0.03% Other Minority

0.5% Native American/ Native Alaskin

2.5%

3.8% African American/ Black

78.1% Caucasian

17.4%

Multi-Ethnic

4.8%

Asian

5.4%

Latino/Hispanic

Total enrollment = 12,768

Source: AAVMC Annual Data Report 2016–2017, https://www.aavmc.org

Any effort to model pet health care after human health care hits a roadblock with paraprofessionals within the veterinary world. This has become a confusing mishmash of job titles and job definitions, shaped by historical choices, inertia, and geographic custom that no longer makes sense, if it ever did. The growing demands of Pet Nation make change inevitable, if uncomfortable.

Walk into a veterinary clinic today and you will see people wearing three different-colored uniforms, not unlike your own medical clinic. Veterinarians wear one color and usually have a stethoscope around their neck. Veterinary assistants or customer service clerks wear a different color, and people wearing a third color (depending on the state you're in) fall somewhere in between, spread across six professional niches with a bewildering array of titles:

- Registered veterinary technician (RVT)
- Certified veterinary technician (CVT)
- Licensed veterinary technician (LVT)
- Licensed veterinary medical technician (LVMT)
- Veterinary technician
- Nurse

Unable to agree on the nomenclature of senior non-veterinarian staff members, employees use the title available locally and hope that it means something to pet owners when they bring their pets to the clinic for care.

I assure you that fewer than 10 percent of pet owners, perhaps fewer than 5 percent, know whether a college degree or accreditation is required for these titles (it is), and even fewer pet owners know if you must pass a national board examination (you do). This means that most pet owners assume that you work at the clinic because you love animals and have learned your skills on the job.

People understand that nurses in human medicine have college degrees and must pass a battery of tests, which inspires confidence that the nurse is trained to give advice and to understand complex medical problems. People spend most of their annual physical exam with a nurse, not a doctor, and rarely complain. In veterinary medicine you may like your _____ (fill in the title), but you don't know her qualifications, or if she has specific qualifications, so you don't rely on her advice or guidance to the same degree as a human nurse.

The first four of the titles noted require a degree in veterinary technology from an AVMA-accredited program, plus passage of the national board examination, known as the VTNE. But if you move from

Ohio (RVT) to Georgia (LVT), and then to Tennessee (LVMT), you have no idea what the differences between titles are, if any. And, if you move to any of the states that do not require credentials, the person handling your kitten can refer to herself as a veterinary technician or nurse, yet lack formal training.

As of 2018, it is estimated that at least 35 percent of credentialed veterinary technicians (RVT, CVT, LVT, LVMT) leave the profession after six years, due to low salaries or the failure of veterinarians to utilize their skills at the level of their training and certification. This keeps veterinary practices from delivering their desired quantity and quality of care. However, veterinarians and paraprofessionals cannot agree on a solution. My Animal Policy Group is coordinating an effort to convert the four credentialed titles to "Registered Veterinary Nurse," but it's a slow process. In 2018, Purdue University unilaterally changed its two-year and four-year degrees in veterinary technology to "veterinary nursing," which will have an impact in Indiana and nationally.

Astonishingly, the only organized opponents to the title change to "registered veterinary nurse" are human nursing organizations. They don't claim that pet owners seeking veterinary care will be confused, or short-changed, but that: (1) they, medical nurses, *own* the word "nurse," and (2) no one else (and no other profession) should be allowed to use this word, even if it's linked to the phrase "registered veterinary." In March 2018, this argument made members of the Ohio House of Representatives Agriculture Committee laugh out loud when the dean of Ohio State's College of Veterinary Medicine, Rustin Moore, DVM, PhD, explained that at least ten different health-care professions in Ohio use the title "Doctor" (he uses it twice), and no one seems to have a problem with the language. And it's not as if medical doctors don't have professional egos! People don't accidentally go to the Cleveland Clinic to neuter their dog, or to a MedVet Hospital in Columbus for a human heart transplant. Stay tuned to see how this plays out, but many pet-care providers hope that the nursing profession will come to its senses, allowing pet owners to understand and to value the expertise of RVNs when they visit a clinic.

BLUEPEARL AND BELLA

Though my brother's dog Bella, a beautiful apricot Shih Tzu, whom he and his wife adopted at the age of four, isn't as famous as Winston, she's certainly been to Fifty-Fifth Street more times than Winston. As a specialty hospital, BluePearl doesn't do vaccinations, trim nails, or express glands. However, if your beloved dog or cat (or English budgie) is desperately ill and needs any of the specialties normally found in a human hospital, they (475 doctors from around the world) will care for it at one of their eighty hospitals. While Bella hasn't sampled all the specialties, she has been treated by seven veterinarians there for different conditions, and, at fifteen years old, is cancer-free and healthy. Her veterinary journey is the story of advanced health care in Pet Nation.

As my brother tells the story, a young college student named Angelo was walking along Fordham Road in the Bronx, in the summer of 2006, when he was stopped by a fellow in his early twenties carrying a paper shopping bag. Though Angelo assumed the man was lost, he noticed that his shopping bag was shaking. To his surprise, the bag contained a small dog, a fluffy, golden-blonde Shih Tzu with big brown eyes, not more than one or two years old. The dog, the man said, was for sale. Angelo didn't know whether she'd been stolen or simply discarded. The transaction was quick and dirty, as they say: $100 cash, no questions asked, no papers exchanged. Angelo simply handed over the money and took her home.

During the next two years, that Shih Tzu, named Bella, delivered two litters (seven puppies) at home. Four of the seven pups that survived were sold for as much as $1,000, a healthy profit margin. Angelo was not the perfect owner, and Bella barely survived the second litter. When Angelo moved to California, he gave Bella to his aunt, whose toddlers treated her like a rag doll, tossing her around their house. A good friend rescued Bella, and when Thomas and Margarita adopted her, she was weak, underweight, and needed to be spayed.

Her life soon changed; it was 2009, and Pet Nation was rolling. She was spayed. Her health improved, and the next few years were medically uneventful. In 2014, when Bella suddenly lost the use of her back legs, her Gramercy Park Animal Hospital veterinarian, Dr. Dale Rubin, said, "She's got to see Dr. Levitin at BluePearl. You can see him tomorrow, and he will know how to treat her. He's the best neurologist in the city." From the moment Bella arrived at BluePearl, her care was comprehensive, considered, and seamless, no different from the care my brother and his wife receive at New York Presbyterian Hospital, one of the five top-rated human hospitals in America. Dr. Levitin spent two hours with her, indoors and out, sprawled on the floor, putting her through a series of movements and routines (with X-rays) to determine the nature of her ailment and to set a course of treatment. He concluded that it was an extruded disk problem, common to Shih Tzus, which can cause them to temporarily "go lame," to limp, to avoid climbing stairs, to resist long walks. However, with a diet and exercise regimen from Dr. Levitin and help up and down stairs and sofas from then on, she recovered.

A few years later, a routine checkup with Dr. Rubin sent Bella back to BluePearl, to Dr. Rocha, a cancer specialist. He found a mast cell tumor on her stomach, conferred with an oncology radiologist, and then handed her off to Dr. Kyle, a specialty surgeon. Dr. Kyle removed the entire tumor, and after quarterly checkups for the next twelve months with Dr. Rocha, Bella was pronounced cancer-free. Apart from a few visits to BluePearl the past two years to see an ophthalmologist, then a dermatologist (which prompted comprehensive, two-page emails from Dr. Abraham and Dr. Seltzer), and the occasional emergency room visit, she's steered clear of the hospital.

THE ANIMAL MEDICAL CENTER (AMC)

A pioneer in the field of veterinary medicine is the Animal Medical Center in Manhattan, a leader in research, treatment, and training, feeding doctors to BluePearl and other hospitals across the country. Founded in 1910 as the Women's Auxiliary, a leading proponent of the humane movement, it became the New York Women's League for Animals in 1912.

As it grew and became a permanent animal hospital, it evolved into a major teaching hospital and the largest nonprofit single animal hospital in the world, treating fifty-four thousand patients each year. The Animal Medical Center, on Manhattan's East Side, currently runs an advanced postgraduate training program in veterinary medicine, with more than one hundred doctors across seventeen specialties.

The same level of care and professionalism found at BluePearl is offered at other specialty practices around the country, such as the Compassion-First hospitals in several states, and VCA, based in Los Angeles, with specialty and general practices throughout the country. It is human-quality health care for pets, and the only restraint on growth for specialty and emergency practices is finding enough veterinarians for their hospitals.

DOGS VERSUS CATS

American pet owners spend more on dogs than cats. As reported by *Today's Veterinary Business* in August 2019, a survey of one thousand pet owners found that the average price to purchase/adopt a dog is $327 and $90 for a cat. On average, American pet owners spend $153/month on a dog, and $95/month on a cat. The *Packaged Facts* 2018 market study revealed that Americans spent $9 billion in 2018 on medications for dogs and cats, and 77 percent of this amount ($6.9 billion) was devoted to dogs.

How do we explain the imbalance? Are dogs more lovable? Are cats healthier? Are cat owners afraid of being scratched? Are dog owners hypochondriacs? Do cat owners believe that cats have nine lives? Does something bad happen inside veterinary exam rooms with cats, which doesn't happen to dogs? Do dogs like hanging out with people (including strangers) and other dogs so much that they enjoy going to the doctor's office? Are cats so dismissive of dogs and other cats (and people, for that matter) that they will not tolerate an hour at the doctor's office? Or are those Subaru and Nissan TV commercials correct that dogs love riding in the car no matter where Mom and Dad are taking them? Has anyone met a cat who likes riding in cars (there must be a reason we don't see them in those charming TV ads)? Is there something to the term "scaredy-cat" (which happens to be the name of the veterinary clinic I use for my cats, Oscar and Chloe)?

We need to understand these subtleties, unless we're convinced that cats heal themselves and don't need comprehensive medical care. Bayer funded a 2010 study that explores the differences between veterinary care for cats and dogs. Consider the following passage in a 2011 *JAVMA*** executive summary of the Bayer study, pertaining to difficulties faced by cat owners:

> *During the pet owner focus groups, it became evident that cat owners found taking their animal to the veterinarian highly stressful for the animal and themselves. They indicated that their cats hid when the cat carrier appeared; aggressively, physically resisted being put in the carrier; cried during the car or bus ride to the veterinary clinic; showed signs of stress and fear in the waiting area,*

---

* *Journal of American Veterinary Medical Association*

*particularly when unfamiliar animals, especially dogs, were pres-
ent; displayed physical signs of tension during the examination;
and acted remote and unfriendly for several days after returning
home. Many cat owners expressed a desire to avoid the difficulties
and unpleasantness associated with bringing their cat to the veterinarian.*

Knowing this, it is easier to understand what a challenge it is to get a
cat to a clinic. Consider the situation of senior citizens, often living alone
in an urban apartment and no longer driving a car. They must herd the
cat into a carrier, take an elevator, walk to the bus stop (perhaps in the
rain or snow), and change buses if necessary, all the while carrying a
howling twelve-pound cat. I'm exhausted just thinking about it.*

Veterinary medicine has a solution but hasn't invested adequately in
providing it. Mobile practices could diagnose and treat cats in their
homes and retrieve them if specialty procedures or testing are required
at the clinic. And we could deploy telemedicine to put the cat owner in
real-time video contact with the veterinarian to begin treatment. Then
combine the two. There are practices in America now delivering these
services, but good luck finding one in your town or city.

Cats are different from dogs, but they share similar internal organs
and skin conditions that require medical care. Veterinary medicine
should recognize the differences between these pets and shape general
practice models around cat behavior, rather than expecting cats to behave like dogs. Dogs like leashes and will follow their owner wherever

---

*Before acquiring Bella the Shih Tzu, my brother and his wife in Manhattan had a black-and-
white tuxedo cat named Pito. He was so averse to veterinary visits and so strong that on a taxi
ride home from the clinic, zooming past Bloomingdale's, the cat shredded the zipper of his soft
leatherette carrying case and leaped through the open "payment" window to the front seat of the
taxi. The Pakistani driver began shouting in Punjabi as he rolled up the windows and Pito ca-
reened around the front of the cab. When they reached their apartment building, their doorman
opened the building's front door just as they opened the taxi door. Pito raced into the building,
down the stairs, and flipped left into the elevator, panting and hyperventilating, home at last.

they go. Cats hate leashes (I've tried them) and are not wired to *follow* anyone anywhere. Carry a cat outdoors with a leash, place her on the ground, and it's anyone's guess what happens next, but she won't march in front of, beside, or behind you. *She* will decide where to go. For good reason, veterinary clinics, including cat clinics, usually require the cat to enter the waiting room in a crate or carrier, to prevent escapes or mayhem in the waiting room. The solution is obvious: we must *bring* health care to the cat, not the other way around.

The news on the health of Pet Nation's cats is encouraging: Swiss researchers at HypoPet AG announced on August 15, 2019, that they are developing a vaccine, HypoCat, which will neutralize cat allergies, a condition affecting approximately 10 percent of all human beings. The vaccine would be administered to the cat, not to its owner, and, if successful, should dramatically reduce cat relinquishment to shelters by owners who no longer can live with them. This also opens the door to more potential cat owners.

THE STATE OF PET HEALTH REPORT

Despite their enthusiasm for their pets, most Americans know little about how the bodies of dogs and cats function, how to care for them at different life stages, and what to do if they are howling, whimpering, or meowing in obvious physical distress (or going silent, when their cries go unanswered). Americans *instinctively* understand the Internet, politics, the movies, popular music, football, and automobiles. Their degree of participation in any of these areas is not a prerequisite to knowledge—they learn by osmosis, primarily through the media, friends, and school. Cats and dogs are different.

Raising a dog or a cat is not the same as raising a child. Most people (80 percent of Americans) have had a sibling, and may be familiar with the basics of child-rearing. However, when people acquire a cat or dog, they typically start from scratch, with little idea of what's in store for them or the animal. Their knowledge base is a patchwork of sources: veterinarian conversations, word of mouth, Internet queries rife with myths, and general-interest pet television shows. There is no cat and dog equivalent to Dr. Benjamin Spock's landmark book, *Baby and Child Care* (1946), that taught tens of millions of American mothers (and a few dads) how to care for an infant. That book's premise, "You know more than you think you do," probably does not hold true for the first-time owners of dogs and cats. There is an astonishing amount of information available on the Internet today, some of it legitimate and supported by science, the balance myth or "folk wisdom." Given these innate information gaps, and the lack of a common language between animal and pet owner, how do people today learn about general pet maintenance and those conditions specific to their pet's breed?

Until recently, Google was the easy answer. Without a national dog or cat registry, googling became the popular layman's tool. However, a question like "How do I get my dog to stop chewing on her paws?" produces more than one hundred answers, some from reputable industry sources (AVMA) and others from random blogs. The process of identifying reliable sources is guesswork.

To remedy this situation, Banfield Pet Hospital created the "State of Pet Health Report." This is a massive, ongoing program launched in 2011, in which "Banfield's research team analyzes data [every year] from more than 2.5 million dogs and half a million cats across our hospitals." Their goal is to give American pet owners and pet-health professionals the latest information to make the best decisions for their pets. The database is organized by breed and health factor, state by state, which veterinarians and pet hospitals across the country consult frequently but which few consumers (pet owners) know about, unless they are clients of a Banfield hospital in their local PetSmart store.

Here Banfield is able to draw upon the vast trove of information they've acquired through their patented pet medical records system, PetWare. This software collects data from every pet cared for in their hospitals so that their research and epidemiology team can analyze data and share their findings, to monitor trends in pet health and disease, and to publish their findings in professional journals and reports. They also release an annual "State of Pet Health" report on their website. The site contains a blend of summary data, trend analysis, "testing" protocols, and preventive and treatment recommendations, all baked into a compact, easy-to-understand format. This report has two primary benefits, one cursory and one exhaustive. Together, they add up to a quick-immersion course in pet wellness.

The first part is the annual overview of dog and cat health, on both a national and state-by-state level, measuring key health factors. This includes an analysis of the twelve most common pet conditions, ranging from arthritis to fleas and ticks to heartworm to obesity. A national map registers the degree of risk for each health factor by state, and provides a tally of the five most common diagnoses, breeds, and pet names for each state, by dog/cat, complete this part.

The in-depth annual report is a more comprehensive study of a single condition or problem. In 2019, for example, it focused on osteoarthritis, following studies on skin allergies and pet obesity in previous years. Starting in 2011, each report would spotlight a common, widespread health issue for dogs and cats, explaining what the condition is, its symptoms and causes, and what you, as a concerned pet owner, can do to treat or to alleviate it. The library of annual reports is available for download on their site.

In 2018, Banfield launched a separate three-year study of more than two hundred thousand dogs across America to identify links between pet activity, behavior, and health, called the Pet Insight Project. It allows pet owners to participate in a research process with their own dog or cat, feeding their own pet stories into a larger body of data. A smart, collar-worn device captures information about each dog's behavior around the clock, which syncs into the Banfield database. This allows their researchers to detect patterns of behavior and early indicators of change in pet health. Millions of health and behavior pairings from hundreds of thousands of dogs inform their analysis of wellness trends, issues, and prevention. The goal is clear: using machine learning, rich data software, and veterinary experience, the Pet Insight Project enables new methods of preventive care for pets.

WHY DON'T MOST AMERICAN PET OWNERS HAVE PET HEALTH INSURANCE?

Pet health insurance has existed since 1980, but, after almost four decades, only 1.2 percent of American pets have coverage. This means that only 2,160,000 out of 185,000,000 American dogs and cats are insured. At least thirteen companies offer pet health insurance, and there is an industry organization for the United States and Canada called North American Pet Health Insurance Association (NAPHIA).

Despite this low number, the number of pets covered by insurance grows each year. There were 18 percent more pets covered in 2018 than 2017, according to NAPHIA. Still, the overall impact on pet health care is limited. These companies provide consumers with analysis of the different types of policies and coverage, analyzing common insurance issues, such as preexisting conditions, deductibles, annual limits, co-pays, and the like. Initially, pet insurance companies only reimbursed owners after payment to the veterinarian, but most now emulate the human health insurance practice of paying directly to the provider.

Given that 98.8 percent of pets aren't covered, why doesn't Pet Nation value pet health insurance? The status quo may change, as the

AVMA instructed its members in 2019 to explain to pet owners how pet health insurance works. Let's consider where we are.

According to a 2019 survey of one thousand pet owners, reported in *Today's Veterinary Business*, roughly 44 percent of pet owners do not even know that pet health insurance exists. For forty years, pet insurers have relied upon veterinarians to help educate pet owners about the value of insurance. This is a common marketing practice, but it has failed, since most veterinarians are scientists who did not attend veterinary school to sell insurance. Even the educational part of this mission feels like "selling," which is not something most veterinarians want to do. The two most effective techniques to date are direct marketing to consumers and the inclusion of pet insurance in employee benefit plans, which is an increasingly popular perk at certain companies (see chapter three).

A bigger problem is the insurance industry clinging to two features of traditional pet health insurance policies: (1) exclusion of coverage for preexisting conditions; and (2) the requirement that pet owners pay the full veterinary bill out of pocket before submitting claims for reimbursement. Companies that address one or both of these limitations are growing.

Historically, pet health insurance was a system (at least in the public's mind) wherein consumers paid premiums to cover two potential events: an accident or end-of-life disease/treatment. Since these are both expensive scenarios, with one inevitable (end-of-life), this aspect of pet health insurance makes sense. However, young families adopting or purchasing their first puppy are often more concerned with the cost of regular, preventive veterinary care rather than potential, future costs. This has motivated pet insurance companies to add wellness coverage for additional premiums, placing them in competition with Banfield Pet Hospitals. More pets enjoy Banfield wellness plans than the combined number of American pets insured by carriers, but the marketplace battle is engaged.

GOLDEN RETRIEVER LIFETIME STUDY

In the 1930s, a highly respected New Jersey veterinarian, Dr. Mark L. Morris Sr., developed his own dog food mix to help patients suffering from kidney disease. This formula was so effective that Burton Hill of the Hill Packing Corporation of Topeka, Kansas, marketed it nationally. The considerable royalties from this product helped fund the Morris Animal Foundation in 1948. Since then, the foundation has invested more than $103 million in more than twenty-five hundred studies in diagnostics, treatments, preventions, and cures that benefit companion animals, horses, and wildlife. One such program is the Golden Retriever Lifetime Study, which started in 2012.

Approximately 60 percent of all Golden Retrievers develop cancer during their lifetime. This dilemma inspired the Morris Animal Foundation to undertake an extensive study, gathering information on more than three thousand Golden Retrievers throughout their lives, to identify the nutritional, environmental, lifestyle, and genetic risk factors for cancer and other major diseases in dogs.

David Haworth, DVM, PhD, president and CEO of the Morris Animal Foundation from 2011 until late 2015, explained to me the genesis of the program and its unique features. The study was originally conceived by Dr. Rodney Page, an authority in canine cancer, who remains the principal investigator, as well as a professor and director of Colorado State University's Flint Animal Cancer Center. During Dr. Haworth's tenure at Morris, they finalized study design and enrolled 3,044 dogs. There's never been a longitudinal study conducted in dogs before, so the correlative findings that *they are not even looking for* will keep scientists busy for decades. "Because cancer (and other diseases) occurs spontaneously in pet dogs (i.e., we don't implant tumors like we do in lab mice), and because dogs share our environment, *and* because their life span is 18 percent of ours, we will harvest incredible insights into the causes and progression of canine and human diseases."

Since all Goldens are so genetically similar, it is much easier to determine which mutations drive disease. The scale of the program proves that this kind of study is both possible and practical in veterinary medicine, which the human health community had previously doubted. As a lifetime study, it takes considerable discipline on the part of the owners to stay with it. Dr. Haworth knows from experience: his Golden Retriever, Bridger, is also a part of the study. As he points out, "The owners who enrolled their dogs in this study, myself included, are extraordinarily motivated, many having lost at least one dog to cancer before. Seven years in, we are still getting data from ninety-eight percent of the dogs originally enrolled."

TECHNOLOGY AND GADGETS

It shouldn't surprise anyone that human health-care technologies are being adapted to pet care. One kind of wearable technology that is increasingly popular is pet trackers. Everyone worries about losing their pets, and trackers help track your pet's movements in real time. Most trackers allow you to set a designated territory for your pets and notify you the moment your pet leaves the area. But other technologies can monitor pet behavior, similar to functions performed by the various human fitness trackers. Some pet trackers will detect licking and scratching, and create health alerts if variations register. Popular affordable models include Whistle GO Explore, Tractive GPS 3G, Findster Duo, and Tabcat cat tracker. Smart collars can collect pet vital signs and behavior data, including temperature, activity, pulse, respiration, positions, calories consumed and burned, and heart-rate variations.

This data syncs into a monitoring service, which can alert owners if an illness or conditions warrant.

Smart litter boxes not only eliminate some of the torture of cleaning litter boxes, but also provide information about household cats. The Litter-Robot brand of litter boxes are self-cleaning, while the LavvieBot is self-cleaning and tracks your pet's usage of the box and changes in weight. Pet Care Monitor from the Sharp Corporation measures your cat's weight and tracks urine volume, frequency, and duration of use. The data is analyzed by an AI program and compared to internal research data that the company sponsored. The Tailio device is placed under the litter box and collects data on your cat's weight, amount of waste, frequency of visits, and behavior in the litter box.

Another common tracker is the Heyrex wearable monitor, which veterinarians use to track a patient's recovery from surgery and response to medication, and to detect changes associated with the early signs of illness and disease. The data collected is then analyzed and delivered to the veterinarian through a device portal. The pet owner can access the data and create journal entries to assist in the diagnosis process. It can be used in short-term therapeutic, long-term monitoring, and postoperative and preventive pet-health management.

THE LAST BREATH

Dani McVety, DVM, is a dynamic veterinarian who graduated from the University of Florida and cofounded Lap of Love Veterinary Hospice, based in Tampa, Florida, three months later. She has built a practice providing compassionate, medically anchored hospice care to pet owners throughout the United States. Lap of Love is a veterinary hospice and mobile euthanasia service network, working with more than seventy veterinarians throughout the country.

This is a demanding practice, laced with emotional and ethical dilemmas. Dr. McVety shared one with her followers and me:

I learned one of the biggest lessons of my professional career a few months after I finished veterinary school from a case I never saw myself. A client requested euthanasia for a twelve-year-old BAR (bright, alert, and responsive) cat from another veterinarian during my evening emergency shift. My colleague attended to the case, which our team was upset about before the history had been taken. The woman said she loved her diabetic cat but could not give him his injections anymore.

My colleague did what most of us would do. She talked to the client at length about the importance of the injections and about rewarding the cat. The client left the practice with her cat in the carrier but returned five minutes later, saying he had escaped somehow and she could not find him. However, the parking lot security camera showed that she had let her cat out and driven away.

I realized how badly we had let the woman and her cat down.

Here's how it began for Dani, fresh out of veterinary school:

While preparing a family for a euthanasia late one night at the emergency clinic, a client looked up at me and said, "Please, can you leave her on my lap? I don't want her on that cold sterile table, I want her right here with me." That wasn't what I was supposed to do, though. Only a few months out of veterinary school at this point, I had been taught that it was best to take her little Chihuahua to the back to begin the process. But her request was too powerful, too meaningful. And it's exactly what I would have asked if I was her.

So I said yes, and delicately ensured the experience was as perfect as it could be. Her little one never left her mom's lap. As they left our clinic, her body was wrapped in the same blanket she was brought to me in. At that moment I knew that's what every pet deserved, to be in the one place they are most comfortable in; their parent's lap. Shortly after, Lap of Love Veterinary Hospice was born in Tampa, Florida. What started as a fulfilling part-time project to help pay back my student loans has grown into a passion for pets, their people, and the doctors that care for them both. To put it simply, I cannot imagine doing anything else.

One of Dr. McVety's favorite sayings is "Death is not the opposite of life, it's the opposite of birth." Unlike human doctors, veterinarians are licensed to perform euthanasia on a patient (see chapter two). This is a weighty emotional burden, and not always performed well or compassionately. Any pet owner, including your author, who has sat with a cat or dog when it is being "put down" knows what I mean. It isn't any easier for the veterinarian or veterinary technician guiding the process.* For many pet owners, the only way they can handle this situation is to say a tearful goodbye at the front desk of the clinic, and then leave while the staff takes your cat or dog to the back of the clinic and performs the procedure. Some owners return to the clinic weeks later to gather the urn holding their pet's ashes.

A difficult challenge for hospice veterinarians is deciding whether to honor a client's wishes to end a pet's life when the veterinarian knows there are alternatives, including adopting out the cat or dog to someone prepared to manage the pet's situation. Do you argue with the pet owner? Shame the pet owner into keeping the pet? Though you know you could find a home for the pet and disagree with the decision, do you

---

* When Pito, the taxi cat described earlier in this chapter, reached the end of his life at seventeen, his excellent veterinarian, Dr. Johnson, at Mercy Animal Hospital, who'd cared for him for many years, said, in tears, "I just can't do it," and handed off the task to a new veterinarian in his practice, who'd never met Pito. The next day, he was cremated at Hartsdale Pet Cemetery in Hartsdale, New York.

simply accommodate the request? These aren't decisions American human doctors have to make, but they are daily grist for Lap of Love's seventy doctors.

HARTSDALE PET CEMETERY, HARTSDALE, NEW YORK

Known as "the Peaceable Kingdom," this is the oldest operating pet cemetery in the world, created in 1896. It is the final resting place for over eighty thousand animals, including dogs and cats, horses, birds, primates, myriad smaller pets, and even a lion cub who lived at the Plaza Hotel. The cemetery creation was a collaboration between Emily Berthet, an accomplished equestrienne, and Dr. Samuel Johnson, a prominent New York veterinary surgeon and proprietor of the first state-of-the-art animal hospital in Manhattan.

Hartsdale is the only pet cemetery listed on the National Register of Historic Places. Its many monuments include the largest aboveground mausoleum ever commissioned for pets, and America's first publicly funded memorial for the dogs of war, designed by the architect Robert Caterson and the sculptor Malvina Hoffman.

In 2013, it was the catalyst for the first state law allowing the interment of human cremated remains in a pet cemetery.

Dani McVety created a national practice in a specialty field that didn't exist in most cities. In 2016, Lap of Love veterinarians guided more than twenty thousand pets at the end of their lives. The vast majority of veterinarians aren't interested in a practice focused on life's end, rather than everything along the way. But as Pet Nation took hold, and pets became the center of life for so many people and families, the old-fashioned method of terminating a pet's life was no longer acceptable. Lap of Love created a new, fresh, sympathetic, and respectful process to take a family and their pet down the last stretch of the road.

There is a science to this process, as Dr. McVety explains, not just counseling a pet owner. "We know the medications to use," she explained to me, "how to use them, and how to adjust dosing and administration based on the disease at hand, the experience the family is expecting, and the personality of the pet. Dogs are not small humans, but cats are not small dogs, either. Our knowledge and appreciation for species differences, especially as they relate to drug usage and interactions, makes us uniquely qualified to contribute to this important conversation in order to achieve the best possible outcome; a peaceful passing."

It's not difficult to imagine Lap of Love soon with hundreds of veterinary partners across America, and competitors popping up. The interesting question, which Dr. McVety has pondered many times, is whether human medicine will ever learn from veterinary medicine and Pet Nation about how we handle our own end of life. Could we take this rough, litigated process and provide our own families with the care and support that Lap of Love gives to its pets and families?

· 8 ·

"IT ISN'T ONLY DOGS AND CATS"

On Christmas Day 1991, a young veterinarian, Dr. Doug Mader, received a call at home from a nurse at his clinic in Los Angeles, informing him that a woman and her seven-year-old daughter had arrived at the clinic after driving from Texas with a nineteen-foot-long reticulated python. For many years, the snake had traveled back and forth across America with the woman's late husband, a cross-country trucker, in the cab of his eighteen-wheeler. The man had been killed in a serious traffic accident, but the python was rescued. The animal had been suffering from encephalitis, a viral brain disease, for several weeks, before mother and daughter traveled to California. The woman begged Dr. Mader to help, "You have to do something, Doctor. I drove all the way from Texas. It was my Christmas present to my daughter. The snake is her only memory of her father." Sixty-three days later, after a complex treatment involving antibiotics, warm fluids, intravenous food and vitamins, and confinement to an incubator to raise its body temperature, the snake recovered and returned to its loving family in Texas. This experience with a python—an animal that terrifies most people—confirmed for Dr. Mader the logic and power of the human-animal bond across all species. For many years thereafter, like clockwork, Monty the Python (yes, that was his real name) sent Dr. Mader a Christmas card.

Now an expert in the field of exotic animals, a veterinarian, author, and educator in Marathon, Florida, he has a unique practice: (a) located in the Florida Keys, his patients, animals of every type imaginable,* come from the sea, the land, and the air; (b) his practice treats both pets (domestic and exotic) and wild animals**(when a dolphin washes up on the beach in Florida in need of medical care, he is the veterinarian local authorities or animal welfare group calls for help); and (c) he has published several medical textbooks on this subject. When Hurricane Irma laid waste to the Florida Keys in 2017, Dr. Mader and his wife, Dr. Gerry Diethelm, his partner in the veterinary practice, lost their home and its contents. As they raced to evacuate the home they knew would be destroyed, they grabbed their dogs, their birds, their snakes, but didn't have time or a way to take their aquarium. "Fish I'd had for ten years, that knew me, that recognized me, that depended on me. Fish that came out of hiding to greet me when I came home from work, I had to leave behind. There was nothing I could do. And when I returned to the ruins of our house, the sight of those fish lying dead in the aquarium was one of the saddest moments in my life, something I will never forget." In Dr. Mader's view, it doesn't matter if your pet is a Cocker Spaniel or a hermit crab. if you take care of them day in, day out, feeding them, protecting them, caring for them year-round, paying attention to

---

* I asked Dr. Mader if there is any animal on earth that he would be afraid to treat and he answered, "No. If you respect the animal, understand them, and show no fear, you can treat them, provided you use the proper professional and safety protocols."

** The week that we spoke, his patients included a mix of domestic and wild animals, including: a three-foot-tall Great American Egret with a broken wing; a fifty-year-old Galapagos turtle (owned by the same family since the 1970s), who went in for a check-up after an injury; and a Florida Keys deer, an endangered species, who'd caught and broken a leg in a fence and needed surgery.

them, responding to their communication signals, they become an integral part of your life.

🐾

IT TAKES ALL KINDS

Have you ever seen: a four-eyed opossum (which, strangely, has only two real eyes); or a crab-eating raccoon, a tropical gourmand that loves crustaceans (oysters, crab, lobster, clams) and the occasional papaya; a binturong, the South American bearcat that smells like popcorn and has little in common with either bears or cats; a furry hyrax, two feet long and ten pounds in weight, genetically related to the elephant and the manatee; or the extraordinary sea apple, a sea cucumber that lives alone in a single-species tank, since the toxins they release at death or when threatened will kill any fish in the aquarium? Unless you are a zookeeper or zoology student, you likely wouldn't identify these rare animals. Yet, for all you know, your next-door neighbor with the heavily landscaped property has a pet tamandua, an arboreal and nocturnal anteater from Ecuador that feeds on ants, bees, and insect larvae, but only at night, which is why you don't know she's there, over the fence, hanging upside down from a eucalyptus tree.

These are a few of the more "exotic" animals that Americans keep as pets—clandestinely and often illegally—for many wild animals found in South and Central American habitats are outlawed, federally or in certain states. There are dozens of species living "beneath the radar" in private homes across America, often without traditional veterinary care, tended by people who are passionate about them and love them as fervently as their neighbors love their chocolate Lab or orange tabby. The nomenclature can be confusing. Effectively, everything but dogs and cats fits under this umbrella, including any rare or unusual pet—an animal that is generally considered a wild species rather than a pet (e.g., a ferret) or an animal that is normally *not kept* within human households (e.g., a goose). The category is elastic, though, since many of the smaller "pocket pets," which, theoretically, fit into a pocket, are much less "exotic" than snakes and spiders. To separate them from cats and dogs, we'll use the term "nontraditional pets," dividing the category loosely into: (a) true "exotic pets" (snakes, large lizards, spiders, monkeys, parrots, turtles, tropical fish); (b) "pocket pets" (hamsters, gerbils, guinea pigs, hedgehogs); and (c) "barnyard pets," comprised of rabbits, chickens, ducks, turkeys, geese, and pigs.

Nontraditional pets—legal and illegal—run the alphabet today, from A for anaconda to Z for zorrilla, sometimes called the striped polecat, a member of the weasel family that emits a foul smell like the look-alike skunk, which discourages adoption. The nontraditional animal category is diverse in size, shape, affect, color, character, origin, and behavior, ranging from animals that most people recognize (parakeets, parrots, tropical fish, hamsters, turtles, and snakes) to the more theatrical species that often appear in media coverage of service animals and airplanes (miniature horses, peacocks, wallabies, wolves, ferenc foxes). Technically, the American Veterinary Medical Association does not endorse the keeping of any exotic pet. Though the AVMA doesn't list the animals by species, they consider primates, venomous snakes, big cats, bats, dangerous large lizards (such as the monitor lizard* or the three-foot-long tegu lizard from Argentina), crocodilians, anteaters, sloths, skunks, raccoons, possums, kangaroos, and others to be off limits: appropriate in their natural habitat or perhaps the local zoo, but not for a private citizen. Still, the pet-crazy American public pays little attention to these guidelines, as we will see in this chapter.

Some familiar animals in this category, such as rabbits, are safe and

---

* There are now three breeding populations of the monitor lizard in the Everglades, one with more than one thousand of these carnivorous, predatory lizards, "first cousins" of the ten-foot-long Komodo dragon found in Indonesia.

cuddly, like characters from children's storybooks, while others are dangerous and invasive, like the Burmese python, which can grow to eighteen feet in length and two hundred pounds, with an estimated population of fifty thousand now living and breeding in the Florida Everglades. Imported from Southeast Asia, with some specimens "liberated" from zoo enclosures by Hurricane Andrew in 1992, the Burmese python has had a devastating effect on the wildlife of South Florida. Rabbits and foxes have gone missing from much of the Everglades. The endangered Florida panther is under attack. Sightings of smaller mammals, like raccoons and white-tailed deer, have decreased by 90 percent in this decade.

Just as the world of cats and dogs changed dramatically during Pet Nation, so, too, has the parallel universe of exotic animals. "Parallel," because nontraditional and domestic animals (dogs and cats) rarely mix in the home. A virtual Noah's Ark now exists in American homes, in city apartments and suburban backyards, and on farms. Many of these species should never have been brought to America in the first place (though they're not about to leave), not necessarily because they pose a physical threat to people or other animals, but because they were not put on this earth to be domesticated or to live in cages.

Owning It

The ownership of nontraditional animals is more complex than the ownership of dogs and cats, and varies from state to state. There are four levels of legal control over true exotic pets: (1) a comprehensive ban on the ownership of all wild and "dangerous" animals (wild cats, large undomesticated carnivores, reptiles, and nonhuman primates) except to select educational and scientific institutions; (2) a partial ban by species; (3) private ownership under a formal licensure or permit scheme; or (4) no regulation whatsoever, except for random permits or licenses, sometimes for as little as $10. The reasons are obvious and well documented: wild animals can be predatory and dangerous, harmful to humans or other animals, invasive (destructive of natural habitats, witness the Burmese python in South Florida), or a health hazard (approximately seventy-four thousand Americans contract salmonella from reptiles each year). Despite these laws, the trade in wild animals and animal parts worldwide is substantial, estimated at $10 billion annually by the US State Department.

The Michigan State University Animal Legal & Historical Center, affiliated with its College of Law, has published this map, which summarizes the private ownership laws for exotic animals by state.

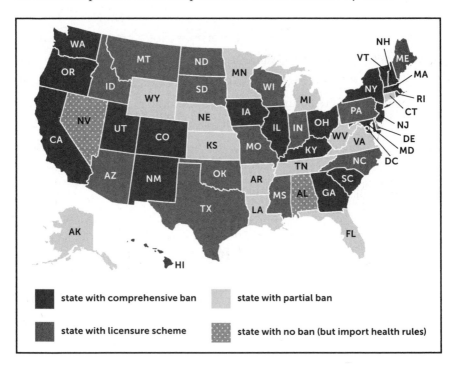

Nontraditional pets live private lives, sharing an enclosure or home with their own species and their owner(s), depending on the species. Both the common exotics (parakeets, parrots, tropical fish, hamsters, turtles, and snakes) and the more rarefied species (e.g., tarantulas) live at home, indoors, out of sight, rarely if ever seen on the street (unless they escape)

or at your local veterinary clinic. Though one occasionally sees large pythons curled around the neck of street vendors or performance artists in some cities, or parrots perched on the shoulder of cyclists, the appearance of a ten-foot python in a public space is cause for alarm for most people.

The ownership of several nontraditional pet categories has accelerated in the past ten years, with some outpacing the growth rate of dogs and cats. This growth has been driven by millennials, who have taken to nearly all classes of pets, but especially fish, birds, and reptiles. This table shows the growth, in the number of households and pets, in the respective categories, since 2012:

	Households %	Pets %
Birds	38%	16%
Fish	35%	32%
Reptiles	23%	13%
Poultry	37%	22%

Meanwhile, these categories have been stable or shrunk in size:

	Households %	Pets %
Ferrets	0%	-33%
Rabbits	1%	-22%
Livestock	-25%	-64%

Care and Feeding

The percentage of American households with nontraditional pets is lower than those with dogs and cats: 63.4 percent of households own dogs, 47.1 percent cats, and 36.9 percent nontraditional pets (in total, including all categories), but the number of nontraditional pet households is growing; 23 percent of all pet owners now have a non-feline or non-canine pet. Numerically, there are more nontraditional pets than dogs and cats, boosted by the high number of freshwater fish. After dogs and cats, the most popular pets are, in descending order: fish (15 percent of households), birds (7.9 percent), rabbits, poultry (chickens, turkeys, ducks, geese), hamsters, guinea pigs, ferrets, turtles, reptiles (4.7 percent), with horses at the bottom of the list, primarily because of the cost and logistics of purchasing and owning a horse.

Number of Pets Owned in the United States by Type of Animal (millions)

Pet	Number
Freshwater fish	139.3
Cat	94.2
Dog	89.7
Bird	20.3
Saltwater fish	18.8
Small animal	14.0
Reptile	9.4
Horse	7.6

Number of US Households that Own a Pet by Type of Animal (millions)

Pet	Number
Dog	63.4
Cat	47.1
Freshwater fish	12.5
Bird	7.9
Small animal	6.7
Reptile	4.7
Horse	2.6
Saltwater fish	2.5

Source: American Pet Products Association's 2017–2018 National Pet Owners Survey

If people study nontraditional animals carefully and provide them with appropriate care, feeding, and living environments—with well-managed expectations, pairing them with the right member of the household—most are harmless and make good pets. The adoption of a nontraditional pet should be a considered process, less automatic or reflexive than the adoption of a dog or cat. Most Americans grow up with dogs and/or cats and have some sense of how to raise and care for them. That is not the case with most nontraditional animals, such as the colorful angelfish, or the beautiful African gray parrot, native to the Ivory Coast and Kenya, which can talk a blue streak and live to one hundred years of age. The myriad questions one should ask about their care and environment are foreign to most Americans and usually answered in practice. How do you create and manage an aquarium for the angelfish; does it need veterinary care and, if so, when? What does the African gray

Most Popular Nontraditional Pets, by State

Alabama: hedgehogs

Alaska: ferrets

Arkansas: ferrets

Arizona: rabbits

Arkansas: hamsters

California: rabbits

Colorado: ferrets

Connecticut: hedgehogs

Delaware: ferrets

Florida: birds

Georgia: hamsters

Hawaii: lizards

Idaho: ferrets

Illinois: snakes

Indiana: ferrets

Iowa: birds

Kansas: ferrets

Kentucky: ferrets

Louisiana: birds

Maine: hamsters

Maryland: hamsters

Massachusetts: birds

Michigan: ferrets

Missouri: hedgehogs

Mississippi: hamsters

Montana: ferrets

Nebraska: spiders

Nevada: lizards

New Hampshire: hamsters

New Jersey: mice

New Mexico: rabbits

New York: hamsters

North Carolina: hamsters

North Dakota: birds

Ohio: birds

Oklahoma: parrots

Oregon: hedgehogs

Pennsylvania: ferrets

Rhode Island: hamsters

South Carolina: rabbits

South Dakota: rabbits

Tennessee: ferrets

Texas: lizards

Utah: hamsters

Vermont: ferrets

Virginia: ferrets

Washington: ferrets

West Virginia: lizards

Wisconsin: ferrets

Wyoming: hedgehogs

eat, where does it sleep, when does it sleep, how do I know when it is sick, does it need an avian veterinarian, what kind of cage does it need, should it be in a cage at all, will it need specialized care when it gets older?

Like all animals, nontraditional pets have needs and behavior patterns specific to their species, whether temperature and humidity control, diet, nesting environment, medical care, sleep habits (diurnal, crepuscular, or nocturnal), compatibility with children, life expectancy (from three years for a hamster to even two hundred for a Galapagos tortoise), and escape habits (the prime offenders being snakes, ferrets, and gerbils). At a minimum, before adopting any nontraditional pet, you should know if it is legal in your state of residence, what activity level it needs, and how long it will live. The African gray parrot can live to one hundred years and needs companionship every day.

The Human-Animal Bond

People who don't own nontraditional pets might wonder if it is possible to form a bond with animals that are far removed from our day-to-day existence. Do people receive the same emotional support and unconditional love from hamsters, turtles, birds, fish, and other animals that others receive from cats and dogs? While the reasons people buy pets vary from species to species, they do overlap. Despite skepticism from critics, the underlying bond between people and nontraditional pets resembles the bond between people and dogs and cats. Likewise, the good and bad reasons for adoption are similar in the two worlds.

But in broad strokes, people adopt animals—domestic or nontraditional—for most of the same reasons. Many people adopt kittens, puppies, hamsters, and bunny rabbits because they are "cute." Some people adopt Labradoodles and neon tetra fish because they are "cool," of the moment, in the media, popular on Instagram and other social media. Others adopt Pit Bulls and pythons because they are potentially dangerous animals and suit an "edgy" lifestyle. Some people adopt domestic or nontraditional pets on a whim, because they are "trending" animals, and then abandon them when their novelty evaporates, and the rigors of responsible stewardship set in. Ultimately, the primary reason that most people adopt and keep nontraditional pets—sometimes for decades—is the human-animal bond.

CATCH ME IF YOU CAN

There are many ways to classify animals—species, size, diet, origin, history, folklore, behavior, geography, intelligence—but we will use a different factor to organize nontraditional pets, considering them from the vantage point of locomotion. That is, do they run, walk, crawl, swim, fly, hop, or some combination thereof? By definition, wild animals are elusive—necessary to evade capture and to sneak up on their prey. Animals do *physical* things that people cannot do, and they do them faster, higher, and more powerfully. Birds fly, people don't. A cheetah's top speed is seventy-five miles per hour. A chameleon skitters away or changes color by adjusting a layer of cells nestled within their skin to affect how light reflects off its skin. Part of the challenge of caring for many nontraditional pets, then, becomes wrangling or corralling them, keeping up with them, preventing them from escaping their pen or cage, sorting out where they're going next.

Crawl (Slither)

Snakes

When we think about snakes, we picture them in motion. They crawl, they slither, they undulate—these verbs embody movement. They don't have legs, so they use their muscles and scales to move in various "wavy" patterns: serpentine, concertina, sidewinding, and rectilinear, each a movement specific to a different species of snake. Their persona is inseparable from this unique, continuous form of locomotion, out of sync with the way people move, first one foot then the next. This helps explain why they are challenging pets to own: some are both dangerous and hard to keep track of, so, to control them, we restrict their movement, containing them in cages, preventing them from doing what snakes do best: crawling. Snakes are a double threat, though, since they also swim. The dangerous green anaconda, which grows to fifteen feet or more in length, can hold its breath under water for ten minutes and swim at ten miles per hour, sustaining a speed of eight miles per hour when pursuing prey, twice as fast as most people walk.

Snakes are "reptiles," a vertebrate class that includes snakes, lizards, crocodiles, turtles, and tortoises. Nearly 4 percent of American households own reptiles, and approximately two million of them keep snakes. Snake owners are focused. Unsurprisingly, they rarely keep other pets, since snakes eat other animals to survive (live or frozen rats, mice, and rabbits). They need special light and heat conditions. Some live for decades. They are escape artists, sliding through tiny spaces. They recognize people and respond to their names. Many people are afraid of snakes but love to wear snakeskin boots, belts, and jackets.* Hollywood movies and the media are partly to blame for America's collective snake "paranoia." Annually, only five to seven people die from snakebites in the United States, roughly one out of fifty million people; you are ten times more likely to die from a bee sting or a lightning strike than a snakebite. Roughly thirty-five thousand people are bitten by venomous snakes each year in America, but almost all recover quickly with medical treatment.

There are nearly three thousand species of snakes, but a handful account for 75 percent of the snakes people keep. They fall into two categories: "starter snakes," which young people can handle safely, and smaller species, like corn snakes, which don't need a large enclosure or special lighting; and "adult snakes," which can be dangerous, requiring

---

*I saw a woman on the New York subway recently who was in all snakeskin, wearing a full-length snakeskin coat, snakeskin boots, and a snakeskin-print dress, and who appeared to be on her way to a job interview in Brooklyn.

Antivenom serum is a medication used to treat venomous snake and spider bites, as well as scorpion and jellyfish stings. It is made by collecting venom from the relevant animals and injecting small amounts of it into a domestic animal. Antibodies then form in the animal's blood and are collected, for injection. Invented in the 1800s, antivenoms have been widely used since the 1950s. They are listed on the World Health Organization's *Model List of Essential Medicines*. Depending on the type of antivenom, they cost $9 to $118 per vial in the developing world versus $2,300 per dose in the United States.

specialized study and commitment, such as the green tree python, king snakes (which eat other snakes and must live alone), milk snakes (often confused with the venomous coral snake), the ball python, the dreaded Burmese python discussed earlier, and others.

A 2015 survey of two thousand pet owners by *Scientific American Mind* concluded that the "central casting" view of snake owners doesn't match their own self-image. Often portrayed as "tough, tattooed, buccaneering, bikers, outsiders," male snake owners who responded consider themselves "neat and tidy" and maintain that they are more likely to regard their snake as "part of my family" than any other class of pet owner. Female snake owners see themselves as "unconventional, novelty-seeking, more open to new experiences than male snake owners or other pet owners, generally." It's all in the way they move and how people choose to bond with them and to care for them.

Spiders

"The itsy-bitsy spider climbed up the waterspout . . ." or so the nursery rhyme goes. Well, not all spiders are "itsy-bitsy." The Goliath bird-eating tarantula, which can be bought online for $60 with next-day delivery, has a twelve-inch leg span, a body that is five inches long, and weighs 6.7 ounces, the size of a grapefruit. Their name comes from an eighteenth-century engraving by the German artist Maria Sibylla Merian that shows this tarantula devouring a hummingbird. In the jungles of Suriname or Venezuela (where people sometimes eat them, roasting them in banana leaves), these spiders rarely eat birds, surviving instead on worms, insects, and amphibians. Like most spiders, the female Goliath outlives the male; she can live to twenty-five, while the male rarely reaches the age of ten.

Highly complex animals, spiders have special talents. They can produce silk, which comes from their abdomens. All spiders make silk, but not all spiders spin webs. They use the silk to climb, to make webs (wherein they trap insects), to build walls in their burrows, to create egg sacs, and to wrap prey.

Almost everything that most people "know" about spiders is wrong, the product of popular wisdom and urban folklore that isn't supported by science. There are more myths about spiders than perhaps any other animal on earth. The Burke Museum at the University of Washington in Seattle, a leading natural history museum and study center, debunks dozens of these myths on their website. Its arachnology department has 170,000 spiders in its collection, as well as 14,000 harvestmen (daddy longlegs), scorpions, and other arachnids; in short, an authoritative resource. There are three kinds of spider myths: general, species-specific, and what they term "just plain weird myths." Here is a sampling:

- **General: False:** Spiders are insects. **True:** Spiders are arachnids. Arachnids have two body parts, eight simple eyes, no antennae, no wings, and four pairs of legs, while insects have three body parts, two compound eyes, two antennae, four wings (or two or none) and three pairs of legs.

- **Species-specific: False:** House spiders belong outdoors, and people who take them from inside the house to the backyard are rescuing them. **True:** House spiders belong indoors. Without their protective indoor habitat, most won't survive outdoors for long.

- **"Just plain weird":** False: Spiders can live in bushy hairdos. This is an urban legend dating to the days of beehive hairdos. **True:** The human body and human hair are not favorable to spider-egg-laying.

Spider collectors include: (a) the hobby collector, often a youth, who catches spiders around the house and then builds a simple, handmade, environment for them; (b) the serious spider aficionado, who keeps non-traditional breeds as pets for many years, such as the Gigantic bird-eating tarantula or the sapphire-blue peacock parachute spider from India that catches insects in midair without a web; and (c) the scientists like the myth busters at the Burke Museum, who know the true story.

The lullaby concludes, "The itsy-bitsy spider climbed up the spout again." This is how most people think about spiders—they will "come again" and they will never go away. They've been on earth for 380 million years, since the first spider, the thin-waisted arachnid, evolved from crablike ancestors. With nearly 50,000 species spread across 3,958 genera and 114 families, there is still much to learn and many more spiders to collect, to keep, and to watch for hours on end.

Fly

Birds

Wild birds travel thousands of miles each year, some flying as high as three thousand to four thousand feet, migrating from South American breeding grounds to summer meadows in North America, "free as a bird," as they say, a symbol of freedom. However, not all birds enjoy this same freedom. Today, there are twenty million birds in America living as house pets in 5.7 million households. They are mostly parakeets, parrots, canaries, African grays, lovebirds, cockatoos, cockatiels, some exotic, some less so ("cousins" of the migratory birds). These feathered pets spend their life indoors, in cages that are only occasionally gilded, singing like canaries, imitating your uncle Morty's New Jersey accent, or just looking beautiful.

Wild or caged, birds are intelligent, beautiful, clever, comical, miraculous creatures. It is no wonder that people keep them as pets, or that they inspired Emily Dickinson to write, " 'Hope' is the Thing with Feathers."

In Bernd Brunner's excellent book *Birdmania*, he explains that people have kept birds in captivity for much of recorded history, from the early days of the Roman empire to Renaissance Italy. In eighteenth-century Germany, caged birds became a cultural obsession, including many of the usual species that people keep today: nightingales, parrots, owls, parakeets, canaries, zebra finches (owls excepted). Brunner profiles the German author and ornithologist, Karl Russ (1833–1899), who wrote several books about birds, including *Foreign Aviary Birds* and *The Speaking Parrots*, and changed the world of interior design forever with the creation of his "bird room." This was a walk-in aviary in his Berlin home in which he studied the more than two hundred species he bred and collected from around the world. There, Russ wrote books and articles about birds and listened to endless birdsong. Bird lovers and their decorators in many countries followed suit, from Northern Europe to Russia to America. Though few people in America keep two hundred species in their home today, there are millions of bird fanciers all over the country.

Though fewer Americans keep birds than dogs and cats (5.7 million households versus 85 million dog and cat households), bird ownership is distributed across all demographic groups. A slightly higher percentage of Hispanics, seniors, and millennials (who seem to like all pets) own birds.

Bird Ownership in America

- 5% of US households own a bird
- 5.7 million households own a bird
- Millennials are the largest segment
- 50% of owners have one bird
- 23% have two birds
- 24% have three or more birds
- 55% of owners would adopt another

Pet Birds in America

- Parakeet: 25%
- Cockatiel: 22%
- Canary: 11%
- Conure: 8%
- African Gray: 7%
- Amazon Parrot: 7%
- Small Parrot: 7%
- Cockatoo: 6%
- Finch: 6%
- Lovebird: 6%
- Macaw: 4%

American Pet Products Association 2018

There are obvious avian advantages for seniors. Birds are easier pets for people with reduced mobility; it isn't easy to walk a Poodle in the rain or snow, but parakeets flit about a cage on their own. They require little space and care; a cage with a half-dozen canaries can tuck into a small apartment. Many small birds, such as canaries and parakeets (which represent one-third of the pet birds in America), require little babysitting and maintenance apart from food, water, and housecleaning. And birds are great company; most birds sing and many talk, excellent companions for people who live alone.

Birds are plentiful in Latin America, where they are more integrated into daily home and commercial life than in America, moving back and forth from outdoor patios to the indoors. Accustomed to an avian-accented lifestyle, a significant percentage of Hispanic households in America keep pet birds.

The millennials' dual love of pets and idiosyncratic lifestyle choices has had far-reaching consequences for society: witness the arrival of millennial-owned dogs in the American workplace. They tend to do things their own iconoclastic way, reasoning, "My parents could never contemplate sharing our house with a squawking Amazon parrot, so, okay, that's fine, I'll rescue that beautiful cockatiel I saw online." They are responsible for much of the growth in the nontraditional pet category since 2012 (birds 16 percent, fish 32 percent, and reptiles 13 percent).

Most small birds are inexpensive to keep and rarely require doctor visits (unlike larger birds); this suits frugal millennials. However, every bird species is different and requires understanding and a specific form of socialization. Larger species, like macaws or eclectus parrots, need regular care, especially at adoption, since birds can carry viruses and illnesses that transmit to humans. Most bird owners take their birds to the vet when they are in distress, injured, or seriously ill.*

---

* Yes, it is possible for avian veterinarians to operate on creatures that weigh an ounce and a half. My brother (the same one with Bella the Shih Tzu and Pito the tuxedo cat) and his wife, Margarita, had thirteen zebra finches over a period of fifteen years. When Torcido, a four-year-old male with a twisted beak, needed surgery, a doctor at St. Mark's Animal Hospital in Manhattan applied a tiny "gas mask" to the bird, set him on a miniature easel, sedated him for fifteen minutes (the maximum time allowable), and performed a delicate but successful operation, giving him an additional six happy years of life before being buried in the garden alongside eleven members of his extended family (the thirteenth finch, Bright Eyes, escaped through an open window one day, flew down Second Avenue, and landed in Rutherford Square with thousands of other birds enjoying the noonday sun—a moment of freedom for Bright Eyes, before meeting his first New York winter).

ON A WING AND A PRAYER

- Birds do the one thing that people have wanted to do for millennia but cannot, which is to fly.

- Of the ten thousand species of birds on this planet, only sixty or so are flightless, like people, including the comical emu, the dangerous cassowary, and the noble ostrich.

- The swift flies for the first three years of its life, sleeping on the wing, mating in midair, never touching the earth or tree limb, flying back and forth from England to Africa, as if it were a holiday jaunt.

- The peregrine falcon roars through the sky at two hundred miles per hour in search of prey.

- Hummingbirds—tiny jeweled, avian helicopters—can fly backward at fifteen miles per hour and spend much of their flight time hovering.

- A Rüppell's griffon, a vulture with a ten-foot wingspan, found in the Ivory Coast, has been reported to fly as high as 35,000 feet. The Himalayan bar-headed goose doesn't bother climbing Mount Everest at 29,035 feet, it simply flies over the top.

- Some birds live to be one hundred years old; it's not uncommon for parrots to live to be forty or fifty.

- African gray parrots are talented talkers, imitating the calls of other birds, some learning as many as nine hundred words, and understanding concepts like shape, number, and color. Having seen a photo of Jane Goodall with a chimpanzee, one famous African gray parrot, N'kisi, greeted her on a visit to N'kisi's home, "Got a chimp?"

Birds don't need to be walked, and most landlords don't classify birds as "pets," a potential bonus for millennials dueling with landlords who ban dogs and cats from their apartments. Allergic to dogs or cats? You likely won't have that problem with birds.

We saw in chapter five that 43 percent of dog owners have more than one dog. Bird lovers are no different, with 47 percent of bird owners keeping two or more birds, and 55 percent considering adopting another bird. They are colorful, particularly within the neutral, off-white minimal homes that millennials favor. Like dogs and cats, birds can become lifelong companions, normally bonding with a single member of the family. With their longer life span—ten years for finches, fifteen years for budgies, twenty for cockatiels, thirty for small parrots, one hundred years of merriment for some parrots—they become an integral part of a family, often outliving their original owners.

THE BIRDS OF MANAGUA

A colorful chapter of my sister-in-law Margarita's childhood in Nicaragua involved birds of all kinds, shapes, sizes, and plumage.

- Emilia: noted below, who survived only one month after Margarita's grandmother, her closest companion, moved to America.

- Rosita: a parrot who "performed" opera, dragging bits of fabric around the house as she sang the same aria from *La Traviata* for hours on end, nonstop, on- and off-key. When Margarita's father went to the hospital for a few days, Rosita (unable to enter the hospital) sang to him from the window ledge of his room, doing her best each day to cheer him up during his convalescence.

- The shop birds (small green parrots) in downtown Managua, who would alert shop owners to potential shoplifters by calling out, "*¡Acqui buscan, acqui buscan, policia, policia!*" meaning "They are looking, they are looking, police, police!"

Birds are playful and sometimes naughty. My sister-in-law's grandmother had a parrot named Emilia, in Nicaragua, who had a perch at the dinner table for thirty years. Emilia would sometimes interrupt Sunday dinner by pretending to "break wind" and then, nodding at the dog sleeping nearby, say, in Spanish *"El perro lo hizo, el perro lo hizo,"* meaning "The dog did it, the dog did it," knowing this was not dinner table behavior. She didn't like a certain government official who occasionally visited their house, and when the man would leave, Emilia would fly after him down the road and drop a messy "party favor" onto his jeep from on high. The man swore that he would kill the bird, but Emilia always eluded him.

If you cannot handle the heartache that accompanies the death of a Labrador Retriever after eight or nine years in the family, a bird is a desirable alternative, considering its longer life span. However, a study performed in 2017–2018 by the American Pet Products Association found that the single greatest drawback to owning a bird, outweighing all the logistical and housekeeping tasks and the occasional cacophony, is the emotional distress and sadness felt by family members when a bird dies—a level of sadness that can be unexpected (especially for first-time bird owners) and which wouldn't occur if there weren't a fundamental bond, a human-animal bond between the two parties. Birds are part of our mythology, part of our cultural and religious history, reaching back to St. Francis of Assisi and his famous sermon to the birds,* and beyond. Birds become part of their owners' day-to-day lives, which is why losing them is no easier than losing a dog or cat.

Poultry

Who would have thought that traditional barnyard animals, especially chickens, that we continue to slaughter for meat and whose eggs we eat for breakfast, would become carefree, pampered pets. Intelligent and

---

* St. Francis had a special relationship with birds, who followed him around and rested on his shoulders or hands as he prayed or walked in the fields. In the sermon recounted in *The Little Flowers of St. Francis*, he said, "My sweet little sisters, birds of the sky, you are bound to heaven, to God, your Creator. In every beat of your wings and every note of your songs, praise Him. He has given you the greatest of gifts, the freedom of the air."

social beings, they provide companionship and can do simple arithmetic, as scientists at the Universities of Padova and Trento have found. Chickens have a certain level of self-awareness. Like dogs, chickens are social beings and do not like to be alone. They will eat from your hand and show affection. Some people even bring chickens indoors. People collect rare breeds and spoil them like Toy Poodles. Twice a year, they go to the vet. Wings clipped, they won't fly away. Chickens are legal in some cities, though roosters are generally banned because of their early-morning neighborhood serenades.

Geese have always made great "watchdogs" on farms, since they are fearless, protective birds. But now they've become household pets, too, along with ducks and turkeys. Turkeys are docile, regal birds that form tight family bonds. Ducks, turkeys, and geese are all exclusively outdoor pets that need grass, feed, and protection from foxes. And they need both human and feathered company.

Poultry is one of the fastest-growing pet categories. According to a 2018 AVMA study, pet poultry ownership has increased 23 percent since 2013, and 1.1 percent of all American households (or 1.3 million households) now have a pet chicken, duck, turkey, or goose. As a society, we continue to eat all four of these birds in great quantities—chickens, geese, ducks, and turkeys—and the eggs they lay, just not the birds we increasingly fall in love with, keep as pets, and bring into the family.

Hop

Rabbits

There are approximately five million pet rabbits in America, all irresistibly cute, almost too cute for their own good. Which partly explains why they've become the third most surrendered animal to shelters, according to the HSUS, which works with the House Rabbit Society to rescue bunnies across America. Founded in 1988, the House Rabbit Society has chapters in most states and many foreign countries. The language in their website mission statement is familiar to anyone who has worked with shelters to rescue dogs and cats over the past thirty years: "Many of these bunnies had run out of time at animal shelters and were scheduled for euthanasia; others had been deemed 'unadoptable' because of age, health, or disposition. House Rabbit Society is able to spend time getting to know each individual bunny and can then match him or her with an appropriate home. We neuter/spay all incoming rabbits, attain any necessary veterinary care, and attend to their social needs." Substitute "dog" and "cat" for "rabbit" and you understand their condition today. The last sentence in the mission statement is especially telling: "We neuter/spay all incoming rabbits, attain any necessary veterinary care, and attend to their social needs." Rabbits that have been spayed live to ten or twelve, five years longer than unspayed rabbits. Rabbits are always fertile, unlike other animals that cycle.

Unfortunately, there is a "mismatch" between rabbits and their target "customer." Many parents consider them perfect starter pets for children, since rabbits are cute and cuddly. However, they need careful socialization, gentle handling, and habitats kept clean; young children are not the perfect candidates for these tasks. They often lose interest or move on to other pets, increasing the distance between child and animal. Rabbit litters are famously large, which people don't always consider at purchase, complicating their life in a home.

There are both domestic and wild rabbit populations, but they are not interchangeable. Like feral cats, wild rabbits do not adapt to domestic life, nor do domesticated rabbits survive in the wild. However, some people abandon rabbits, assuming that they will do fine with their "wilder" cousins in the meadow.

Yes, rabbits hop, a function of their anatomical structure. Their muscular and powerful hind legs allow them to run fast. In the wild, preyed on by other animals, they can hop at forty to fifty miles per hour, covering distances with a single bound. Their spine is flexible and designed to accommodate hopping. They do walk and run, but prefer to hop, a fast and economical way to get around.

Run

Ferrets

When someone says, "We'll ferret out the information," it means that they will "dig up" the information; they'll find it with careful, detailed, relentless searching, and they won't give up until they find it. The word "ferret" comes from the Latin *furittus*, meaning "little thief," a reference to the ferret's habit of finding small items and then hiding them away.

Today, ferrets spend more time indoors than out, as they've become a popular American pet. A quick reading of Internet literature, though, would make you wonder why, unless you "dig" a bit deeper. A post on fluffyplanet.com, "17 Steps to Ferret-Proof a House," discusses things to do before bringing home your first ferret. This involves blocking electrical outlets, protecting computer cords and surge protectors, eliminating potential food and chemical hazards, and ensuring that the ferret won't find easy escape routes.

Like the much-maligned spiders discussed earlier in this chapter, there are many popular misconceptions about ferrets, which have twisted their public profile, contributing to the high number of ferrets in American shelters. Contrary to conventional wisdom, ferrets: are not silent; can be trained; can learn to use a litter box; needn't be caged full-time if your house is ferret-proof; do need veterinary care, including vaccinations; are not wild animals, having been domesticated two thousand five hundred years ago; are mammals, the domesticated form of the European polecat; are legal in many states; are not as stinky as people think, especially if they've been neutered; are intelligent; like to play; are crepuscular (alert at dusk and dawn); shouldn't be kept outdoors; should not be declawed; and are hypoallergenic.

In many ways, the ferret's journey from the farm and the outdoors into the home replicates that of dogs. Domesticated in Europe long ago, skilled at going down holes and "ferreting out" prey, they were primarily used for hunting rodents, rabbits, and moles. In 1390, a law was passed in England allowing only the aristocracy to own and keep ferrets for hunting. They were brought to America in the seventeenth century, used for hunting, and then, from 1860 until World War II, employed to guard granaries, much like the dogs and cats we met in chapters one and two.

Good pets? Certainly, if you train and socialize them. They are affectionate, quiet, as playful as any other household pet, bond with their owners, and sleep eighteen hours a day. Well tended, they can live ten to twelve years. There are more than one million pet ferrets in the United States today, the most popular pet on social media in several states.

Hamsters, Guinea Pigs, Gerbils, and Hedgehogs

Sometimes it doesn't matter how cute you are. This grouping of small mammals—pocket pets—that scurry about on four short legs isn't welcome everywhere in America, especially in the great states of California and Hawaii.

Hamsters

I believe that people are in denial, or simply uninformed, about hamsters. Cute and cuddly, easy to maintain, small enough to earn their nickname of pocket pets, they are routinely bought for children as a perfect starter pet. Yet, through no fault of their own, they are poorly "designed" for children under the age of eight, since they do bite, can be aggressive when handled roughly (as children can do), sleep during the day when children are awake, fight with other hamsters, can carry salmonella and other viruses, and don't live long (two to three years), which is potentially devastating for a child who's grown attached to them.

Effectively, they've become inexpensive, disposable "mass market" pets. Yet they are social and friendly if you take good care of them and spend time with them. The words that keep spinning round the hamster wheel are "cute, cuddly, fluffy, inexpensive, low-maintenance, independent, self-reliant, calming." After all, maybe hamsters are better suited for adults than children.

Guinea Pigs

Guinea pigs, on the other hand, are the rock stars of small, nontraditional mammals. Ignored by most historians, they pulled off one of the most impressive social-climbing feats in the past millennium. For centuries, guinea pigs were foodstuffs for the Inca people of Peru. Then, in the late 1500s, after the Spanish conquest of Peru, guinea pigs were imported to Europe (Francisco Pizarro sailed to Peru in 1509 in search of gold and found guinea pigs instead). In Europe, they assumed a new identity, that of an exotic New World animal, adored by the upper class. In a single generation, they said adios to the kitchen stove and became beloved house pets. Guinea pigs were suddenly chic, popular, owned by the wealthy, though their reproductive habits soon expanded their presence into the middle class.

They eventually came to America, where they've become popular pets. Approximately nine hundred thousand households have a pet guinea pig, numbering 1.5 million animals. The Spanish were right. Guinea pigs purr when petted and make great pets—good for children, friendly, less fragile or temperamental than hamsters, easy to manage, hardy (they live to six or seven), and gymnastic superstars, performing an act called "popcorning" by jumping repeatedly into the air, running forward and backward, always consummate showmen. They figured it all out five hundred years ago: "Who wants to end their life in a stewpot high in the Andes, when they can enjoy the good life in loving homes all over the world."

Gerbils

Desert animals, gerbils are prohibited in California, which has plenty of desert, and Hawaii, which doesn't. The powers that be in both states decided that if gerbils (burrowing animals with considerable energy) were released into the wild, they could establish feral colonies and damage native crops and wildlife. They are socially curious and nonviolent, additional reasons that these states should welcome them. Innately theatrical, they communicate by thumping their back legs and whistling, a veritable one-man band.

Hedgehogs

How the mighty hedgehog has fallen! They were a sacred animal for the ancient Persians, because they consumed agricultural pests. The Greeks, who created the concepts of civilization and the body politic, praised them, "The fox knows many tricks, the hedgehog one good one" (its ability to roll up into a ball). And now they're barred from entering California, Hawaii, Georgia, Pennsylvania, New York City, and Washington, DC. In some states, hedgehog owners need breeding licenses. What have they done to be shunned?

What exactly is a hedgehog? A small, spiny mammal the size of a cantaloupe, it is not related to the hog and does not live in hedges. Unlike porcupines, their quills do not easily detach from the body. When threatened, the hedgehog rolls up into a ball and the quills face outward in a defensive position. Sadly, hedgehogs have many drawbacks. They squeal and snort. They love sweets, and eat too much, developing fatty liver. They suffer some diseases common to humans, including cancer, and can transmit salmonella and ringworm to people. Like cartoon characters, they sometimes contract "balloon syndrome," when gas is trapped under their skin and they inflate, blowing up like a beach ball to twice their normal size. In Africa and Eurasia, they are traded for witchcraft and traditional medicine; the Bedouins believe that hedgehog meat can cure arthritis, rheumatism, and male impotence. Hedgehogs got the short end of the stick.

Like ferrets, however, the main reasons that hedgehogs are banned in California is that they are a flight risk and could pose a threat to native wildlife. After enduring challenges worthy of the Book of Job, it's easy to understand why they roll up in a ball and are so darn hard to unfurl. It's probably not worth it.

Swim

Ornamental Fish

The website of the Roger Williams University Feinstein School of Social and Natural Sciences, in Providence, Rhode Island, defines "ornamental fish" as "fishes that are kept in home aquariums, or for aesthetic purposes. . . . These fishes encompass a wide variety of species, of many shapes, sizes, and colors. Ornamental fish are usually kept in tanks or other aquarium systems. Water quality is extremely important in aquaculture, because the fish are dependent on the caretaker for their health. Diagnostic services are offered on a case-by-case basis for various species of ornamental fish."

According to a 2017–2018 National Pet Owners Survey by the American Pet Products Association, there are 139.3 million freshwater fish and 18.8 saltwater fish kept in home aquariums in the United States. That means there are more ornamental fish in America than either cats or dogs, with 15 percent of American households (12.75 million households) keeping fish. It is not a hobby for seniors, as 73 percent of fish owners are under the age of fifty.

Fish are popular with young men. Two of three people who keep fish are male, with the ages twenty-five to forty-five representing 60 percent of total ownership. Beyond the human-animal bond, people like fish because they are relaxing. Watching these bright, beautifully colored animals glide through water helps fish owners chill. The relaxation factor is more important to older keepers, while the decorative aspect is paramount for younger people.

The Chinese have been breeding ornamental fish for over one thousand years, beginning with goldfish (koi), which are prized for their markings. There are four thousand to five thousand species of ornamental fish. The annual global trade in ornamental fish is approximately $4 billion, with certain rare goldfish selling at retail for as much as $15,000.

In chapter four of the 2009 study *Manual of Exotic Pet Practice*, Stephen M. Miller and Mark A. Mitchell, discuss an "unusual paradox in that [ornamental fish] are both well known and unknown to veterinarians. These animals," the authors write, "are well known because they can be seen every day in the home aquarium, ornamental pond, pet store, and public aquarium, while at the same time they are unknown because knowledge regarding their health care is limited (e.g., in the areas of antibiotic residuals, antibiotic resistance, emerging diseases, antiquated or undocumented diagnostic and surgical techniques, and pain management issues)."

The process of keeping fish is more technical than most forms of pet-keeping. Maintaining a fish tank requires disciplined monitoring of the aquarium water's pH levels and balancing its mix of ammonia, nitrate, and phosphate. Replicating a fish's environment requires a level of skill that is absent with keeping other pets.

There are 12.7 million American households that spend considerable time and money caring for 160 million fish and blissfully chilling out. These are not temporary relationships, since most people who keep fish keep them for many years. Who can say that a person loves a ninety-year-old goldfish any less than their neighbor loves their pet Chow Chow? It is simply a different relationship. It speaks to the diversity of Pet Nation that its leading characters range from 120-pound Malamutes to majestic macaws to the tiny, multihued neon tetra fish, 1.5 million of whom are imported to America every month of the year.

Walk

Turtles

Considering their method of locomotion and a top walking speed of three miles per hour, it is fitting that turtles are the last animal in our survey. They walk slowly, but they keep going. Sometimes, for a long time. Jonathan, a giant tortoise living on the island of Saint Helena, born in 1832, is considered the oldest living land animal in the world.

There is an ongoing dialogue, sometimes emotional, between people who adopt, keep, and love turtles (a few million Americans) and those who believe that it is somehow wrong to own turtles. Both parties have a hard "shell," like turtles, though both agree that wild turtles should never become house pets.

The Internet is filled with articles discouraging turtle ownership. Many of the points that HSUS and PETA make vis-à-vis turtles are true, e.g., turtles do live for decades and require a lifetime of specialized care; they carry salmonella; you don't have to touch a turtle to get sick; it is illegal to buy or sell a turtle smaller than four inches in length.

However, there are just as many articles extolling the virtues of turtles and the joys of owning them. There are several turtle species that make excellent pets and plenty of turtles in need of homes and rescue. Good turtle stewardship is a question of care, study, adoption from responsible sources, and avoiding species like the red-eared slider turtle, one of the most abandoned animals in America. There are multiple turtle species that are endangered, and several groups, like the Turtle Conservancy, working to protect them.

EXOTICS AREN'T SO EXOTIC ANYMORE

The animals discussed in this chapter include the most popular non-traditional pets, but they are only a fraction of the animals in this world. There are tens of thousands of species across the different animal classes: birds, fish, reptiles, small mammals, poultry. Though most of these animals are not seen in public, like cats, they are growing in number, variety, and popularity.

Millennials are adopting more pets in every category, especially fish and reptiles. Families continue to buy hamsters, guinea pigs, rabbits, the small animals "intended" for children, often more complex in management than people expect, along with egg-laying chickens. The animal mandala keeps turning. As the black-market trade in nontraditional pets continues to flourish, both for endangered and/or dangerous animals (e.g., panda, snow tiger, rhinoceros), state governments, particularly California and Hawaii, have become more involved in the regulation of nontraditional animals, including those kept as pets.

The Convention on International Trade in Endangered Species of

Wild Fauna and Flora (CITES), in 1975, created a divide between the legitimate and illegitimate animal trade. With 175 signatory countries, it created three tiers of protected animals, including the most endangered animals that cannot be sold, those limited by permits, and some with country-specific regulations. Unfortunately, as Alex Mayyasi wrote for *Priceonomics*, in 2014, "Poachers and traffickers can camouflage their activities as the legitimate (if not exactly celebrated) trade of bred-in-captivity animals, which makes the nontraditional animal trade much more difficult to regulate." As discussed earlier in this chapter, there are layers of laws regulating activity with these animals, and attempts at ownership, and authorities are increasing surveillance and enforcement.

Fortunately, there are multiple, reputable channels of distribution in the nontraditional pet category, whether online, shelter, or retail, such as PetSmart and Petco—safe places to adopt or to shop for healthy animals, from A to Z.

Depending on where you live, it isn't easy to find veterinarians with a specialty in exotics. Only six of the thirty veterinary schools in the country teach this as a discipline. Dr. Mader, in Marathon, Florida, operates an innovative internship program for students specializing in exotic veterinary medicine. They receive hands-on training with a wide variety of animals that come for treatment at his hospital, and experience the overlap between domestic pets and the wild animals found in the Florida Keys.

Currently, only Nationwide offers insurance coverage of nontraditional pets. This will change, as more millennials adopt nontraditional pets, more companies extend pet insurance to employees, and the awareness of these animals in society increases. This is critical, since many people don't take their nontraditional pets to the vet on a regular basis.

Every nontraditional pet is an animal, part of the earth's tapestry, worthy of love and respect, different one from the other, and different in many ways from dogs and cats, though profoundly similar in others. They all make us better. They change us and enrich each day of our lives, and whether they stick around after sixty-three days of veterinary care like Monty the Python, two years like the jittery hamster, or seventy-five years, if we're truly blessed, with an African gray parrot, they form one more link in the human-animal bond chain that crisscrosses our country.

·9·

PET NATION
Is There More to Come?

If you don't subscribe to *L'Osservatore Romano*, the Vatican newspaper, you may have missed a curious debate about pets involving the pope and an interview with a journalist from his native Argentina, in 2015. A surprising controversy that goes to the heart of this book, it stirred up a hornet's nest around Francis I, who chose his name in honor of Saint Francis of Assisi, the patron saint of animals.* A warm, humble, and approachable man, the pope loves animals, no? A simple question with a complex answer.

How did the pope get involved in this imbroglio? Did his papal promotion come with a pack of Italian Greyhounds that chase him around the Vatican, begging for biscotti, drowning out his sermons with incessant barking? Was his childhood in Buenos Aires—where parrots live much better than dogs—bereft of pets?

---

* The Grotto in my native Portland, Oregon, greets visitors with a classic bronze statue of Saint Francis, surrounded by a lamb and a wolf, who looks remarkably like a modern dog.

The pope's reaction to Pet Nation in interviews and sermons is confounding, to say the least:

1. "Care for pets is like programmed love. I can program the loving response of a dog or a cat, and I don't need the experience of a human, reciprocal love." He characterized this trade-off as *worrisome*.

2. Troubled by how people spend their money, he commented that "after food, clothing, and medicine, the fourth item is cosmetics and the fifth is pets. That's serious." He expressed a "worry that people sometimes have feelings, powerful feelings, toward animals, and yet remain indifferent to the suffering of our human brothers and sisters."

3. From a sermon in Rome on June 2, 2014: "It might be better, more comfortable—to have a dog, two cats, and the love goes to the two cats and the dog. Is this true or not? Have you seen it? Then, in the end this marriage comes to old age in solitude, with the bitterness of loneliness."

Pope Francis is a global leader who presents a surprising, yet powerful argument challenging the foundations of Pet Nation, human-animal bond research, and the social capital of pets. It's one thing to attack gratuitous sex and violence in Hollywood movies, religious leaders do that regularly. But Francis I's arguments against pets rest on faulty premises. How, for example, can you lump pets—living, breathing, intelligent creatures—in with cosmetics? Is it fair to fault Pet Nation for spending money on our animals? Are pets a means of superficial, instant gratification, as he suggests? Is loving a pet harmful to the development of meaningful human relationships? I doubt that his namesake saint would understand these ideas.

My Irish Catholic mother won't appreciate this from her perch in heaven, but her hero, whose *Time* magazine photo never left her coffee table, is plain wrong . . . so wrong that it's difficult to comprehend what he was thinking. But I'll take him at his word in this final chapter, as we examine the future of Pet Nation.

Three arguments challenge the very notion of Pet Nation and my view that the success of Pet Nation should motivate Americans to expand the number and reach of pets. Recall the recommendations at the end of chapter four concerning the human-animal bond and social capital of pets. If we take the science and studies to heart, we should encourage as many households in America as possible to have pets (hopefully 100 percent), and the total number of cats and dogs should increase from 185 million to 330 million, matching the number of people in the United States.

Let's consider these contrary views:

LOVE IS ZERO-SUM

Pope Francis believes that to enjoy, engage, and love a dog or cat inevitably depletes the pet owner's capacity to enjoy, engage and love humans, especially those in need. But love or engagement is not zero-sum. More of one does not mean less of the other.

The zero-sum argument has superficial, yet unrealistic appeal: the world would be a better place if people would only spend the time they currently devote to their precious puppy or kitty volunteering instead at a homeless shelter to help folks in need. But this call for sacrifice applies to any activity outside the workplace. Why are you painting, hiking, playing competitive sports, visiting friends, reading romance novels, sampling new restaurants in the neighborhood, or traveling to places unknown, when you could be volunteering at a homeless shelter? Why does the pope single out *pets*? If he wants people to spend more time helping the needy, he should make the case for it on the merits without disparaging the time they spend playing with a dog or cat, or buying them a toy.

There is no evidence I can find that establishes, or even hints, that pet owners are less generous or less philanthropic than non–pet owners. Whether it's measured in dollars, volunteer hours, or social activism, where's the proof that pet owners lag behind the rest of society? People who volunteer at shelters or spend their weekends driving homeless dogs to rescue homes a thousand miles away understand the concept of altruism. The research we considered in Perth, San Diego, Portland, and Nashville demonstrates that pets connect strangers, helping them meet new people, perhaps helping others in times of need, with or without pets.* Pets *add* to the human equation, not *subtract*. Moral behavior is judged by how you treat not only strangers but friends and acquaintances, too, including those one meets while walking a dog.

A dad or mom watching their young daughter roll in the grass with an eight-week-old kitten is certainly capable of loving them both. Laughing at the kitty's acrobatics doesn't "fill up" Mom, leaving no room to melt at her daughter's antics. Does the pope's theory of human capacity prevent us from emotional multitasking, so that we can't enjoy a slice of apple pie, then walk to a soup kitchen and serve lunch for the homeless? By all accounts, Francis of Assisi didn't limit his animal outreach to one bird, or one squirrel. He loved all the creatures he encountered. Let's get this pope a Corgi and see if his mood doesn't improve.

The pope's blunt criticism of married couples choosing to have a pet instead of a child is also unfair. He assumes that the two decisions are derivative, when, in my experience, there's no reason to connect them.

---

*Service dogs help people in *chronic* need in dozens of ways (veterans with PTSD, autistic children, the blind). A key element of this pet-human success story is the mysterious human-animal bond, so any attempt to limit contact between healthy people and pets could backfire, short-circuiting new, pet-based solutions to help those with severe physical, emotional, or psychological challenges.

It's a serious choice for a couple to decide not to have kids. But is this the typical conversation: "Okay, it's either a baby or a Siamese kitten, honey, you flip the coin"? Do couples who choose not to have children often adopt or purchase a pet? Yes, but it's not necessarily one choice *measured against* the other choice. A decision to get a pet before starting a family doesn't mean that the couple chose to own a pet *instead* of having a child. For the 42 percent of American adults who are single, this is an even more tangled subject. There's no obligation to have children, or even to get married, or to have a pet. Otherwise, nuns would be in hot water. I learned enough in school to know that Catholic theology has grounded itself for centuries in free will regarding both simple and complex choices.

ANIMAL DISCRIMINATION

Some people don't like children, others don't like animals. They resist the expansion of Pet Nation, primarily because of their aversion to cats and dogs. This is a form of bias or discrimination that is tolerated in most circles and not condemned like other forms of social discrimination (race, ethnicity, sexuality, religion). For example, we don't allow people in public places to discriminate against different ethnic groups, but people are allowed to discriminate against pets. If one store in a shopping mall allows pets to accompany customers, why permit other stores to prohibit them? What's different about a person being accompanied by a cat or dog (who means the world to them), versus a friend of a different color, race, or ethnicity? I'm sure most readers have never considered this and would assume the difference is obvious, but is it? What if the store owner isn't concerned about sanitation or noise but simply doesn't like pets? Health issues or discomfort for other customers are the safe hooks upon which to hang a "Pets Not Wanted" sign, but, then, many people don't enjoy the behavior of small children in public art museums.

The analysis gets more personal when we compare pets to children, which happens frequently. A store owner could never post a sign that reads, "Children Are Not Welcome" or, even worse, admit that "I don't like kids, so I don't want them in my store." The same isn't true for pets. If an establishment is open to the public, should we leave it to the proprietor (a private citizen) to decide who enters the public shop? Let's say a store owner attended Auburn University and loathes the University of Alabama because the Crimson Tide regularly beats his Auburn football team. What would happen if the owner posted this sign: "No University of Alabama graduate, or anyone wearing an Alabama cap or T-shirt, is welcome in the store"? Setting aside whether that's legal, would it be wrong? And if it is wrong or illegal, should it be any different for people with pets?

As Pet Nation expands and it becomes more common to take pets everywhere—except restaurants and places where safety considerations justify restrictions on access—do we doubt that pet owner demands will increase, or that they will march into a shop with their Cocker Spaniel and dare the owner to stop them? Do pet owners risk a backlash if they don't respect some safe havens for non–pet owners? If the pet industry supported a broad attack against pet barriers, political and legal, effectively arguing that pets should be treated like children, wouldn't industry open a door to the most effective claim for abolishing the rule against noneconomic damages we explored in chapter six? The argument would need to be crafted carefully in terms of the pet owner's right of association, and not a separate theory of discrimination against pets. It's not an easy choice for Pet Nation. Pet Nation may regret advancing these arguments, so we cannot be certain how this will unfold.

Will restaurants that welcome children, but not pets, be able to maintain this policy over the long term? With airlines, the tolerance for service animals (compelled by federal laws) opened the door to pets of all sizes and shapes to board passenger planes, regardless of whether they are service dogs. Or will these battles dissipate because store owners, restaurant owners, and others discover, as airlines have, that business improves when Pet Nation is welcomed?

The rights of non–pet owners is an awkward issue, but it is unlikely to become a public battle unless a business owner takes a highly inflammatory stand against cats or dogs. Non–pet owners will not welcome counterattacks from pet owners, which could be intense and unfriendly. It will be interesting to see whether Pet Nation weighs in uniformly for greater public access. Supporters could clamor that all dog owners *must* support the cause, but it's unclear if a majority of pet owners support unlimited access. Cat owners may not care about the plight of dog owners, so the test is whether a sizeable majority of dog owners vote to tear down "Dogs Not Wanted" signs. As with many things in Pet Nation, this landscape is evolving.

TOO MANY PETS?

The safest ground on which to challenge Pet Nation is the third argument: that the introduction of too many pets, especially behaviorally challenged pets, will cause "untenable" problems in society. I haven't yet seen commentators make these arguments publicly, but it's easy to imagine some of their concerns. Chronic piles of dog treasures* (the Parisian "I just stepped in it" routine) on city sidewalks come to mind, or furniture in stores or on patios chewed to bits. Dogfights, or worse,

---

* In Latin America, they say that stepping in these "treasures" brings you good luck—hence their Spanish nickname, *tesoros*.

an unprovoked attack by a dog on a third party, are never welcome in civil society. Yet each of these problems can be corrected or prevented by a responsible dog owner, so the problems should be manageable.

Should society hold people responsible for the behavior of their pets in public spaces that were once off limits? Why not? That is, pet owners could be cited (with financial fines) when their dogs misbehave. Let store owners or members of the public snap pictures on their smartphones and send them to the "pet police." Make it clear that pets are welcome but misbehavior will be punished. Lawyers would line up to be appointed the pet judge (doubtless the next big reality show).* Thankfully, the kinds of problems or discomfort caused by dogs are limited and can usually be remedied. It is no different from a parent paying for a vase their child breaks in an antiques shop. We don't allow these incidents to justify banishment of all children from stores, so why should a similar breach expel an entire species of pets? Private or public restraining measures should be sufficient.

🐾

OTHER CHALLENGES?

As we aim for an additional fifty million to seventy million dogs in the United States (and the same number of additional cats), can we produce enough dogs to meet demand? Chapter five explored some potential solutions for dogs, so we will wait to see if political opposition to commercial breeding recedes, once humane standards are accepted. If not, will potential dog owners, or current dog owners seeking additional dogs, be satisfied with a cat? Some shelters already counsel potential

---

* Virtually every other *Judge Judy* episode has one dog case, covering multiple Pet Nation issues, such as ownership, dog bites, or veterinary care or the lack of it.

dog adopters to consider a cat, especially if the adopting family's life-style better matches the household needs of a cat. For example, you can leave a cat with someone to feed it for a weekend getaway, and the house will look the same when you return. Cats fend for themselves during the day, particularly in the bathroom department, unlike dogs, who must be let outside to find relief. These options have never been marketed to a large audience of potential cat owners. But we do know that shelters have scores of cats waiting for adoption if consumer prefer-ences change. If these two solutions fail, then the progress of Pet Nation will stall, unless foreign dog breeders fill the breach, which, as we learned in chapter five, is the most complicated scenario of all dog-sourcing strategies.

Then there's the challenge of allowing pets in rental homes and apartments. Can private and/or political efforts convince landlords to welcome pets, or allow more than one per unit? This policy shift is critical, especially for lower-income Americans in many cities who only have the option of rental housing. Sometimes the bond is so strong that pet owners will pass up good housing options to remain with their be-loved animal. A friend shared a story about a well-known homeless man with a big, beautiful dog living under a bridge, in downtown Napa, California. He turned down an apartment in public housing because they wouldn't accept his pet. He remains under the bridge today. These stories could be avoided if deposits covered the actual costs for repair-ing pet-related damage when a tenant vacates. Studies show they do and that pet owners will accept these charges. But the HABRI-Michelson Found Animals survey, shared in chapter three, determined that young adults, young children, and middle-age adults cause more damage to rental units than dogs or cats. Fears of property damage are a barrier to pet ownership based upon myths we can overcome.

A persistent challenge facing landlords, however, remains the liabil-ity or property insurance companies that refuse to insure pet-friendly premises because of fears of property damage or injuries to other tenants. Insurance plans are driven by data and actuarial analysis, which assign an economic value to risks. These calculations lead to problems being solved, enabling landlords to understand the relative costs and benefits of pet-friendly policies, and insurance companies to compromise and raise premiums in exchange. These same calculations may lead state housing agencies to finance developers building or renovating low-income properties that allow for pets. The benefits to the community greatly outweigh the risks.

Can we produce enough veterinarians and paraprofessionals to provide health care for another 120 million cats and dogs? Human medicine cannot catch up with societal needs for health professionals, despite dramatic growth in the number of care providers. We would be foolish to expect veterinary medicine to enjoy easier success. We must build more American veterinary schools, increase class sizes, and expand accreditation of foreign universities, initiatives which are already working. This will increase the number of veterinary graduates and, perhaps, allow us to develop a new tier of professionals—call them "veterinary nurse practitioners"—to provide additional health care. Like human medicine, veterinary medicine should embrace telemedicine, or digital care, which opens the door to millions of patients being treated who are currently outside of the system, especially cats.

To offset the fear that the costs of expanding Pet Nation will outweigh the benefits, we need more studies like the one performed by George Mason University researchers, discussed in chapter four. They identified $11 billion in annual savings in health-care costs from people owning pets. These savings could be used, at least in part, to promote more pets for more Americans, with further savings expected.

As pets become more entwined in the daily lives of Americans, inside and outside of our homes, we should institute pet registries, by breed, like the models operating in Sweden and the Czech Republic, which are mandatory for pet owners. This would enhance Pet Nation in various ways, from enforcing the laws to gathering data, informing pet owners of public health alerts or other news, and facilitating micro-chipping of pets to ensure their return when lost. In a country of 330 million people and 185 million dogs and cats, this would be a massive undertaking. We could start with one state, as a pilot, perhaps with financial support from the pet industry in the start-up phase, to demonstrate how this could work and the possible benefits. With proper incentives, we might see five to ten states bidding to test a pet registry.

Any discussion of the potential to expand American ownership of pets must examine why non–pet owners choose *not* to have a dog or cat. In 2012, the American Humane Association conducted a comprehensive study of this question, partially funded by PetSmart Charities. The fifteen-hundred-person online survey studied three groups: (1) persons who had never owned a cat or dog; (2) persons who previously had owned a cat, but not within the past twelve months; and (3) persons who previously had owned a dog, but not within the past twelve months. This survey provides a road map Pet Nation could follow to convince non–pet owners to take the leap.

The survey found that four factors play a role in their decisions: the cost of pet ownership; lifestyle changes (mainly pet-care responsibilities interfering with travel); maintenance and clean-up requirements; and grief over the loss of a former pet. Costs and grief are unique issues for each individual, so it would be hard to prescribe a mass remedy for them. Fortunately, online channels are lowering costs for products and services. Similarly, the lifestyle barrier is less of a challenge, now that a wide range of professional service providers will care for cats and dogs while owners are away. It's easy to access these services at reasonable prices. For example, it only costs $35 a day to hire a live-in house sitter for two cats in Scottsdale, Arizona. The clean-up requirements associated with cats, such as litter box smells, have been reduced significantly by new technologies that remove odors and simplify the handling of litter boxes.

The greatest opportunity to increase pet ownership identified by the

American Humane study rests with the demographic group identified as the *least* likely to acquire another pet in their lifetime: *seniors*. The time between the 2012 study and 2020 represents eight more years of baby boomers reaching senior status. Baby boomers are the foundation of Pet Nation, with a significantly higher level of pet ownership than their predecessors. Greater ease of pet ownership, particularly from Internet access to services and products, improves the odds that a new wave of seniors will find a way to continue to enjoy the benefits of the human-animal bond. And consider the pioneering work of the Pets Peace of Mind nonprofit group, which brings pets into hospices while arranging for adoptions when the owner passes, helping to address concerns of seniors that they should not keep pets.

It's hard to imagine Pet Nation slowing down. Pets aren't a fad, and their appeal shows no signs of fading. If dogs become a luxury item, then the marketplace will force changes to spur commercial breeding. With millennials driving new apartment developments across America to welcome pets, why would Generation Z and the next generation (both of whom grew up with pets) change course?

Health-care shortages will be a pinch point, but a more likely script is that new categories of caregivers will arrive on the scene if veterinary medicine doesn't address the problem. Pet Nation sees this playing out in human health care, so pet owners won't be shocked, or even troubled, if the scenario repeats in pet health care. However, the new corporate groups acquiring veterinary practices won't sit by and watch their markets shrink. These players will invest in alternative providers of pet health care if existing models fail to adapt. Pet Nation forced pet health care to adapt once already, so why wouldn't new adaptations follow?

Serious questions aside, let's not forget that dogs and cats, and puppies and kittens and other pets, are fun. It's as simple as Kurt Vonnegut's explanation, "I let the dog out, or I let him in, and we talk some. I let him know I like him, and he lets me know he likes me." They light up a room and greet a pet owner after a long day at work in a way that never grows old. Pet Nation unfolded because Americans took the time, and had the freedom, to discover the human-animal bond. Social media spread the news, and people everywhere realized what amazing friends we have in our pets, and how much fun it is to share our pets with the world. We read about the good things pets do for people, and the joy and laughter they create, because that's what pets do. Trouble happens, but not that often. Francis of Assisi had it right, so there's still hope for his namesake, Francis I.

I've heard a phrase since I was a child in Oregon: "The barn door's already open, and those cows are gone." Hokey, yes, but the point was that once an idea, particularly a good idea, escapes through an open door, there's no getting it back. That's the story of Pet Nation. More Americans experience it every day. If someone tells you they don't like pets, don't say, "Move on, or get over it," tell them where to find a dog or cat and enjoy one for themselves. Nine times out of ten, Pet Nation will soon have another member!

ACKNOWLEDGMENTS

Pet Nation is a book that needed to be written, and I'm grateful for the vision and commitment of my agent, Kitty Cowles, and the Avery team at Penguin Random House, led by Caroline Sutton as editor in chief. Caroline and her assistant editor, Hannah Steigmeyer, took on the formidable task of guiding this first-time author, and you may be the judge of how well they did. Caroline and Hannah were delightful and highly professional as field marshals. Their patience, humor, and belief in *Pet Nation* made such a difference.

Three of my children (Annelise, Jillian, and Caitlin) appear in the text as passionate pet owners. Meredith and Mark Patrick weren't able to share anecdotes, but I assure you they appreciate the magic of pets in our lives. Each of my kids grew up with a dad who tried cases and dove into political campaigns, and I know they were as surprised and amused as I when life took its turn toward all things pet.

My wife, Natalie Langley, PhD, is an accomplished researcher and author in the field of forensic anthropology (picture weathered bones found in a shallow grave in a field), and an anatomy professor at Mayo Clinic in Scottsdale, Arizona. She understands what it takes to be an author and encouraged me every step of the way. Thanks to her, I knew what I was getting myself into, since it's no walk in the park to balance a full-time workload with the demands of researching and writing a book. Natalie was a brilliant (and relentlessly candid) sounding board, and deserves credit for my growing appreciation of the unique genius of kittens and cats. We each diligently serve as staff for Chloe and Oscar.

The world of pets, particularly pet health care, has been the professional surprise of my life, and introduced me to scores of thoughtful and passionate people. They've put up with my style and advocacy around the country for more than fifteen years, and I wish I could thank each of them. A few folks must be recognized: Scott Campbell; John Payne; Ralph Johnson; Kelly O'Brien; Steve Feldman; Jason Johnson; Eleanor Green; Dave DeYoung; Francisco Trigo; Kristen Peck and her Zoetis team; Pete DeBusk; Julie Funk; David Haworth; the NAVC trio (Tom Bohn, Pete Scott, Gene O'Neill); Kerri Marshall; Bob Lester; Lisa Perius; Andy Bane; Elizabeth Green; Audrey Wystrach; Thomas Kerr; and Andy Maccabe. I'll stop there, but so many more have made such a difference in my career and understanding of the power of pets.

My Animal Policy Group team actually made this work possible, not just in managing work life alongside producing a book but with the research and scope that anchors *Pet Nation*. My executive assistant, Zen St. Clair, and researcher, Victoria Ramassini, were stellar. Special thanks goes to my dear friend, colleague, and co-conspirator from the start of the Animal Policy Group, Ali McIntyre. Ali is a force of nature, and as good a friend and business partner as one could have. Without her there is no *Pet Nation*.

Finally, I come to my brother and best friend, Thomas. It seems we've shared the same sense of humor, irony, and perspective for most of our lives, stretching back to a sleepy Oregon farm town, McMinnville (now the stylish Pinot Noir capital of America), palm-lined Stanford University, and our journeys throughout the world (in my case, absorbed in law, politics and pets; in his case, fashion). The rhythms and glory of being a pampered pet in America approach perfection in the Manhattan lifestyle of his and Margarita's treasured Shih Tzu, Bella. Thomas introduced me to my agent, Kitty Cowles, and collaborated as my research, writing, and analytical partner from the first notions of *Pet Nation* through publication. We've had great fun and managed the ride without a single argument!

NOTES

Chapter 1:
In the Backyard No More: The Transformation of Pets in American Society

3–4   a different story, in which two beautiful cats became the fulcrum for a modern Seattle wedding: Elyse Wanshel, "Couple Holds Wedding 'Kitten Hour' Instead of Cocktail Hour," *HuffPost*, November 16, 2018, https://www.huffpost.com/entry/wedding-kitten-hour-cocktail-hour_n_5bedff4fe4b0510a1f2f2005

6   "Animals make us human": Temple Grandin and Catherine Johnson, *Animals Make Us Human: Creating the Best Life for Animals* (Boston: Houghton Mifflin Harcourt, 2007).

14   He couldn't get elected dogcatcher: Amy Kolb Noyes, "Can't Get Elected Dogcatcher? Try Running in Duxbury, VT," NPR, March 24, 2018, https://www.npr.org/2018/03/24/595755604/cant-get-elected-dogcatcher-try-running-in-duxbury-vt.

18   When they're feeding dogs and cats vegan foods, they're making dogs and cats abide by their own personal philosophical beliefs: Sarah Zhang, "Why Is Buying Pet Food So Hard?" *The Atlantic*, August 6, 2018, https://www.theatlantic.com/science/archive/2018/08/vegan-pet-food-wild-earth/566723/.

23   6 percent of dog owners: https://www.aspca.org/about-us/press-releases/how-many-pets-are-lost-how-many-find-their-way-home-aspca-survey-has-answers/

23   Only 58 percent of microchipped pets: https://avmajournals.avma.org/doi/abs/10.2460/javma.235.2.160

27   Unsurprisingly, a "host of dog-oriented enterprises": https://www.latimes.com/nation/la-na-amazon-dogs-seattle-20190621-story.html

27   a poll of 3,500 dog parents: https://www.bustle.com/p/choosing-a-pet-over-a-partner-is-way-more-common-than-you-think-9350319

Chapter 2:
How Pets Went Viral

39   The word "euthanasia" is derived from the Greek prefix eu, meaning "well, easily" and thanatos, which means "death": Aaron J. Atsma, "Thanatos," Theoi Project, last modified 2017, https://www.theoi.com/Daimon/Thanatos.html

42   "In our atomised societies, ever more adults are single, don't identify with their jobs and don't belong to a clear economic class, religious grouping or trade union": Simon Kuper, "Trump, Johnson and the New Radical Tribes of Politics," *The Financial Times,* July 24, 2019.

42   You might blame it on Lassie: "Lassie," Wikipedia, last modified June 12, 2019, https://en.wikipedia.org/wiki/Lassie

46   People all over the world fell in love with canine heroes like Lassie, Strongheart, Rin Tin Tin: "Rin Tin Tin," Wikipedia, last modified September 19, 2019, https://en.wikipedia.org/wiki/Rin_Tin_Tin

46   Her creator, Elizabeth Cleghorn Gaskell: "Elizabeth Gaskell," Wikipedia, last modified October 4, 2019, https://en.wikipedia.org/wiki/Elizabeth_Gaskell.

49   People laugh when little dogs or ten-pound cats go after big dogs: Alyssa Castle, "12 Famous and Lovable Dogs from Movies and TV," Alyssa Castle from World of Angus, August 26, 2019, https://www.everythingzoomer.com/arts-entertainment/2019/08/26/famous-dogs-from-movies-and-tv/

59   "Alone together": Sherry Turkle, *Alone Together, Why We Expect More from Technology and Less From Each Other* (New York: Basic Books, 2009), xxi.

Chapter 3:
The Whole Damn Country Has Run Amok: The Pet Land Grab

86   "I worry about the fenced-in lives of dogs today": Grandin and Johnson, *Animals Make Us Human*, 41.

94   the staggering number of pets flying on American planes each day: Scott McCartney, "On U.S. Planes, the Dogs Are Winning," *The Wall Street Journal*, August 8, 2018, https://www.wsj.com/articles/on-u-s-planes-the-dogs-are-winning-1533734133.

96   "When we travel, the pugs come along whenever possible because, to us, they are family": Steve Eder, "Pups Onboard: Why Trains Are a Great Way to Travel with Your Dog(s)," *New York Times*, June 19, 2018, https://www.nytimes.com/2018/06/19/travel/dogs-train-travel.html.

96   "I've always thought a hotel ought to offer optional small animals": Anne Tyler, *The Accidental Tourist* (New York: Knopf, 1985), 157.

102   "The positive behavioral effects of prison animal programs include enhanced empathy, emotional intelligence, communication, patience, self-control and trust": Julia Jacobo, "Prison Animal Programs Are Benefitting Both Inmates and Hard-to-Adopt Dogs in Florida, Experts Say," ABC News, February 2, 2019, https://abcnews.go.com/US/prison-animal-programs-benefitting-inmates-hard-adopt-dogs/story?id=60600864

103   with few exceptions, live animals of any kind are not permitted on the premises of a grocery store, a restaurant, or any other food establishment: Rebecca F. Wisch, "FAQ: Dogs in Restaurants," Michigan State University College of Law,

Animal Legal & Historical Center, 2019, https://www.animallaw.info/article/faq-dogs-restaurants.

108 **These are serious medical issues that demand analysis, public policy, and controls:** Jason W. Stull, VMD, PhD; Jason Brophy, MD MSc; J.S. Weese, DVM DVSc, "Reducing the Risk of Pet-Associated Zoonotic Infections," *Canadian Medical Association Journal* 187, no. 10 (July 14, 2015): 736–43. http://www.cmaj.ca/content/187/10/736.

Chapter 4:
The Secret to Pet Nation: The Human-Animal Bond

115 **Friedman study on coronary heart disease:** Friedmann, E. and Thomas, S. A. 1995. Pet ownership, social support, and one-year survival after acute myocardial infarction in the Cardiac Arrhythmia Suppression Trial (CAST). *American Journal of Cardiology* 76, no 17 (December 15, 1995): 1213–1217.

116 **Herzog maintained that human-animal bond research lacked rigor and adequate sample sizes:** Harold Herzog, "The Impact of Pets on Human Health and Psychological Well-Being: Fact, Fiction, or Hypothesis?" *Association for Psychological Science, Current Directions in Psychological Science* 20, no. 4 (August 2011): 236–39, https://www.researchgate.net/profile/Harold_Herzog2/publication/241645032_The_Impact_of_Pets_on_Human_Health_and_Psychological_Well-Being_Fact_Fiction_or_Hypothesis/links/547630490cf29afed6141f07/The-Impact-of-Pets-on-Human-Health-and-Psychological-Well-Being-Fact-Fiction-or-Hypothesis.pdf

120 **When engaged with a dog or cat or horse, does something happen in the human brain that explains improved health or pleasure factors, or a stress reduction:** C. J. Charnetski, S. Riggers, and F. X. Brennan, "Effect of Petting a Dog on System Function," *Psychological Reports*, 95, no. S3 (December 1, 2004): S1087–91, https://doi.org/10.2466/pr0.95.3f.1087-1091

120 **No field of human-animal bond research draws greater interest than the study of an animal's impact on autistic children and their families:** Sigal Zilchal-Mano, Mario Mikulincer, and Phillip R. Shaver, "Pet in the Therapy Room: An Attachment Perspective on Animal-Assisted Therapy," *Attachment and Human Development* 13, no. 6 (October 19, 2011): 541–61, https://doi.org/10.1080/14616734.2011.608987

120 **the long-term benefits of autism-assistance dogs for both the individual with autism and the surrounding family and caregivers:** Sophie S. Hall, Hannah F. Wright, Annette Hames, and Daniel S. Mills, "Dogs De-stress Families with Autistic hildren, New Research Shows," *Science Daily, Journal of Veterinary Behavior: Clinical Applications and Research* 13 (July 20, 2016): 46–54, https://www.sciencedaily.com/releases/2016/07/160720094602.htm

120 **The pet effectively lowers the burden on the parents serving as the sole focus:**

M. Grandgeorge, S. Tordjman, A. Lazartigues, E. Lemonnier, M. Deleau, and M. Hausberger, "Does Pet Arrival Trigger Prosocial Behaviors in Individuals with Autism?" *PLOS ONE* 7, no. 8 (August 1, 2012): e41739 ("Discussion," paragraph 1), https://doi.org/10.1371/journal.pone.0041739

120 frequent contact with dogs helps improve the social skills of autistic children: Beth Ellen Barba, "A Critical Review of Research on the Human/Companion Animal Relationship: 1988 to 1993," *Anthrozoös* 8, no. 1 (April 27, 2015): 9–19, https://doi.org/10.2752/089279395787156509

121 "The beauty of the horse is that it can be therapeutic in so many different ways": Julie Rovner, "Pet Therapy: How Animals and Humans Heal Each Other," NPR, March 5, 2012, https://www.npr.org/sections/health-shots/2012/03/09/146583986/pet-therapy-how-animals-and-humans-heal-each-other.

122 increasingly, nurses and doctors are welcoming dogs into hospitals to relieve patient stress: Elisa Sobo, PhD; Brenda Eng, RN, MN, CPNP; and Nadine Kassity-Krich, MBA, BSN, RN, "Canine Visitation (Pet) Therapy, Pilot Data on Decreases in Child Pain Perception," *Journal of Holistic Nursing* 24, no. 1 (March 1, 2006): 51–57, https://journals.sagepub.com/doi/10.1177/0898010105280112

122 animal-assisted therapy can lower stress levels in schizophrenia patients: P. Calvo, J. R. Fortuny, S. Guzmán, C. Macías, J. Bowen, M. L. García, and A. Bulbena, "Animal Assisted Therapy (AAT) Program as a Useful Adjunct to Conventional Psychosocial Rehabilitation for Patients with Schizophrenia: Results of a Small-scale Randomized Controlled Trial," *Frontiers in Psychology* 7 (May 6, 2016): 631, https://doi.org/10.3389/fpsyg.2016.00631

123 Why not pair shelter dogs who need loving homes with paramedics during their shifts, when they need to relax and to be calm: Mark Tenia, "Unique Program Pairs Pets and Paramedics to Relieve Provider Stress," *Journal of Emergency Medical Services*, September 5, 2018, https://www.jems.com/2018/09/05/unique-program-pairs-pets-and-paramedics-to-relieve-provider-stress/.

124 the benefits of placing cats and dogs in a household to expose children to a wider range of microbes and bacteria than they normally encounter: University of Alberta Faculty of Medicine and Dentistry, "Pet Exposure May Reduce Allergy and Obesity" *Science Daily*, April 6, 2017, https://www.sciencedaily.com/releases/2017/04/170406143845.htm

124 By watching fish, seniors have been recorded as eating more food and having better weight gain outcomes than those who don't have access to these aquatic beauties: Linsey Knerl, "How a Furry Friend Can Add Purpose and Health to Lives of Older Loved Ones," *Delaware Online*, March 27, 2019, https://www.delawareonline.com/story/sponsor-story/five-star-senior-living/2019/03/27/how-pet-can-add-purpose-and-health-lives-older-loved-ones/3279672002/

126 the link between service dogs and combat veterans suffering from PTSD: Dr. Maggie O'Haire and Megan Huckaby, "Study Shows Service Dogs Are Associated with Lower PTSD Symptoms Among War Veterans," *Purdue University*

News, March 2, 2018, https://www.purdue.edu/newsroom/releases/2018/Q1 /study-shows-service-dogs-are-associated-with-lower-ptsd-symptoms-among -war-veterans-.html

127 **The research indicates that pets in the classroom may help improve academic performance and social skills in children:** HABRI, "Publication of Largest-Ever Study on Pets in the Classroom Indicates Positive Impact on Academic and Social Behavior," *Human Animal Interaction Bulletin*, August 28, 2019, https://habri .org/pressroom/20190826

128 **interaction with a therapy dog before surgery—placing a child's pet in the hospital room for a few hours before the child enters the operating room—can significantly reduce their anxiety level:** Lori Marino, "Construct Validity of Animal-Assisted Therapy and Activities: How Important Is the Animal in AAT?" *Anthrozoös* 25, no. S1 (April 28, 2015): S139–51, https://doi.org/10.2752 /175303712X13353430377219

129 **97 percent of the doctors believe that owning a pet delivers quantifiable health benefits:** HABRI, "Family Physician Survey," Human Animal Bond Research Institute, 2014, https://habri.org/2014-physician-survey

130 **Cat and dog behaviors in these studies were nearly identical:** Kristyn R. Vitale, Alexandra C. Behnke, and Monique A.R. Udell, "Attachment Bonds Between Domestic Cats and Humans," *Current Biology* 29, no. 18 (September 23, 2019): 864–65, https://doi.org/10.1016/j.cub.2019.08.036

130 **The social capital of pets is the human-animal bond writ large:** Lisa Wood, "The Pet Connection: Pets As a Conduit for Social Connection?" *Social Science & Medicine* 61, no. 6 (September 2005): 1159–73, https://www.sciencedirect.com /science/article/abs/pii/S0277953605000535

Chapter 5:
Dog Shortages and Canine Freedom Trains

154 **The dogs travel north in air-conditioned vans to shelters:** Greg Allen, "With Rescue Dogs In Demand, More Shelters Look Far Afield for Fido," NPR, January 1, 2015, https://www.npr.org/2015/01/01/374257591/with-rescue-dogs-in -demand-more-shelters-look-far-afield-for-fido

158 **For the first time ever, the mainstream media had covered this issue:** Kim Kavin, "Does America Have Enough Dogs for All the People Who Want One?" *Washington Post*, February 8, 2017, https://www.washingtonpost.com/news/animalia /wp/2017/02/08/does-america-have-enough-dogs-for-all-the-people-who-want -one/#targetText=It 20determined%20that%2044%20percent,than%209.2%20 million%20by%202036

159 **the mysteries and economics of puppy production in America:** Kim Kavin, *The Dog Merchants* (New York: Pegasus Books, 2017), 4–20, 66–112.

159–160 **a wickedly effective epithet they applied to all commercial dog breeders:** Kim Kavin, "When 'Puppy Mill Rescue' Blurs the Line Between Saving and Selling

Dogs," HuffPost, July 14, 2019, https://www.huffpost.com/entry/national-mill
-dog-rescue-puppy-mills_n_5d07cdd2e4b0953278381e02

165   It erodes public confidence: https://www.nationalgeographic.com/news/2017/02
/wildlife-watch-usda-animal-welfare-trump-records/

166   credible findings that spay and neuter procedures, particularly neuters of large
dogs, pose major health risks due to the loss of access to hormones: Leeann Du-
Mars, DVM, ABVP, "The Spay/Neuter Controversy," Pet Medical Center and
Spa, February 28, 2017, https://petmedicalfresno.com/wp/2017/02/28/spayneuter
-controversy-dr-leeann-dumars-abvp/

166   Increased risks of joint disease, cancer, and obesity: Nicole Noga, "UC Davis
Study Shows the Negative Effects of Neutering," The California Aggie, April 4,
2013, https://theaggie.org/2013/04/04/uc-davis-study-shows-negative-effects-of
-neutering/

166   Hip dysplasia, knee ligament damage, mast cell tumors, cancer of blood cell
walls, lymphatic cancer: Pat Bailey, "Neutering Health Effects More Severe for
Goldens Retrievers than Labradors," Human & Animal Health, July 14, 2014,
https://www.ucdavis.edu/news/neutering-health-effects-more-severe-golden
-retrievers-labradors/

166   Scandinavian pet owners manage sexually intact dogs—in public and private—
with seemingly few problems: Alexandra Horowitz, "Dogs Are Not Here for
Our Convenience," New York Times, September 3, 2019, https://www.nytimes
.com/2019/09/03/opinion/dogs-spaying-neutering.html

171   illegal importation of dogs is a serious problem: NAIA Official Blog, "Careless
Rescue Importation Exposes People to Zoonotic Disease," National Animal Interest Alliance, July 9, 2018, http://naiaonline.org/blog/shelter-rescue/careless
-rescue-importation-exposes-people-to-zoonotic-disease/#.XZ-eDC2ZPjA

172   the practice endangers public safety, leading to cases of rabies and other diseases: J. H. McQuiston, T. Wilson, S. Harris, R. M. Bacon, S. Shapiro, I. Tre-
vino, & N. Marano, "Importation of Dogs into the United States: Risks from
Rabies and Other Zoonotic Diseases," Zoonoses and Public Health 55,
nos. 8–10, (October 2008): chapter 6, 421–26, https://doi.org/10.1111/j.1863
-2378.2008.01117.x

172   the risks to American communities from dogs carrying canine brucellosis, rabies,
and other vector-borne diseases: Ben Thompson, "Group Stops Bringing Dogs
from Puerto Rico for Now," Boston Globe, November 26, 2017, https://www
.bostonglobe.com/metro/2017/11/26/group-stops-bringing . . . to-rico-for-now/
aSZloTqw23Tq77XnxQpC9O/story.html?s_campaign=8315

Chapter 6:
The Good, the Bad, and the Ugly: Legal and Political Fights Are Just Beginning

183   PETA's worldview of suffering pets in homes also collides with evidence that pets
enjoy their relationship with their owners: C. L. Coppola, T. Grandin, and

R. M. Enns, "Human Interaction and Cortisol: Can Human Contact Reduce Stress for Shelter Dogs," *Physiology & Behavior* 87, no. 3 (March 30, 2006): 537–41, https://doi.org/10.1016/j.physbeh.2005.12.001

183 **2011 study in Skara, Sweden, found that dogs' oxytocin levels, the hormone that promotes attachment between individuals and stimulates interactive social behavior, significantly increased three minutes after they begin interaction with their owners:** J. S. J. Odendaal and R. A. Meintjes, "Neurophysiological Correlates of Affiliative Behaviour between Humans and Dogs," *Veterinary Journal* (May 2003): 165, 296–301, https://www.ncbi.nlm.nih.gov/pubmed/12672376

183 **PETA's medieval vision ignores the fact that the relationship between people and pets is mutually beneficial:** L. Handlin, E. Hydbring-Sandberg, A. Nilsson, M. Ejdebäck, A. Jansson, and K. Uvnäs-Moberg, "Short-term Interaction between Dogs and Their Owners: Effects on Oxytocin, Cortisol, Insulin and Heart Rate—an Exploratory Study." *Anthrozoös* 24, no. 3 (April 28, 2015): 301–15, https://doi.org/10.2752/175303711X13045914865385

188 **It's been more than a decade since any jurisdiction has considered this idea, and the flame appears to have flickered out:** R. Scott Nolen, "After More than a Decade, Has Pet Guardianship Changed Anything?" *JAVMA* News, March 18, 2011, https://www.avma.org/News/JAVMANews/Pages/110401a.aspx

191–2 **According to *Feline Behavior*:** Bonnie V. Beaver, *Feline Behavior: A Guide for Veterinarians.* Saunders (1992).

194 **New York's passage of a declawing ban in July 2019:** Dani Matias, "Cats Can Keep Their Claws; New York Bans Declawing," NPR, July 23, 2019, https://www.npr.org/2019/07/23/744436827/cats-can-keep-their-claws-new-york-bans-declawing

199 **Violent criminals often launch their careers by abusing animals:** "The Link Between Cruelty to Animals and Violence Toward Humans," Animal Legal Defense Fund, accessed July 15, 2019, https://aldf.org/article/the-link-between-cruelty-to-animals-and-violence-toward-humans-2/

199 **adults convicted of violent crimes, particularly against women, have previously abused animals as youths or adults:** J. Febres, H. Brasfield, R. C. Shorey, J. Elmquist, A. Ninnemann, Y. C. Schonbrun, and G. L. Stuart, "Adulthood Animal Abuse Among Men Arrested for Domestic Violence," *SAGE Journals* 20, no. 9 (October 15, 2014): 1059–77, https://doi.org/10.1177/1077801214549641

199 **Studies of women in domestic violence shelters:** D. S. Wood, C. V. Weber, and F. R. Ascione, "The Abuse of Animals and Domestic Violence: A National Survey of Shelters for Women Who Are Battered," *Society & Animals* 5, no. 3 (January 1, 1997): 205–18, https://doi.org/10.1163/156853097X00132

199 **Another study of violent adult male criminals:** Febres, et al., "Adulthood Animal Abuse Among Men Arrested for Domestic Violence," *SAGE Journals.*

200 **so that women are not afraid to leave their house or apartment where they are being violated, for fear that their pet will be left behind to suffer:** Wood, et al., "The Abuse of Animals and Domestic Violence," *Society & Animals*, 5.

200   This provision of the Farm Bill establishes grants for domestic violence shelters to create programs to provide emergency and short-term shelter and housing assistance for domestic violence victims with pets, service animals, emotional-support animals, or horses: Pet and Women Safety Act of 2017 H.R. 909., 115th Congress (2017) (USA).

200   HABRI playing a key role, to support shelters throughout the United States: HABRI, "New Coalition to Support Legislation Protecting Victims of Domestic Violence and Their Pets," Human Animal Bond Research Institute, July 23, 2018, https://habri.org/pressroom/20180723

204   demonstrate how vulnerable Pet Nation is to repeat abuse by opioid addicts who are desperate to obtain drugs routinely used each day in veterinary practices: Wes Rapaport, "Pets Used as Opioid Drug Pawns Could Prompt Legislative Changes," KXAN, October 6, 2018, https://www.kxan.com/news/pets-used-as -opioid-drug-pawns-could-prompt-legislative-changes/

205   The Hoarding of Animals Research Consortium: Gary Patronek, *Public Health Reports* 114.1 (1999): 81.

Chapter 7:
Pet Health Care Will Never Be the Same Again

217   The most visible change in the veterinary profession during the span of Pet Nation is its wholesale transformation from a male to a female profession: Greg Kelly, "Veterinary Medicine Is a Woman's World," *Veterinarian's Money Digest*, May 7, 2017, https://www.vmdtoday.com/news/veterinary-medicine-is-a-womans-world

217   A male-dominated profession in the seventies and eighties, with classes nearly 90 percent male, American veterinary graduates are now 80 percent female: Jeanne Lofstedt, DVM, "Gender and Veterinary Medicine," *Canadian Veterinary Journal* 44, no. 7 (July 2003): 533, https://www.ncbi.nlm.nih.gov/pmc /articles/PMC340187/

230   Pet health insurance has existed since 1980, but, after almost four decades, only 1.2 percent of American pets have coverage: Paul Sullivan, "Pets Are Like Family. But as Health Costs Rise, Few Are Insured That Way," *New York Times*, October 12, 2018, https://www.nytimes.com/2018/10/12/your-money/pets-health -costs-veterinarians.html

Chapter 8:
"It Isn't Only Dogs and Cats"

294   the private ownership laws for exotic animals by state: "Map of Private Exotic Pet Ownership Laws," Michigan State University Animal Legal & Historical Center, accessed September 17, 2019, https://www.animallaw.info/content/map -private-exotic-pet-ownership-laws

245   23 percent of all pet owners now have a non-feline or non-canine pet: American

Pet Products Association, "2017–2018 National Pet Owner's Survey," Insurance Information Institute, accessed August 15, 2019, https://www.iii.org/fact -statistic/facts-statistics-pet-statistics#targetText=Sixty 2Deight%20percent %20of%20U.S.,year%20the%20survey%20was%20conducted

247 **Most Popular Nontraditional Pets, by State:** Meghan Cook, "The Most Popular Pets that Aren't Cats and Dogs," *Insider*, July 19, 2018, https://www.insider.com /the-most-popular-pets-in-every-state-2018-7

251 **the "central casting" view of snake owners doesn't match their own self-image:** Karen Simring, "What Your Pet Reveals About You," *Scientific American Mind*, September 1, 2015, https://www.scientificamerican.com/article/what-your-pet -reveals-about-you1/

251 **not all spiders are "itsy-bitsy":** "Goliath Bird-Eating Tarantula," accessed September 26, 2019, https://en.wikipedia.org/wiki/Goliath_birdeate

252 **Almost everything that most people "know" about spiders is wrong, the product of popular wisdom and urban folklore:** "Spider Myths: Everything that 'Everyone' Knows about Spiders Is Wrong!" Burke Museum of Natural History and Culture, University of Washington, accessed September 29, 2019, https: //www.burkemuseum.org/collections-and-research/biology/arachnology-and -entomology

254 **people have kept birds in captivity for much of recorded history:** Bernd Brummer, *Birdmania: A Remarkable Passion for Birds* (Vancouver, British Columbia: Greystone Books, 2017), 7.

259–60 **Intelligent and social beings:** Colin Barras, "Despite What You Might Think Chickens Are Not Stupid," BBC Earth, January 11, 2017, http://www.bbc.com /earth/story/20170110-despite-what-you-might-think-chickens-are-not-stupid

262 **there are many popular misconceptions about ferrets:** Kristine Lacoste, "25 Ferret Myths and Misconceptions," *Petful*, November 15, 2012, https://www.petful .com/misc/ferret-myths-misconceptions/

267 **an "unusual paradox in that [ornamental fish] are both well known and unknown to veterinarians:** Mark A. Mitchell, Thomas N. Tully, *Manual of Exotic Pet Practice* (Saint Louis: Saunders Elsevier Inc., 2009, pages displayed by permission of Elsevier Health Science).

275 **"poachers and traffickers can camouflage their activities as the legitimate (if not exactly celebrated) trade of bred-in-captivity animals, which makes the nontraditional animal trade much more difficult to regulate":** Alex Mayyasi, "The Exotic Animal Trade," Priceonomics, February 20, 2014, https://priceonomics .com/the-exotic-animal-trade/

INDEX

Note: Page numbers in *italics* refer to illustrations.

Accidental Tourist, The (Tyler), 96
activities, pet-friendly, 98
acupuncturists, veterinary, 26
adoptions of pets
    and alienation/social isolation of people,
        59, 72, 132
    changes in routines for, 70
    costs associated with, 144–45, 173
    and decision to get a pet, 20–22
    digital tools enabling, 58, 70–71
    media pets' impact on, 49
    in mid-twentieth century, 140–41
    motivations for, 248
    from shelters, 143, 156, *156*
    and sources for dogs, 195–96, *195*
advertising featuring pets, 62–63
Air Carrier Access Act (1986), 92
airplanes, animals traveling on, 93–95, 137,
    278–79
Alfred State University, 106
Allen, Laurel, 88
allergies
    and animals on planes, 95
    prevention of, in children, 124
    and workplaces with pets, 82
Amazon, 43, 72
American Humane Association, 95n, 283
American Kennel Club (AKC), 156
American Society for the Prevention of
    Cruelty to Animals (ASPCA)
    and dog breeders, 160–61, 164, 174,
        197
    founding of, in 1866, 7, 115
    fund-raising of, 145, 196–97
    mission of, 196–97
    spay-and-neuter campaigns of, 167
Americans with Disabilities Act (ADA), 105,
    115

American Veterinary Medical Association
    (AVMA)
    on declawing cats, 193, 194
    exotics policy of, 194, 242
    and pet health insurance, 231
    and revenues from pharmaceuticals,
        198–99
    on shortage of veterinarians, 215
    on sterilization of dogs, 167
    task force on human-animal bond, 115
Amish dog breeders, 161
Amory, Cleveland, 31
Amtrak, 95–96
animal abuse, 196–97, 199–205, *201*, *202*,
    204
animal-assisted therapy
    and cancer patients, 119
    in health-care settings, 122–23
    organizations providing, 115, 116
    in prisons, 101–3
animal colorers, 25
Animal Medical Center (AMC), 224
Animal Policy Group, 2, 89, 221
animal rights lawyers, 25
animal shelters. *See* shelters
Animals Make Us Human (Grandin), 86–87
animal-welfare laws, 115, 163, 173, 269–70
annoying animals, 11
Antech, 212
Antisocial Personality Disorder, 199
antivenom serum, 251
anxiety, 123, 127
apartments, 21–22, 39, 89–92, 136, 281–82,
    284
apathy/antipathy toward pets, 10–11
Apple, 43
Arizona Department of Corrections, 103
Ashe, Dan, 164–65

Atlanta, Georgia, 90
attachments of animals, 129–30
attitudes about animals, changes in, 8, 34, 35, 37
Austin, Texas, 90, 91, 100–101
Austin Beer Garden and Brewing Co., 100–101
autism, 119, 120–21
availability of pets. *See* dog shortages

baby boomers, 84, 89, 194–95, 284
Bailing Out Benji, 161
bakeries, 104, 111
Banfield Pet Hospital, 211–13
    as corporate-owned practice, 214
    Pet Insight Project, 229–30
    and pet lobbying effort, 2
    "State of Pet Health Report," 228–29
    wellness care at, 231
BARK, 83
Barker, Bob, 145, 165
Barking Hound Village, LLC v. Monyak, 178–79
bars, dog-friendly, 100–101
Bed Bath & Beyond, 104
beds shared with pets, 5, 16–17
Behnke, Alexandra, 129
Bell, Alexander Graham, 42, 42n, 54
Bergh, Henry, 115
Best Buy, 104
best-friend status of pets, 5, 28–31, 76
Bethencourt, Ryan, 18
Birdmania (Brunner), 254
birds, 245, 245, 246, 246, 253–59
BluePearl, 209, 212, 214, 223–24
Boise, Idaho, 90
books, paperback, 42–43
Bordetella (kennel cough), 111
Bornhorst, Breeanna, 121
Boston, Massachusetts, 89
brands and branding, 52–53, 62–63
breeders, commercial, 159–65
    addressing dog shortage through, 149, 153, 160, 172–73, 197
    and ASPCA/HSUS, 160–61, 164, 174, 197
    criticisms of, 160–62, 189–90
    and demand for purebred puppies, 164
    and federal regulation, 164–65
    and import/export of dogs, 170
    and industry standards, 162, 163, 164, 168–69, 173, 174
    and land-grant universities, 168–69

and market forces, 284
as only scalable solution, 153
and pet stores, 164
and physical challenges of purebred dogs, 190
public relations problems of, 160, 173, 190
and puppy mills, 159–64, 190
transparency in, 162, 169, 173, 174
BringFido, 96–98
Brinkley, Elizabeth, 159
Brunner, Bernd, 254
Buber, Martin, 30
Buffington, Tony, 18
Bulldogs, 109
Bureau of Land Management (BLM), 103
Burke Museum at University of Washington, 252, 253
Bustad, Leo, 115, 117

California, food trends in, 17
Campbell, Scott, 211–12
cancer, 119, 122, 125–26, 232–33
cardiovascular disease, 122
Carnarvon, George Edward Stanhope Molyneux Herbert, 52
cartoon animals, 49–50
Catholic churches, 107
cats
    ability to bond with humans, 129–30
    advantages of, 281
    and animal therapy in prisons, 102–3
    of author's youth, 141–42
    cafés featuring, 99–100
    and cat lovers, 142
    declawing, 190–95, 192
    and dog shortage threat, 144, 281
    euthanization of, 38, 191
    health care for, 38–39, 224–27, 282
    and "kitten hour" (in lieu of cocktails), 4
    and litter boxes, 234, 283
    money spent on, 142, 224–25
    prevalence of, 246
    and rodent control, 190–91
    in shelters, 144, 281
    status of, 38–39
    stray cats, 38, 144, 191
cat-scratch fever, 110
cat towers, 17
celebrities, animals as, 64–65
Center for Animal Welfare division of USDA, 164

Centers for Disease Control and Prevention (CDC), 109, 110, 125, 171, 172
Cetacean Community v. Bush, 186
Charlotte, North Carolina, 89
Chewy, 21, 72
chickens, 259–60
Chihuahuas, 109
children
  allergy prevention in, 124
  animals' impact on development of, 118
  couples having pets in lieu of, 276–77
  couples having pets prior to, 5, 20
  in hospital settings, 123
  and pets in the classroom, 127–28, 137
  pets' status as, 5
  on-screen companions of, 50–51
  and small animals, 261, 263–64, 269
Christmas stockings for animals, 66
churches, 107
cities, dogs living in, 85–86
civic engagement, 132
Clark, Katherine, 200
Clark, Nigel, 47
classrooms, pets in, 127–28, 137
Clower, Terry, 129
clubs, private, 107
Cohut, Maria, 125
Coleman, Cathy, 121
college campuses, pets on, 89, 105–6
Colorado Correctional Industries, 103
Columbus, Ohio, 90
commerce, 60–61, 69–72
commercial breeders. *See* breeders, commercial
commitment to pets, 60, 71
commonality as aspect of pet ownership, 67
communication of pets, 61
companionship of animals
  best-friend status of pets, 5, 28–31, 76
  emergence of idea of, 37
  See also human-animal bond
Compassion-First hospitals, 224
computers, personal, 56
control of pets, 67
Convention on International Trade in Endangered Species of Wild Fauna and Flora (CITES), 269–70
cortisol
  of dogs after engaging with owners, 183
  of humans after engaging with dogs, 120, 123, 126

of veterans with PTSD, 127
and workplaces with pets, 84
court rooms, federal, 107
cruelty to animals, 196–97, 199–205, *201, 202, 204*
Czech Republic, 282

daily lives of pets, 78
Dallas, Texas, 90
damage caused by pets, 11, 134, 279, 281–82
Dawkins, Richard, 68
daycare for dogs, 81
deaths of owners, pet care following, 28, 284
deaths of pets, 39, 139, 259, 283. *See also* euthanization
declawing cats, 190–95, *192*
Delta Airlines, 94
Delta Foundation (now Pet Partners), 115, 116
dementia, 122
Denver, Colorado, 89, 90
developing countries, 76, 93
diabetes, 125–26
Diaz, Manny, 92
Diethelm, Gerry, 240
dinner conversation, pets as topic of, 10
discrimination against animals, 277–79
disease-detection, pet assisted, 125–26
Disney, Walt, 45, 50
Disney characters, 49–50
Disney World, 170
dissections of animals in research settings, 114
divorces/separations, 28, 40
dogcatchers, 6n, 14
Dog Merchants, The (Kavin), 159
Dog Parks: Benefits and Liabilities (Allen), 88
dog runs and dog parks, 86–88, *87, 88,* 137
dogs
  alone time of, 86–87, 150
  arrival in North America, 75
  barking of, 11
  beds shared with, 16–17
  benefits of having, 40
  bites from, 14–15n, 109, 134
  cancer in, 232–33
  in cities, 85–86
  daycare for, 81
  dislike of, 10–11
  dog-free households, 78
  doghouses, 16, 38

dogs (*cont.*)
  domestication of, 76–77
  emotional welfare of, 86–87
  events/festivals centered around, 86, 98
  exercising with, 129
  faithfulness of, 52, 61
  foreign, 170–72, 281
  "handbag dogs," 111
  leashed, 87
  lifespans of, 152
  in military service, 115
  money spent on, 224–25
  multiple-dog households, 150, *150*
  off-leash, 11
  outdoor lives of, 76
  ownership rates for, 39–40, *246*
  owners' responsibility for, 11, 280
  population of, 40, 57, 59
  protection offered by, 76
  purebred, 70, 160, 164, 189–90
  in shelters, 157, 158, 195–96, *195*
  socialization of, 150
  sources of, 195–96, *195*
  strays, 6n, 107, 154, *195*
  ubiquity of, 13, 78–79
  walking with, 132–33
  and waste on sidewalks, 108, 134, 279
  working dogs, 27, 37–38, 49, 115
  See also dog shortages
dog shortages, 139–74
  anticipated shortfall of dogs, 153, 156, 280
  and ASPCA/HSUS lobbies, 197
  and breeders, 149, 153, 159–65, 172–73,
    197 (*see also* breeders, commercial)
  and cat adoptions, 281
  economic implications of, 147–48
  and foreign dogs, 170–72, 281
  and land-grant universities, 168–69, 173
  and laws of canine supply and demand,
    140, 141
  in local shelters, 143, 144
  media coverage of, 157–58
  and need for puppies, 153, 165
  public awareness of, 190
  and source of misconceptions, 145
  and sources for dogs, 156
  and spay-and-neuter campaigns, 145, 158,
    165–67
dog shows, 37, 42–43
Dog Starter Kits, 21
dog walkers, 71–72, 85, 133
Dog Whisperer, The (television series), 63

domestication, 76–77
domestic violence, 199–201, *201*, 202–3
dopamine, 126
Dumb Friends League in Denver, 7n, 144
Durrell, Gerald, 60
dysfunction in American society, 40–42

economics of pet ownership
  and dog shortage threat, 147–48
  growth in pet economy, 24, 32–33, *33*, 35
  people who work for/with pets, 25–26
  pet food spending, 17, 19, *19*, 33, *33*
  and pets in the workplace, 26–27
  size of pet industry, 73
  and socioeconomic status of owners, 10
  and working dogs, 27
Eder, Steven, 95–96
electricity, 42–43
email, *56*
encyclopedias, 42–43
endorphins, 123
equality, 9–10, 66–67, 78, 86
Europe, status of animals in, 7, 76
euthanization
  of animals in shelters, 140, 145, 149, *156*,
    157, 158
  of author's childhood dog, 141
  and declawing cats, 193, 194
  declining rates of, 38
  emotional hardship of, 39
  ethical dilemmas in, 235–38
  and hospice care, 234–38
  process of, 39
  "to put down" term, 210n
  of stray cats, 38, 191
  of stray dogs, 6n
  and transfer of pets from Southern to
    Northern shelters, 155
  and veterinarians' services, 210
events/festivals, dog-centered, 86, 98
exercising with a dog, 129
exotic and nontraditional pets, 239–71
  and antivenom serum, 251
  AVMA's policy on, 242
  birds, *245*, *245*, 246, *246*, 253–59
  care and feeding of, 245–48
  categories of, 242
  consumers' passion for, 241–42
  definition of, 241–42
  and domesticated animals, 243
  ferrets, *245*, 246, 262–63
  fish, 124, 240, *245*, *245*, 246, *246*, 266–68

Index

gerbils, 265
Guinea pigs, 246, 264–65
hamsters, 246, 263–64
health care for, 246–47, 256n, 270
hedgehogs, 265–66
and human-animal bond, 239–41, 248,
   259, 271
illegal trade in, 269–70
invasive species, 243
ownership laws for, 243–44, *244*, 270
poultry, 246, 259–60
prevalence of, 245–46, *246*
private existence of, 244–45
rabbits, *245*, 246, 260–62
reptiles, 245, *245*, 246, *246*, 249–51
spiders, 251–53
trends in, 245, *245*
turtles, 246, 268–69

Facebook, 43, *55*, 58, 62, 65, 67–68
factory employees, 84
Fair Housing Act, 92, 105
"Fairness to Pet Owners" bill, 198
Feldman, Steven, 119
ferrets, *245*, 246, 262–63
Fields, Nathaniel, 200
financial aspects of pet ownership
   average annual spend on pets, 32
   costs associated with pet adoptions,
      144–45, 173
   and decision to forgo pets, 283
   and decision to get a pet, 21
   health-care services spending, *33*, 213,
      224–25
   pet food spending, 17, 19, *19*, *33*, *33*
fish and aquariums, 124, 240, 245, *245*, 246,
   246, 266–68
Food and Drug Administration (FDA),
   103–4, 203
food and nutrition of pets, 17–20, *19*, *33*, *33*
food establishments, 103–4, 111
foreign dogs, 170–72, 281
Fort Lauderdale, Florida, 89, 90
France, Anatole, 30
France, tolerance of animals in public, 78
Francis I, Pope, 273–76, 285
Francis of Assisi, Saint, 259, 259n, 273, 276,
   285
Frasier (television series), 51–52
Frederick, King of Prussia, 29
Freud, Sigmund, 29
Friedman study, 115

Fuller, Kristen, 126
funeral parlors, 105

Gaskell, Elizabeth Cleghorn, 46–48
Generation Zs, 136, 214–15, 284
genetic predisposition for liking animals, 11
gerbils, 265
German Shepherds, 48, 109
Geronimo, Danielle, 123
Golden Retriever Lifetime Study, 232–33
Goodby v. Vetpharm, Inc., 179
Good Dog Foundation, 122
Goofy (Disney dog), 49–50
Google, 43, 57
Grandin, Temple, 6, 86–87, 142
Great Britain, 202–3
grocery stores, 103–4
Grumpy Cat, 64
"guardianship" legal standard, 188–89
guide dog trainers, 25
Guinea pigs, 246, 264–65

Half-brothers, The (Gaskell), 46–47
Hall, Sophie, 120–21
hamsters, 246, 263–64
"handbag dogs," 111
happiness of pet owners (and pets), 34–35
Hart, Benjamin, 166
Hartford, Connecticut, 90
Hartsdale Pet Cemetery, New York, 237
Haworth, David, 232–33
health care, effect of pet-engagement on,
   128–30
health insurance for pets, 81, 230–31, 270
health risks associated with animals, 108–11,
   172
hedgehogs, 265–66
Herbert, George Edward Stanhope
   Molyneux, 52
Hernandez, Charles, 127
heroic portrayals of pets, 45–48
Herzog, Harold, 116
Hidden Life of Dogs, The (Thomas), 150
Hitchens, Christopher, 31
hoarders, 205–7
Hollywood Walk of Fame, 48
Home Depot, 104
Homer, 29
hookworm, 110
Horowitz, Alexandra, 166, 167
horses, 103, 121, 246, *246*
hospice care, 234–38

hospitals, 107–8, 111, 122–23, 128
hotels, pet-friendly, 96–99
Houellebecq, Michel, 60
House Rabbit Society, 261
housing, pet-friendly, 21–22, 39, 89–92, 136, 281–82, 284
Hughes, Randy, 63
human-animal bond, 113–38
  across all species, 239–41
  and allergy prevention, 124
  chemical foundation for, 126
  defined, 113–14
  doctors' perspectives on, 128–30
  and exotic/nontraditional pets, 239–41, 248, 259, 271
  milestones in, 115
  as motivation for adoption, 248
  as mutually beneficial, 60, 138
  positive effects of, 116
  research supporting, 116–30, 138
  and rise of Pet Nation, 285
  and seniors, 124–25, 284
  and service/emotional support animals, 276n
  social advances that enabled, 114
  term, 115, 117
Human Animal Bond Research Institute (HABRI)
  and doctors' view of pet ownership, 128–29
  and domestic violence victims, 200
  founding of, in 2011, 115
  on human-animal bond, 113–14
  mission of, 118–19
  and pet-friendly apartments, 90
  Pets in the Classroom Study, 127
  and preoperative anxiety, 128
Humane Society of the United States (HSUS)
  and dog breeders, 159–62, 164, 174, 197
  fund-raising of, 145, 196–97
  mission of, 196–97
  and rabbits in shelters, 260–61
  on turtles, 268
human population, size of, 12–13, 30, 38, 40, 57, 58–59
hunting, 76–77
Huxley, Aldous, 29

I and Thou (Buber), 30
icebreakers, pets as, 133
identity, branding as expression of, 62
IKEA, 104

"Impact of Pets on Human Health and Psychological Well-Being" (Herzog), 116
importation of dogs, 170–72
indoors lives of pets
  and beds shared with pets, 5, 16–17
  dogs' role in creating homes, 60
  and domestication of dogs, 76–77
  in shared public/private spaces, 77–79
  transition from outdoors to, 75–76, 77
  See also public places
Instagram, 43, 53, 55, 64–65, 66
insurance companies, 281–82
International Association of Human Animal Interaction Organizations (IAHAIO), 117–18
Internet and digital tools
  BringFido, 96–98
  commerce on, 69–72
  emergence of, 56
  entertainment on, 68–69
  media pets, 44–53, 44n
  and memes, 53–54, 68–69
  Petfinder, 58, 70, 72
  and rise of Pet Nation, 43–44
  Rover, 71, 85
  sales of pets on, 164
  See also social media
iPhones, 57, 59

Jiffpom the Pomeranian, 64–65
Johnson, Rebecca, 126
Journal of the American Veterinary Medical Association, 23
Justice v. Gwendolyn Vercher, 184

Kavin, Kim, 159
Kelly, Kim, 124
Kimpton Hotels, 97, 98
"kindness to animals" construct, 7
"kitten hour" (in lieu of cocktails), 4
Knerl, Linsey, 124
Koneko cat café, 99–100
Kuper, Simon, 42

Lackland Air Force Base, 115
Lagerfeld, Karl, 28, 31, 65
Landau, Elizabeth, 127
land-grant universities, 168–69, 173
Lap of Love Veterinary Hospice, 234–38
Larch Cat Adoption Program (formerly Cuddly Catz), 102–3
Lassie, 42, 44, 46–48, 53, 64

Las Vegas, Nevada, 89
laws on animal-welfare, 115, 163, 173,
    269–70
lawsuits for emotional damages, 176–81
legal and political battles, 175–208
    animal abuse, 199–205, *201, 202, 204*
    animals from breeders vs. shelters, 189–90
    declawing cats, 190–95, *192*
    "guardianship" legal standard, 188–89
    hoarders, 205–7
    money in pet industries, 196–99
    noneconomic/emotional damages, 176–81
    opioid abuse, 203, 205
    "personhood" of animals lawsuits,
        184–88
    sources of dogs, 195–96, *195*
Levinson, Boris, 115
litter boxes, 234, 283
Little Rascals, The, 50
livestock, *245*
Lloyd, James, 215
loneliness/social isolation in America, 59, 72,
    132
long-term-care facilities, 122
Lorenz, Konrad, 115, 117
loss of pets (fates unknown), 139
lost and found pets, 22–24, 233
love
    best-friend status of pets, 5, 28–31, 76
    of humans, for pets, 28–30, 273–77
    offered by pets, 61
    Pope Francis on, 273–76
    zero-sum fallacy, 275–77
    See also human-animal bond
Lovecraft, H. P., 31
Low, Ken, 105

Macintosh computers, 56
Mader, Doug, 239–40, 270
Madison, Wisconsin, 90
mail carriers, 14, 14–15n, 109
Manhattan, New York, 79n
Man Meets Dog (Lorenz), 115, 117
Manual of Exotic Pet Practice (Miller and
    Mitchell), 267
Marie Antoinette, Queen, 16–17, 16n
marketing featuring pets, 62–63
marriages, 40–41
Marriott Hotels, 98–99
Mars, Incorporated, 117, 118, 212
Marshall, Kerri, 212
Mars Veterinary Health, 213

*Matter of Nonhuman Rights Project, Inc. v.
    Lavery,* 184–85
Mayo Clinic's Caring Canines Program,
    122
Mayyasi, Alex, 270
McCain, John, 105
McCartney, Scott, 94
McCune, Sandra, 118, 133
McVety, Dani, 234–38
media, 62–69
media pets, 44–53
    and adoptions of family pets, 49
    with attitude, 51–52
    and branded merchandise, 52–53
    cartoon animals, 49–50
    companions of children, 50–51
    definition of, 44n
    heroes, 45–48
    perceptions of pets reframed by, 45
memes, 53–54, 68–69
mental health, 128
Meow Parlour, 100
Miami, Florida, 91
Michelson Found Animals Foundation, 90
Mickey Mouse, 50, 52, 53
microchips, 22–24, 62, 283
Millan, Cesar, 63
millennials
    attention given to pets by, 20–21
    choice to acquire dog before parenthood,
        5, 20
    commitment to pets, 30, 71, 146
    and declawing cats, 194
    and dog runs/parks, 88
    and exotic/nontraditional pets, 245, 254,
        255, 256, 269, 270
    marriage trends of, 40–41
    "pet-friendly" as standard for, 98, 112
    pet-friendly rentals demanded by, 79, 89,
        90, 284
    pet-friendly workplaces sought by, 80–81,
        83, 84, 136
    and pet health-care industry, 212, 214–15,
        216
    and purebred dogs, 190
    rate of pet ownership among, 20
    and sources for dogs, 196
Minneapolis, Minnesota, 90
Mississippi State College of Veterinary
    Medicine, 153–55
Moore, Bob, 149
Moore, Rustin, 221

Moore Information polling data, *150*,
    151–52, *151*, *152*, 195, *195*
Morrill, Justin, 168
Morris, Mark L., Sr., 232
Morse, Samuel, 54
multiple pet households, 5, 34, 134–35, 150,
    150
My Life as a Dog (Hargrove), 52

Naruto v. Slater, 187
Nashville, Tennessee, 90
National Animal Interest Alliance (NAIA),
    172
National Cat Day, 99
National Institute of Child Health and
    Human Development, 118
National Institutes of Health (NIH), 115, 118
National Veterinary Associates (NVA), 214
Nationwide, 83–84
Native American Tribal Councils, 107
Neaves, Tonya, 129
New York City, 10
New York Times, 95–96, 166
noneconomic/emotional damages, 176–81
Nonhuman Rights Project, Inc. v. Presti, 185
Nonhuman Rights Project, Inc. v. Stanley,
    185–86
North America, arrival of dogs in, 75
North American Pet Health Insurance
    Association (NAPHIA), 230
Northern Virginia Therapeutic Riding
    Program in Clifton, Virginia, 121
Norway, animal welfare in, 166

Odyssey, The (Homer), 29
O'Haire, Maggie, 126–27
O'Hara, Kerry, 83–84
Oklahoma City, Oklahoma, 89
opioid abuse, 203, 205
Oregon Humane Society in Portland, 143
organic food movement, 17–18
Orlando, Florida, 90
oxytocin, 120, 123, 126, 133, 183

Page, Rodney, 232
paramedics, shelter dogs paired with, 123
"parenting" of pets by pet owners, 30
partners, animals' reactions to, 27–28
parvo, 171
PAWS Act, 200
People-Pet Partnership, 117
personal space, pets' invasions of, 11

Perth study, 130, 131–33
pest control, 37, 76, 190–91
"pet" (term), 6–7
PETA (People for the Ethical Treatment of
    Animals), 181–207
    about, 181–82
    goal of banning pets, 182–84
    and "personhood" of animals lawsuits,
        184–88
    on turtles, 268
pet adoption counselors, 26
Pet Care Trust, 127
Petco, 72, 211
pet culture, 9–11
    daily lives of pets, 14–16, 78
    and decision to get a pet, 20–22
    and divorces/separations, 28
    equality in, 9–10, 66–67, 78, 86
    and food standards, 17–20, *19*
    lifestyles of modern pets, 15–16
    and lost and found pets, 22–24
    in nineteenth and twentieth centuries,
        14–15
    and number of pets, 12–13, *12*, *13*
    and sleeping quarters of pets, 16–17
    and trust placed in animals' instincts,
        27–28
Petfinder, 58, 70, 72
pet-food testers, 25
pet-free people/households, 10–11, 78, 83,
    108, 277–79, 283
Pet Insight Project, 229–30
Pet Leadership Council, 146, 148, 149
Pet Nation
    equation leading to, 69
    role of commerce in rise of, 69–72
    role of media in rise of, 62–69
    role of media pets in rise of, 44–53
    role of technology in rise of, 42–43, 54–61,
        72–73
    and social dysfunction, 40–42
pet owners
    and best-friend status of pets, 5, 28–31, 76
    boomers as, 284
    decreased health-care costs of, 129, 282
    demographics of, 151–52, *151*, *152*
    divorces/separations of, 28, 40
    and finances (*see* financial aspects of pet
        ownership)
    Generation Zs as, 136, 214–15, 284
    happiness of, 34–35
    having pets in lieu of children, 276–77

having pets prior to children, 5, 20
health of, 132
love for pets, 28–30, 273–77 (*see also* human-animal bond)
moral behaviors of, 275–76
need to increase number of, 134–35, 283–84
and others' irritation with pets, 10–11, 279–80
"parenting" of pets by, 30
pet care following deaths of, 28, 284
pet-friendly housing desired by, 21–22, 39, 89–92, 136, 281–82, 284
pet-friendly workplaces sought by, 80–81, 83, 84, 136
policies that encourage pet ownership, 135–38
polling data on, *151, 152*
and reasons for American pets obsession, 66–67
relationships with pets, 28–30
responsibility for pets, 11, 280
terms referring to, 67
trust placed in animals' instincts, 27
See also millennials
Pet Partners (formerly Delta Foundation), 115, 116
pet psychics, 26
pet registries, 137, 282–83
Pets.com, 62–63
pet selfies, 58
Pets for Paramedics, 123
Pets in the Classroom Study, 127–28
PetSmart, 72, 211, 212
Pets Peace of Mind, 284
pet stores, 164, 196
pet trackers, 26
PetWare medical records system, 229
pharmaceuticals, revenues from, 197–99
Philadelphia, Pennsylvania, 89, 90
philosophical framework underlying human-animal dynamics, 114
Phoenix, Arizona, 89, 90
photos of pets, 58
Pit Bulls, 109
Pluto (Disney dog), 49–50
point of view of animals, humans' understanding of, 114
policies that encourage pet ownership, 135–38
political battles. *See* legal and political battles

population of pets in America
estimated size of, 5, 57
increases in, 7, 12–13, *12, 13*, 32, 57, 59
lack of data on, 147, 149
misconceptions of, 145, 149 (*see also* dog shortages)
polling data on, 149–52, *150, 151, 152*
Portland, Oregon, 89, 90
postal workers, 14, 14–15n, 109
post-traumatic stress disorder (PTSD), 122, 126–27
poultry, *245, 246*, 259–60
Prince (author's dog), 140–41
prisons, animal therapy in, 101–3
product purchases for pets, 60–61, 69–70, 72
profits from pet industries, 196–99
property damage, 11, 134, 279, 281–82
protection
animals' need for, 114
offered by dogs, 76
public places
airplanes, animals on, 93–95, 278–79
cafés and bars, pets in, 99–101
and discrimination against animals, 277–79
dog-centered public events, 86, 98
dog runs and dog parks, 86–88, *87, 88*
hotels, pet-friendly, 96–99
pet-free spaces, 103–8, 111
planes and trains, pets on, 93–96
and public-health risks, 108–11
and social connection, 85–86
unavoidability of dogs in, 78–79
workplaces, pets in, 26–27, 80–85
Puppies Behind Bars, 101
puppy mills, 159–64, 190. *See also* breeders, commercial
PuppySpot, 70, 72, 169
Purdue University College of Veterinary Medicine, 118
Putnam, Robert, 130–31
pythons, 239–40, 243, *245*, 251

rabbits, *245, 246*, 260–62
rabies, 109, 110–11
Raleigh, North Carolina, 90
relocation experts, 25
rental housing and apartments, 21–22, 39, 89–92, 136, 281–82, 284
reptiles, 245, *245*, 246, *246*
rescue organizations, 172
reservations, Native American, 107

responsibility for pets, owners,' 11, 280
restaurants, 98, 103–4, 111, 278
retail stores, animals in, 104–5, 137, 277–78
Rice University, 105–6
Richmond, Virginia, 90
Rin Tin Tin, 48–49
rodent control by animals, 37, 76, 190–91
Rottweilers, 109
roundworm, 110
Rover, 71, 85
Rovner, Julie, 121
Royal College of Nursing, United Kingdom, 122
Rubin, Dale, 223
Russ, Karl, 254

safety in neighborhoods, 133
salmonellosis, 111
Salois, Matthew, 215
Salt Lake City, Utah, 90
San Diego, California, 90
San Jose, California, 90
schizophrenia patients, 123
schools, pets in, 127–28, 137
Schultz, Howard, 63
Schulz, Charles, 51
Seattle, Washington, 89, 90
Seattle Animal Shelter, 4, 143
Selfish Gene, The (Dawkins), 68
seniors, 119, 124–25, 254–56, 284
service and emotional support animals
    on airplanes, 94–95, 137, 278–79
    certifications for, 21–22
    on college campuses, 105
    and human-animal bond, 276n
    legislation supporting, 115
    and pet-friendly housing, 91–92
    in restaurants, 111
    and veterans with PTSD, 126–27
services for pets, 71–72, 98, 283
Shank-Rowe, Ryan, 121
shelters
    adoption process at, 70–71, 143, 154
    adoption rates at, 156, 156
    advocates for adopting from, 189–90
    cats in, 144, 281
    cost of adopting animals from, 144–45
    dog shortages in, 143, 144
    and dogs sold in pet stores, 164
    euthanization of animals at, 140, 145, 149, 156, 157, 158
    lost animals retrieved by owners from, 23

misconceptions about volume of animals in, 149
    no-kill, 158
    outcomes for dogs in, 157, 158
    paramedics paired with dogs from, 123
    percentage of dogs adopted from, 195–96, 195
    rabbits surrendered to, 260
    sterilization practices and policies of, 147, 166, 167
    transfer of pets from Southern to Northern, 154–55, 189
Shipwreck Guide to Dorset and South Devon (Clarke), 47
Simpson, Missy, 166
sitters for pets, 71–72
Slater, David, 187
smartphones, 43, 59, 215
Smith, David, 153–54, 156, 157
snakes, 239–40, 243, 245, 249–51
Snoopy, 51, 53
social capital engendered by pets, 86, 130–33, 274, 275
social media
    as agent of change, 55
    animal celebrities on, 64–65
    animals' accounts on, 5, 66
    and branding, 62
    Facebook, 43, 55, 58, 62, 65, 67–68
    Instagram, 43, 53, 55, 64–65, 66
    memes on, 53–54, 68–69
    prominence of animals on, 65–68
    reasons for pet obsession on, 66–67
    and rise of Pet Nation, 57
    and sense of community, 67–68
    Victorian-era predecessors of, 43
    YouTube, 43, 53, 68
    See also Internet and digital tools
social skills, 128
society and social life
    and civic engagement, 132
    connection as by-product of pets, 1, 6, 85–86
    dysfunction in, 40–42
    instability in, 41
    isolation and loneliness in, 59, 72, 132
    and opportunities for pets created by social distance, 41
    social capital engendered by pets, 86, 130–33, 274, 275
Society for the Prevention of Cruelty to Animals (SPCA), 7, 123

spay-and-neuter campaigns, 145, 147, 165–67, 189
spiders, 251–53
staphylococcus, 110
Starbucks, 63
"State of Pet Health Report," 228–29
state parks, 105
status of pets in America, 5, 7–8, 38–39
Steele, Apryl, 144
Stetter, Mark, 170
Strand, Patti, 172
stress
    and animal-assisted therapy, 122–23
    and autism, 121
    and cortisol levels, 84, 120, 123, 126, 127, 183
    effects of pet-engagement on levels of, 120, 121, 126
    of family in hospital waiting rooms, 122–23
    in mental-health patients, 123
    in work places, 84
Strickland v. Medlen, 177–78
Strongheart, 48, 49, 53
Subaru, 63
Sweden, animal welfare in, 166, 282
Swift, Taylor, 65

TAILS (Teaching Animals and Inmates Life Skills), 102
Taine, Hippolyte, 31
Take Your Dog to Work Day, 83
talent agencies for pets, 26
Target, 104
tax credits/deductions for pet ownership, 136
Taylor, Elizabeth, 64
technology
    and alienation/social isolation of people, 59
    health tracking, 233–34
    and opportunities created for pets, 41, 59
    and pet health-care industry, 214–15
    pet trackers, 233
    and rise of Pet Nation, 43–44, 54–61, 69, 72–73
    Victorian-era predecessors of modern, 42–43
    See also Internet and digital tools; social media
tele (Greek word for "far"), 41
telegrams, 42–43
telephone, 42–43

Texas, 14n
text messaging, 59, 67
therapy dogs, 125. *See also* animal-assisted therapy
"three-dog night" (term), 76
Tilikum v. Sea World Parks & Entertainment, 187–88
Toto (*Wizard of Oz*), 50–51
Towne, Zeb, 14
tracking technology for pets, 233
trains, animals traveling on, 95–96
transportation, 93–96, 137
trust
    perceptions of trustworthiness, 133
    placed in animals' instincts, 27–28
Turkle, Sherry, 59
turtles, 246, 268–69
typewriters, 42–43, 56

Udell, Monique, 129
United Kingdom, animal-welfare law in, 115
University of Pennsylvania's School of Veterinary Medicine, 203
US Department of Agriculture (USDA), 164–65, 171, 173
US Military Working Dog Teams National Monument, 115

VCA, 212, 214, 224
vegan food for pets, 18
Vest, George Graham, 28
Vetere, Bob, 32
veterinarians and health care services, 209–38
    and animal abuse, 201–3, *202*, 205
    and ASPCA/HSUS lobbies, 197
    Banfield Pet Hospital, 211–12, 214, 231
    BluePearl, 209, 212, 214, 223–24
    for cats, 38–39, 224–27, 282
    and consumers' expectations, 213, 214–15, 216
    and declawing cats, 190–95, *192*
    defining characteristics of, 210
    demographics of, 217–19, *217*, *218*, *219*
    and dog shortage threat, 148
    earliest, 216
    for exotics/nontraditional pets, 246–47, 256n, 270
    gender imbalance in, 217
    and Golden Retriever Lifetime Study, 232–33
    and health tracking technology, 233–34

veterinarians and health care services (*cont.*)
  and hospice care, 234–38
  and microchips, 22–24, 62, 283
  mobile practices, 226
  money spent on, *33*, 213, 224–25
  and noneconomic/emotional damages,
    180, 181
  and opioid abuse, 203, 205
  organization of, 213–15
  and paraprofessionals, 219–22, 282, 284
  and Pet Insight Project, 229–30
  and pet insurance, 81, 230–31, 270
  and revenues from pharmaceuticals,
    197–99
  rise of corporate veterinary groups, 214, 284
  shortages in, 197, 215–17, 282, 284
  and specialty medicine, 210, 213, 214,
    223–24
  and "State of Pet Health Report," 228–29
  telemedicine options in, 226, 282
  training of health-care providers, 215–22,
    217, 218, 219
  wellness care, 210–11, 213, 231
veterinary schools
  and Animal Medical Center, 224
  applications for, 214
  at Big Ten schools, 90n
  call for more, 282
  demographics of, *217, 218, 219*
  earliest, 216
  and exotic/nontraditional pets, 270
  gender imbalance in, 217
  small number of, 197, 215, 216, 282
Vetsource, 199
Victorian era
  changing attitudes toward animals during, 7
  descendants of technology from, 42–43
violence (interpersonal) and animal abuse,
    199–201, 202–3

Vitale, Kristyn, 129–30
Voltaire, 29
Vonnegut, Kurt, 284

walking with dogs, 132–33
Wall Street Journal, 94
Walmart, 104, 198
WALTHAM Petcare Science Institute, 117
Wanshel, Elyse, 3–4
warmth offered by dogs, 76
Washington Post, 157–58, 159
Weatherson, Harry, 209
weight loss, 129
Welser, Jen, 212–13
Wesely, Jennifer, 102
West, Gil, 94
Westminster Kennel Club Dog Show, 43
Wharton, Edith, 60
WHIP (Wild Horse Inmate Program), 103
Wild Earth, 18
Winston (French Bulldog), 209
Wizard of Oz, The, 50–51
Wood, Lisa, 131, 133
Woodruff, Kimberly, 153–54, 156, 157
working animals
  decline in need for working dogs, 37–38
  and human-animal bond, 114
  job market for, 27
  popularized by media pets, 49
  See also service and emotional support
    animals
workplaces, pets in, 26–27, 80–85, 136

YouTube, 43, 53, 68

zero-sum nature of love, fallacy of,
    275–77
Zhang, Sarah, 18
zoos, lessons from, 169